The Detroit Pistons 1988 -'89

by Roland Lazenby

Photographs by Kirthmon Dozier
of *The Detroit News*

A FULL COURT PRESS BOOK

TAYLOR PUBLISHING COMPANY
Dallas, Texas

Design by Karen Lazenby

©1988, Full Court Press, Inc.
Taylor Publishing Company
1550 West Mockingbird Lane, Dallas, Texas 75235

ISBN 0-87833-646-X

Printed in the United States of America

Contents

Preface

The timing couldn't be better. Just as the Detroit Pistons have joined the royalty of the NBA, they've taken up residence in their own palace.

It would be difficult to think of a better setting for Coach Chuck Daly and his court as they seek to continue the fairy tale they started last spring. In the last chapter, the Pistons conquered the Celtic kings and broke their spell.

Now we find our heroes about to set out on the 1988-89 quest for the NBA's holiest grail. It is sure to be an exhilirating journey. They face dungeons and dragons and Hawks and the most feared of all, Magic, the scorcerer.

On their side, they have honor and courage and strength in numbers. They have Isiah to lead them. And Daddy Rich to guide them. Beyond that they have a heck of a home crowd to get them through the tight spots.

To help you decipher this action, we offer you this book, the first in a series of yearly Pistons guides. It is the work of a number of people. At the top of the list is Matt Dobek, the Pistons' public relations director who authored the Pistons' profiles and compiled the statistics. He and his assistant, Debbie Mayfield, provided all the help and support to make the project possible.

We also have to thank Arnie Hanson, our publisher at Taylor Publishing Company, who recognized that the Pistons' story would make a great book. For editorial guidance, we must thank our editors, Tim Orwig and Ricky Lovegrove at Full Court Press, and Philip Tate at Taylor Publishing.

The heart of this book is the photography, which The Detroit News graciously agreed to provide. Linda Rauhut-Robak produced excellent prints from the newspaper's lab. Bob Giles, the executive editor; Mark Hass, the assistant managing editor for local news and photography; and Greg Anderson, the assistant director of photography, all made sure the effort came off without a hitch.

The book design and production are the work of Karen Lazenby and Lisa Harrison at Full Court Press with supervision from Kathy Ferguson, the art director at Taylor Publishing.

With the efforts of such a fine group, we hope this will be the first of many Pistons guidebooks to come.

Roland Lazenby
Kirthmon Dozier

Detroit fans had the pleasure of watching the Pistons rip the Celtics in the Eastern Finals.

Joe Dumars scrambles for a loose ball against the Lakers.

SHAKE ME, WAKE ME

Deep in the sleep of their summer nights, the Detroit Pistons had a choice. They could grope for the nightmare or the dream. The dream, of course, is that sweet vision of Game Six of the 1988 Eastern Conference Finals, of Red Auerbach stoically leading his defeated Boston Celtics from the Pontiac Silverdome floor amidst an outbreak of Detroit delirium. Few clubs have had the pleasure of celebrating an Eastern championship over one of Red's teams. Just the kind of memory that makes for blissful summer slumber.

The nightmare, on the other hand, is a gripper. Game Six of the NBA Finals in the Forum. A minute remaining in regulation with the Pistons holding a 3-2 edge in games and a 102-99 lead over the Los Angeles Lakers. A mere 60 seconds from an NBA title, the franchise's first ever. For the first real instant all season, the window of possibility has opened to a Detroit championship. Then comes Byron Scott's 14-foot jumper to bring L.A. within one, 102-101, at 52 seconds. Detroit struggles for the right shot on its possession and fails when Isiah Thomas misses an 18-footer. At 14 seconds, Lakers center Kareem Abdul-Jabbar positions for a sky-hook from the baseline, and the Pistons' Bill Laimbeer is called for a foul. Kareem makes both free throws, giving L.A. a 113-112 lead. The Pistons have the ball and a chance to win it. At eight seconds, Joe Dumars takes the shot for Detroit, a six-foot, double-pumper.

The nightmare lingers a bit on this instant, with the ball hanging in midair. It misses, the rebound slipping through Dennis Rodman's frantic hands, and with it, Detroit's best opportunity in three decades. Byron Scott controls the loose ball. The Lakers escape.

"I thought I could get it to the hole," Dumars said afterward. "I thought there was an opening, but then they converged on me. They just cut me right off."

A dream, then a nightmare.

Still, there is little question that triumph was the dominant theme of Detroit's 1987-88 season. "I've been a very blessed young man," point guard Isiah Thomas said after the Game Seven loss to Los Angeles. "Though we didn't win the championship, the good far outweighs the bad."

Yes, 1987-88 ultimately became a time to count blessings. They could be found in everything from a club-record 54 regular-season wins to banner field-goal percentages and gate receipts. It was all quite a haul considering that the season had begun with an irritation that bordered on despair. And, despite the loss to the Lakers, it ended with a crescendo of hope. Harry Chapin once wrote, "It's got to be the going, not the getting there, that's good." The Pistons, it seems, can subscribe to that line of thinking. Theirs was a complete effort. They held nothing back. The going was good. And when it was all over, they had arrived.

THE IRREGULAR SEASON

The regular season opened under the shadow of the disappointing loss to Boston in the 1987 playoffs. Thomas had made the mental error in Game Five allowing Larry Bird to steal the last-second pass that led to Boston's winning layup. Then when the Celtics won the series in seven games, Thomas and Dennis Rodman became embroiled in the well-publicized dispute questioning Bird's abilities. That, of course, blossomed into a media incident that further deepened Isiah's disappointment. The death of his father just before training camp only added sorrow to his frustration.

Fortunately, the Pistons' early play distanced them from their problems. They broke out at a strong pace, averaging 116 points per game through early November. From there, they upped their offensive output, blasting Golden State 131-108 on November 20 and whipping Chicago 144-132 in overtime a night later.

"They are a great offensive team,"

Dantley possesses a strong inside game.

Chicago Coach Doug Collins said of the Pistons after his team's loss. "They have a lot of ways to beat you."

Small forward Adrian Dantley, who led Detroit with 45 points, agreed: "We don't have to rely on any one guy on any night. Isiah is the catalyst. Tonight just happened to be my turn to score."

Thomas had hit a three-pointer to send the game into overtime. But the Pistons as a team had come to the realization that no one player would carry them. "It's much easier now because we have an array of talent, people who can go out and do other things," Thomas said. "I'm not the guy who always has to deliver the basketball, and it takes a lot of pressure off me.

"My assists may come down," he acknowledged, "but in the overall scheme it helps the team. We have eight guys who can score in double figures, eight guys who can really pass the ball. That makes our team much better."

Across the league, the Pistons were recognized as an excellent team, built from mediocrity in seven seasons by General Manager Jack McCloskey. Thomas, taken in the first round of the 1981 draft, had been the singular talent around which the other components were added. The hiring of Coach Chuck Daly in 1983 was the other key move. He was the architect of the team's eight- and later nine-man rotation.

Laimbeer, a role-playing center out of Notre Dame, had arrived in a 1982 trade with Cleveland. In Detroit he had worked to expand his limited range into a unique set of skills. Vinnie Johnson, a pure scorer out of Baylor, was another Pistons veteran who fit nicely as an accelerator off the bench. Dumars was an unselfish, complete player drafted out of McNeese State in 1985. The '86 draft brought John Salley out of Georgia Tech and Rodman from Southeast Oklahoma State. After playing through their rough spots as rookies, both developed into floor-running forwards, remarkable in their flexibility and utility. Power forward Rick Mahorn had been acquired from

Isiah Thomas is caught in traffic during a December game with the Trailblazers.

Dantley passed his own milestone December 8 when he scored his 20,000th NBA point in a win over the Portland Trailblazers.

Washington, where he was seen as something of a brute. But in Detroit he expanded and developed his game and earned a new-found respect in the process. The next-to-last element was Dantley, a legitimate superstar brought in from Utah for the 1986-87 season. He was well-traveled, with stops in Los Angeles,

Buffalo and Utah, seemingly never comfortable in his role until he found a home with the Pistons and became their leading scorer.

This gang of eight continued their high-output, versatile offense on November 27, beating San Antonio, 143-111, to give Daly his 200th Pistons victory before a Silverdome crowd of 30,743. For five seasons, Daly had molded this team first around, then beyond Thomas' talents. "I've always felt he doesn't get enough credit simply because I'm on his team," Thomas said of the 57-year-old Daly. "It's assumed we're going to have a certain number of wins just because I'm playing. Like, when we were winning games with Kent Benson and Earl Cureton, people acted as if we were supposed

to do that. They didn't realize how much Chuck brought out of his players."

Dantley passed his own milestone December 8 when he scored his 20,000th NBA point in a win over the Portland Trailblazers. The only real negatives in this pre-Christmas stretch were personal. Veteran center Darryl Dawkins had been acquired before the season in hopes that he could return to form and become a solid backup. However, he abruptly left the team December 12 to deal with the trauma of his wife's suicide.

On the court, the Pistons were in the midst of a club-record 10-game winning streak that would be capped the day after Christmas by a 110-75 devastation of the New Jersey Nets in the Silverdome. The streak pushed

Detroit General Manager Jack McCloskey honors Dantley for his 20,000th career point, recorded December 8.

Thomas does Dallas during Detroit's December win streak.

Detroit to a 17-5 record, the best start in the franchise's history, good enough for only a half-game lead over Atlanta in the Central Division.

They would run up an 11-1 record during December, enough to win Daly NBA coach-of-the-month honors. But from there, the hot streak cooled with the weather. The Pistons lost 10 of their next 17 games and fell behind Atlanta by three games. That, in part, may have contributed to Dantley and Laimbeer missing the All-Star team selection in January.

"We've got a lot of balanced scoring on our club," Laimbeer replied when asked why he wasn't selected. "Nobody's statistics really stood out."

Yet Dantley had been hot, averaging 22.3 points per game by hitting 51.7 percent from the floor. "I guess my numbers weren't strong enough," he told reporters. "Some of the guys they picked didn't have strong numbers either, and they aren't playing on winning teams. [Kevin] McHale is having a good season, but he missed 16 games [after foot surgery]. But it's the coaches' decision. They decided to pick a guard for the seventh spot instead of a forward. That was the bottom line."

Detroit's January 27th home game with Indiana marked Laimbeer's 600th consecutive game, the longest streak among active players. (The all-time record is 906 games set by journeyman pro Randy Smith during the 1970s.)

The upswing from this low stretch began with a January 29 win over the Celtics at the Silverdome before an NBA-record crowd of 61,983, breaking the previous record of 52,745 also set in the Silverdome in February 1987. The 125-108 victory was Detroit's seventh consecutive at home over Boston.

Despite the upturn, February brought more turmoil and change. Dantley missed a string of games with ankle and leg injuries and was replaced by Dennis Rodman, who played superbly. Al Davis, managing general partner of the Los Angeles Raiders, heard the Pistons were being dubbed the "Raiders of the NBA" because of their physical style, so at mid-month he sent sweaters and various gifts displaying the Raiders' silver and black logo.

The real gift, however, came from Phoenix on the 26th—center James Edwards in a trade for Ron Moore and a 1991 second-round draft choice. "I couldn't be happier," declared Edwards, who suddenly found himself working for a playoff contender.

When Detroit visited the Lakers at the Forum on the 21st, they took their Raiders image with them. In the second quarter, Laimbeer inadvertently hit Abdul-Jabbar in the head. Immediately the two centers faced off.

"He told me, 'Don't be hitting me in the head,' " Laimbeer said of Kareem afterward. "I told him, 'Get out of my

Rick Mahorn had his best regular season ever.

face.' I have a technique where I slap the ball away. This time he got his head in the way and ran into my hand."

The Pistons lost, 117-110, despite 42 points from Thomas, but it did little to slow their regained momentum. They won their next six. Much of the turnaround could be traced to Thomas, who had averaged a little more than 18 points while shooting 42 percent from the field for the first 39 games. Somewhere around the 40th game, Isiah came alive, upping his field goal accuracy to 49 percent while averaging 20.2 points and leading the Pistons on a 22-6 run. By February 28, they held a comfortable five-game lead on the Hawks in the Central.

In March, they hit full stride, and by the Ides, they had piled up a club-record 16 consecutive wins at home. They would extend the streak to 18. "I guess when you look back at this [record] at some point it will be very nice," Daly said. "It means that we've been doing a good job of protecting our home territory, something we've talked so much about. We're going to have to do that to win the division, or try to catch Boston. All in all, it's a nice tribute to our guys."

The Celtics, meanwhile, were way ahead in the Atlantic Division and charging toward the home-court

Detroit's John Salley rides out a loose ball against Atlanta.

Dennis Rodman brought enthusiasm to the line-up in February.

advantage in the Eastern playoffs. Following three to five games at their heels gave the Pistons plenty to think about.

During this stretch, Thomas turned his attention to the playoffs. He began staying after practice working on his shot and lifting weights. "I want to raise my game to the next level," he explained to reporters. "When I talk about raising my game, I'm talking about improving my concentration, being fundamentally sound so that good things happen naturally. The last few games my shot has been falling, and everything else has just fallen into place."

On the 26th, he scored 36 in a win over the Suns. "I feel good about my shooting, and my teammates have been setting good screens for me," he said afterward.

"Isiah just took over the game," then-Phoenix Coach John Wetzel said. "We didn't have much luck shutting him down."

Laimbeer was another major March contributor. Averaging just 11.5 points on 9.7 shots per game, the center had spent his time racking up substantial numbers of assists— five, six, seven per game. "Sometimes people have to make sacrifices offensively," he said of the change, "and I don't mind being one of them. It doesn't bother me if I score six or 26 points. I'm into passing these days."

14

Salley works a pump fake against New Jersey April 16, the day Detroit clinched the Central Division crown.

Still, he found a big game just when they needed it most, scoring 27 points to subdue the streaking Utah Jazz, 103-98, in the Silverdome March 9th. His outburst came just one night after he had been punched in the eye during a scuffle with Indiana's Steve Stipanovich.

The scruffs and scrapes were part of the game. The Pistons' real problem came at the end of the month when backup center William Bedford checked into a substance abuse program. His action was announced the morning of March 30, and that night they lost a key home game to the Hawks in the Silverdome, 103-102, ending their 18-game home winning streak. "It's something that has happened that is unfortunate," Thomas said, "but if he's looking for sorrow or pity on my part, no. It's well documented in our society what drugs do to your mind and your body."

Not to mention your playoff hopes.

Yet those hopes were safer than they had ever been in Pistons history. They couldn't quite eclipse Boston for the home-court advantage in the Eastern Conference, but the Pistons did wrap up their first-ever Central Division title. At the same time, they broke the one million mark in attendance, becoming the first team in NBA history to draw mega numbers. With the vast Silverdome as their temporary home, the Pistons also held the previous record of 908,240, set in 1986-87. They accomplished both feats April 16 with a 114-96 win over the Nets. The same day, the New York Knicks beat the Hawks, giving Detroit the title.

"It's a tremendous accomplishment for this organization and illustrates once again what tremendous fans Detroit fans are," said Dan Hauser, the Pistons vice-president of marketing. "We've given them an excellent team to support and we expect that they will continue to turn out in the future."

That Saturday night in the team training room, several players gathered to wait for the score of the Atlanta-New York game. When the news came, they greeted it with champagne. "It's a championship," Thomas shouted as he popped a cork. "Someone go tell my wife I'm going to be a little late tonight."

Daly arrived fresh from his radio show, and his players quickly soaked his tailored suit in bubbly. He had seen the celebration routine on TV before and had heard the champagne would burn his eyes. "It does," the coach said after the experience, "but it's worth it. We finally did it."

In his tenure, veteran guard Vinnie Johnson had lived through some of the low times with the Pistons. "It's great for this organization after 30 years of not winning anything to finally win it," he said. "I'm proud I was a part of it."

The Central Division title, however, was just another part of getting there.

REVERSING THE PLAYOFFS

The Pistons had begun the regular season by establishing their offense, but they reversed field a bit for the playoffs. Instead, they sent a message across the league about their defensive prowess. It didn't get anyone's attention right away. The NBA had been under the domination of the Lakers and Celtics so long, it almost seemed as if no other franchise really mattered.

The Pistons struggled through a

Bill Laimbeer and Washington's Moses Malone go for the tip during Detroit's playoff series with the Bullets.

The Pistons struggled through a best of five series with the Washington Bullets before winning the fifth game, 99-78. Next came the Chicago Bulls with league MVP Michael Jordan.

best of five series with the Washington Bullets before winning the fifth game, 99-78. Next came the Chicago Bulls with league MVP Michael Jordan. Finally, in this second-round series, people began to take notice of Detroit's defense. They opened with a 93-82 victory over the Bulls in Game One in which their defense made half the difference. The other half was 23 points from Dantley. "We've double-teamed Dantley everywhere except from the bench with [coach] Doug Collins," Chicago assistant John Bach said afterward. "Dantley's a threat that has to be handled."

Yet when the Bulls double-teamed, Dantley simply fired a pass to the open man. "He has been smart enough to get rid of the ball," Bach said of Dantley. "Frankly, if he were being more selfish and holding onto the ball more, he'd be easier to play. But he recognizes that he's playing with other guys who can spot up and score."

The "other guys," however, didn't come through in Game Two. Led by Sam Vincent's 31 points, the Bulls nailed down a 105-95 victory at the Silverdome. The Pistons shot 31 percent from the floor in the first half and never recovered. "You expect your shooting average to go down because of playoff intensity," Daly said the next day. "But I didn't expect anything like this."

The only real positive aspect of the loss was the emergence of backup center James Edwards, who had remained out of the limelight since his arrival from Phoenix. But he made

Detroit's team defense shackled Michael Jordan's offense during the second-round series with Chicago.

Dantley gets position against the Bulls' Charles Oakley.

seven of nine shots from the floor to lead Detroit back in the second half. Daly remarked afterward that he hoped Edwards would continue to find his pace. "That would be an added dimension that would really help us," the coach said. At the time, even Daly didn't realize how much. But in retrospect, this home loss to Chicago marked the turning point in Detroit's season. Somehow it awakened the Pistons as a team, sending them on a tear.

The Game Two defeat meant Detroit had lost the home-court advantage. His team faced the next two games in Chicago, and Daly was left to worry. "What I'm looking at now is a five-game series," he said, "and we're going in as the visitors to try to steal one."

Instead of one, they stole two. Again, the burglar tools were defensive. Game Three was a 101-79 blowout marked by a scuffle between Jordan and Laimbeer. The Detroit center was charged with an offensive foul on Jordan, and moments later they squared off. "I set a pick and I guess he wasn't looking," Laimbeer said. "After he swung at me, I pushed him." Nothing was landed, but the decision clearly went to Detroit. Jordan said the offshoot was a shattering of his concentration. "I wasn't able to get into my flow after

that," he told reporters.

That, of course, was just fine with the Pistons. Even better, Sam Vincent had lost his hot hand from Game Two, making only three of 12 from the field. The Detroit offense had become a matter of getting hot again, and everyone knows that no one gets hot faster than Vinnie "The Microwave" Johnson. He had been shorted out during the late going of the regular season but fired up the Pistons in Game Three with 23 key points.

Then for good measure, Johnson hit seven of 10 from the floor in Game Four to keep the offense moving. That and more superb defense on

Jordan gave the Pistons a 96-77 win and a 3-1 lead.

"It's great to come through when the team really needs me," Johnson said. "The guys were looking for me, and that's a great feeling in itself, knowing they look for you to come through when the pressure's on. I've felt as if my shot has been there all along, but there have been games when it hasn't fallen. But now it is, and it couldn't happen at a better time."

Jordan's fortunes were headed in the opposite direction. "Detroit is playing very well with some great defense," he said. "We just can't score. Detroit does a great job on me. They didn't let me penetrate and I kept giving up the ball."

Another big factor for Detroit was Isiah's toughness. He caught an elbow from Jordan under the right eye early in the third quarter and had to be led to the locker room partially conscious. The room, however, was locked, so Thomas returned to the bench and re-entered the game five minutes later. Despite the injury, he played inspired defense and scored 11 more points in pacing Detroit to the win.

"I can't say enough about Isiah," Daly told reporters afterward. "He got knocked out, basically... I thought, frankly, he probably wouldn't return to the game. The next thing I know he's coming back to the bench. He struggled a little after that, but then, boy, did he show up at a crucial time."

The series returned to the Silverdome that Wednesday May 18, where the Pistons ripped Chicago in Game Five, 102-95. Suddenly the season became a matter of waiting to see who would win the Atlanta-Boston shootout. As Dantley explained, if the Hawks won, the Pistons had home-court advantage. Then again, if Boston won, the Pistons had a chance to right last year's wrongs. The heck with righting wrongs. The Pistons decided to root for the Hawks and the home-court advantage. As things turned out, they got the best of both options.

BEATING THOSE OLD BEANTOWN BLUES

They wasted little time getting things straight. Bird and the Celtics had escaped the Hawks in a classic Boston Garden showdown Sunday, May 22, and three days later the Pistons were in town with a week's rest and an issue or two to settle. Much of the pre-game hype centered on the fact that Detroit hadn't beaten the Celtics in the Garden in 21

straight games dating back to December 19, 1982, Isiah's second season in the league.

Beyond that, there were the memories of the painful 1987 playoff loss to the Celtics. But the Pistons were eager to put all such talk aside, to keep their focus on getting to the championship round. "This year we're more confident being in the Eastern Conference Finals," Joe Dumars said. "We're not just happy to be here. This is a step you have to go through to

Dumars scrambles against Dennis Johnson and the Celtics.

Dumars penetrates for an assist against Boston.

get to the finals."

Much was made of the great Celtics mystique, but the Pistons remained fixed in their determination. "I don't care if we have to play the Little Sisters of the Poor to get to the finals," Thomas quipped. "That's what it's all about."

Quickly folks realized they weren't just talking. Game One in the Garden had a strange atmosphere. The air seemed almost dead, the fans unusually subdued. The teams dogged each other through the first three quarters with neither seemingly capable of seizing opportunity. Laimbeer hurt his shoulder in the third quarter, and Edwards once again was a factor, with six points and six rebounds in 22 minutes. Thomas, however, was the major force for the Pistons with 35 points and 12 assists, much of them in the critical fourth quarter when Detroit pulled away.

It was a strange but welcome sensation to see the Boston fans leaving the Garden early. Late in the game, Thomas fed Rodman for a breakaway slam. Then the Pistons point guard finished things off with a jumper and two free throws for a 104-96 win. The Garden jinx was finally dead.

"Isiah was tremendous," Daly said afterward. "He kept making big shots over big people."

"Some bad things happened to us," Thomas explained, "and I felt I had to take charge. It feels really good. Really good... I've got a lot of respect for Boston, and we know they can come back. But this puts us in a good position. They're the team trying to catch us now."

Daly, nevertheless, quickly doused the post-game elation. "Let's not forget that it's a seven-game series," he said. "Boston looked really tired. It looked like Atlanta took a lot out of them."

For Game Two the next night, the Pistons kept the blade to Celtic throats. Boston owned a 53-46 lead at the half, but Vinnie had hit six of 10 from the field to keep Detroit close. The Pistons were called for 16 fouls in the first two quarters, including

Reserve center James Edwards came into his own during the playoffs.

three each on Mahorn and Thomas. Dantley scored nine in the third, and the Pistons stayed within reach, entering the fourth period down, 81-78.

They took the lead, 84-83, two minutes into the quarter and continued apace. This time the spotlight belonged to Edwards, whose series of fallaways and turnarounds disheartened Boston's defense. He scored eight points and left the Garden crowd staring in disbelief. Dantley hit two free throws for a 101-100 lead with 45 seconds left. A Danny Ainge basket and another Dantley free throw brought

the score to 102 all at the end of regulation.

Thomas scored seven in the first overtime, including a clutch, seemingly insurmountable three-pointer for a 109-106 lead with seven seconds left. The Garden crowd swallowed the reality that their boys were about to fall behind 0-2. Just about that time, Kevin McHale scooped up a loose ball and hit his dubious three-pointer, his only trey of the season. Dantley screamed that his foot was on the three-point line. But referees Jack Madden and Mike Mathis and alternate Bill Saar said they didn't see the foot placement in the scramble. TV replays were inconclusive, but it didn't matter anyway. Tied at 109, the game went into a second overtime. There, the home boys prevailed 119-115.

"If they didn't see it, what the hell are we paying them for?" Daly asked of the officials afterward. "We could have really been in the driver's seat. But now we have to go back and just keep playing hard. We're not intimidated."

Joe Dumars certainly wasn't. The steady, well-rounded guard picked Game Three at the Silverdome for his offensive display. He scored 29 points (12 of 21 from the floor) in pushing the Pistons to a 98-94 win that wasn't as close as the score. "I hit the first shot and it felt good," he said in the interview room afterward. "I hit the second one. The third one, I didn't think it was going in, but when it did, I really felt good. That's when I thought I was in my rhythm. I take the same shots every game. Today, they just fell."

The Celtics surged in the third quarter, but again Edwards came on to subdue them with four baskets in the last four minutes of the period. "This is my once-in-a-lifetime chance," the 7'1" center said afterward. "I've been in the league 11 years and it's winding down for me. This is my chance to get my championship ring."

The other unsung hero was the team defense. Through the nine previous playoff games, the Pistons had held teams led by the likes of Jordan and Bird to an average of 91.8 points. Only once in 13 playoff games had a Detroit opponent shot better than 50 percent from the floor. "We're really working hard and our defensive pressure is good," said an obviously pleased Daly. "It has to continue to be as good or get better."

The Celtics were shooting just 43 percent, with Bird well below that at 35. Much of the credit for the Boston star's problems went to Dantley. "Adrian is doing a great job, playing very hard," Dumars told reporters. "It's the hardest defense I've seen him play, as a matter of fact. But it's still a team thing."

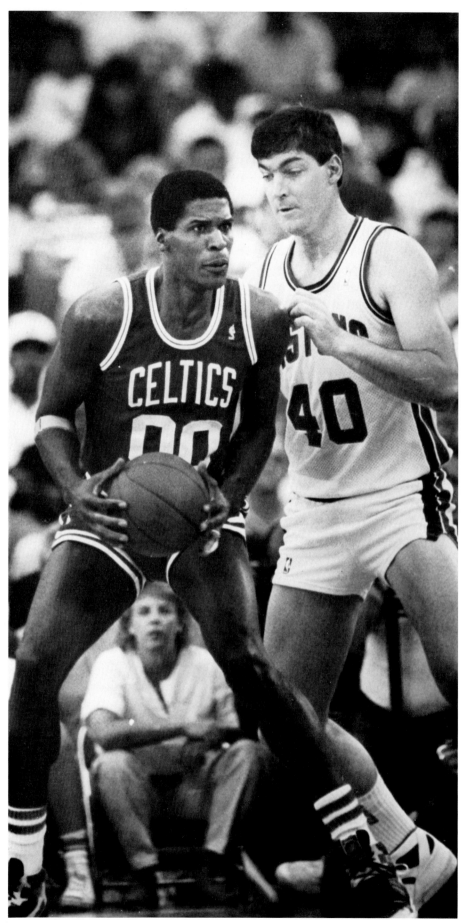

Laimbeer works against Boston's Robert Parish.

Dantley played down his success. "I'm just playing hard, playing physical," he said. "I'm giving it all I've got, that's all."

Thomas, however, was ever fearful of awakening the Celtics. "Our defense has been good," he said. "But when players such as Bird and Jordan go up to shoot, all you can do is hope they miss. They're that good."

His fears proved well-founded. Not that the Celtics underwent an offensive awakening. All they did was draw on their mystique to steal Game Four at the Silverdome, 79-78, deflating Detroit hopes in the process. Suddenly, the series was even at 2-2, and the Pistons had lost their hard-earned home-court advantage.

From start to finish, Game Four had been an offensive nightmare. During a 10-minute stretch of the first half, they missed 20 straight shots. They shot 16.7 percent from the floor during the first quarter, and finished at 33.3 percent for the game. They scored 10 in the first and 10 in the fourth quarters, tying record lows. And still they could have won it, but Dumars' last-second shot fell short amid calls for goal-tending against Boston center Robert Parish.

Daly could only think that the series should have been a 4-0 sweep. "I've got a rash of emotions... anger, disappointment, mad," he said.

The Pistons carried that disappointment back to Boston, where Thomas told reporters Boston was the better team. The Pistons, he said, had yet to prove themselves. Their downturn and Daly's rash continued through the first half of Game Five. By intermission, Isiah Thomas had three fouls and the Celtics owned a 54-40 lead. When the lead extended to 56-40 early in the third period, Daly switched gears and attacked with Rodman, Salley, Dumars, Thomas and Dantley.

"I decided that we had to get some speed on the floor and pressure the ball," Daly explained. "When we get into our running game, we're a different club."

Their speed did the trick. The comeback stunned Boston with its swiftness, as Detroit took the lead at

Boston's Kevin McHale became frustrated with Detroit's double-team.

23

The Celtics were frustrated enough to fight after their Game Six loss in the Silverdome.

Vinnie Johnson and Rodman celebrate the Eastern Championship.

71-70. During a timeout, Daly told his players they could be part of one of the greatest comebacks in NBA history.

"You never say die with us," Rodman said afterward. "We can get down, but our defense sparks us and we can run off 10 or 12 straight points. It was unbelievable—just great defense in the second half. It was our night."

Regulation ended tied at 92, but McHale had fouled out. With him gone and Bird slumping, the Celtics had no firepower. Dantley, Thomas, and Salley all scored in the overtime as Detroit went on an 8-0 run and won going away, 102-96. Thomas had scored 35 points with eight rebounds.

"This is the proudest I've ever been of a Detroit Pistons' team," the point guard said in the locker room. "I've been in the league seven years and I've worked my tail off to get to this point. I want this next game more than anything in the world except my baby [his wife Lynn was expecting their first child]. I want this next win. I want to go to the finals."

In the hours leading up to Game Six, Daly had quipped that the Celtics were like a snake. You had to sever their heads to make sure they were dead. Building on that line, Laimbeer showed up for the Friday night practice before the Saturday game with a sickle.

The outcome was the dream game, a 95-90 victory. And Vinnie Johnson was the man for the Pistons, with 24 points on 10-of-15 shooting from the floor. "I'm more excited about beating the Celtics than winning the Eastern Conference," he said with a glow. "It feels great!"

The celebration became a Pistons' hug-in. Thomas hugging Dantley at midcourt. Dumars squeezing Salley, and Daly putting the bear on his assistants. Even for a team that hadn't celebrated a championship in more than three decades, the pressing of the flesh, the high fiving, the loud jiving, was substantial.

"A.D. said he's buying me a deep-dish apple cobbler tonight," Dumars said with a huge grin. "We never eat

Salley is a fan favorite.

dessert all year. Tonight, it's everything."

After doing his share of whooping, Thomas turned reflective. "To beat the Celtics, you need to beat three things," he explained to a group of writers. "The mind-set, the team and the five great players. Through determination, effort and never giving up, we finally did that."

He was asked if the triumph was the way he imagined it would be.

"Yeah..." he said after thinking a moment. "Exactly. I guess when your dreams meet your reality, it's what? Fantasy?"

MOTOWN VS. SHOWTIME

And what do you call it when your dreams meet the L.A. Lakers? Catastrophe? Most of the basketball world considered the possibility that the Pistons would be eaten alive. Magic Johnson and entourage seemed particularly determined to repeat as NBA Champions, to make themselves the first team in 19 years to do so.

Of course, Isiah made it known that he, too, was determined to win a championship. Yet all this profession of determination was tempered a bit by the sight of Magic and Isiah holding hands and kissing before each tipoff. Their display of brotherly love would wear a bit thin as the series intensified.

Detroit wasted little time casting doubt on L.A.'s repeat plans. Dantley made 14 of 16 shots from the floor in Game One at the Forum, enough to lead the Pistons to a shocking 105-93 win and a 1-0 lead in the series.

Suddenly, the Los Angeles press noticed that the Lakers bore a remarkably striking resemblance to the Celtics: i.e. old and tired.

Despite his best defensive efforts, Lakers forward A. C. Green watched helplessly as Dantley deployed his one-hand set shot. "It's so slow, you almost fall asleep," Green said of Dantley's shot. "He's got a slow release on it. You don't expect him to shoot it because of the timing, he's out of rhythm. You expect him to pass. And he has it back far enough, it's difficult to reach. He's developed that shot over his career."

After watching Game One, Lakers Coach Pat Riley said it would be difficult to stop Dantley. "Adrian seems so committed," Riley said. "So dedicated to a mission. That's the beauty of players who have been on struggling teams. When they see a chance to be a champion, they get that special commitment."

Dantley, however, seemed to take offense at that notion. Just because he had played for weaker teams before coming to the Pistons didn't mean that he hadn't given 100 percent. "Everybody talks about the playoffs being the time to turn it up a

"Adrian seems so committed, so dedicated to a mission. That's the beauty of players who have been on struggling teams. When they see a chance to be a champion, they get that special commitment."
—Pat Riley

notch. Not me," he said. "I'm already full-force."

For their part, the Lakers were humiliated. "It was an embarrassing loss for us," Riley told reporters the next day. "The players came in this morning a little angry, a little upset

and I hope they get worse. We're going to have to bring an attitude different than the one they took into Game One."

And like the Bulls and Celtics before them, the Lakers had gotten a taste of Detroit's playoff defense. Much of the credit for the Pistons' defensive success was given to assistant coach Ron Rothstein, who left the Pistons after the season to become head coach of the Miami Heat, one of two new NBA teams.

"To say I am the architect of the defense...is a misnomer," Rothstein said. "There is nothing tricky about it, absolutely nothing. We have not written the book on it. It's been done before and it'll be done again. Good defense requires that you defend off the dribble, defend low-post people and help each other, and what nobody talks about is we are an excellent defensive rebounding team. But you're only as good as your people, and you're only as good as your people want to work at it."

Daly and his staff obviously didn't want the euphoria to stagger the team. They immediately sensed the danger of false security. "The onslaught will be unbelievable," the head coach predicted of the Lakers in Game Two. "They'll attack in every way. Usually, when something like this happens, Pat [Riley] comes up with some big move or something unusual. So, we spent all night trying to figure it out. Nothing came to mind."

With an appropriate sense of timing, the league announced the All-NBA teams the day after Game One. For the first time since his rookie season, Thomas made neither the first nor second team. "I knew coming into this year I wouldn't make the first team or the second team because it's not decided by the players and coaches," he said. "I knew I wasn't going to have a good statistical year simply because of the fact of how I was going to have to play in order for my team to get to the championship. We couldn't be selfish. Statistics is everything that people judge on. I think this is the worst statistical year that Adrian Dantley has ever had,

[Bill] Laimbeer has ever had, Vinnie Johnson has ever had, myself.

"So, in terms of statistics, they mean very little. But in terms of overall team play, the most important thing we wanted to do was get to the championship. And the only way to get here, you have to be unselfish and sacrifice yourself. In the years I made the team, we didn't get to the championship. This year we did. That should tell you something."

Although Magic Johnson had the flu, the Lakers charged back the next night and evened the series at 1-1

with a 108-96 win. James Worthy scored 26 for Los Angeles while Scott had 24 and Magic 23. "I don't think there's any doubt that Earvin Johnson showed the heart of a champion," Riley said afterward. "He was weak. Very weak. But this is what I call a hope game—you hope you get through it—and we got through it."

Dantley led the Pistons with 19. And Thomas finished with 13 after spending much of the game on the bench in foul trouble. "I'd like to say I'm satisfied with a split," Daly said, "but I'm not really. We had a chance

> **"Statistics is everything that people judge on. I think this is the worst statistical year that Adrian Dantley has ever had, [Bill] Laimbeer has ever had, Vinnie Johnson has ever had, myself.**
>
> **"So, in terms of statistics, they mean very little. But in terms of overall team play, the most important thing we wanted to do was get to the championship."**
>
> **—Isiah Thomas**

to win the basketball game. Now we've got three at home. It'll be interesting to see if we can hold serve in our home territory."

The Lakers broke serve and more that Sunday, returning a high, hard one past the Pistons, 99-86. The main damage was done in the third period when the Lakers shot 64 percent and outscored Detroit 31-14 to break open a one-point game. Finally, Daly had seen enough and was ejected by referee Earl Strom in the fourth quarter for protesting a call. "He has the whistle and he's the boss," the coach quipped afterward.

"Today's the first time in a long time that we felt we were beaten," Laimbeer said. "In all the Boston series, we felt we won all six games. And we felt we outplayed the Lakers in the first two games of the series even though we lost Game Two. This is the first time since Game Two against Chicago we felt someone beat us rather than us just blowing it."

Once again, Magic shone despite his illness. His 18 points, 14 assists and six rebounds pushed the Lakers right along. They also got a tremendous game from A.C. Green, who had eight rebounds and scored 21 points by hitting nine of 11 from the field. Beyond that, he found the defensive answer to the Dantley riddle. The Pistons' forward had only

Dantley penetrates against the Lakers and dishes off.

The agony.

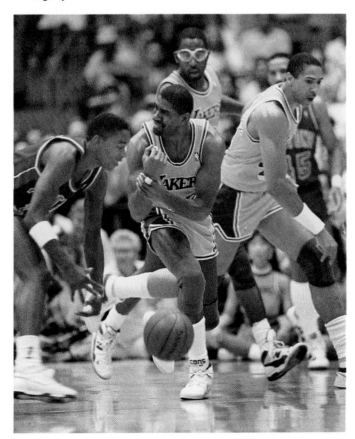

Isiah swipes the ball from his buddy Magic Johnson.

Laimbeer battled Kareem.

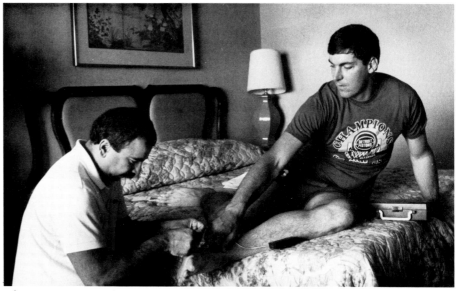

Laimbeer gets ankle treatment from team trainer Mike Abdenour during the Lakers series.

14 points, and scored just two in the second half.

"They just whipped us," Dantley said. "They were just better than us today. I know one thing: I got hammered today, and I only went to the free-throw line once."

The Dantley situation was largely responsible for Daly's ejection from the game. "I was upset really a little bit earlier," Daly said. "I thought Dantley was fouled on several plays going to the basket and didn't get a call. We were struggling to get to the line and then on that particular play, I thought they had camped in the lane five or six seconds. We didn't seem to get a call that maybe could sway it a little bit our way. I argued profusely and he ejected me and that is his right."

The Pistons stormed back to take Game Four, 111-86, and the love affair between Isiah and Magic turned into a scrap. Daly had been concerned that Johnson's smiling demeanor was stripping his players of some of their intensity. Those worries departed as the Pistons, particularly Dennis Rodman, focused their efforts on shutting down the Lakers point guard.

His frustration was obvious in the runaway fourth quarter. Johnson knocked Isiah to the floor with an elbow, and Thomas leaped back up in his face. Immediately afterward, the writers wanted to know if the friendship was off. "It was nothing personal —just business," Thomas replied.

"That's all it is," Magic agreed. "It's business."

Would it be forgotten? reporters asked.

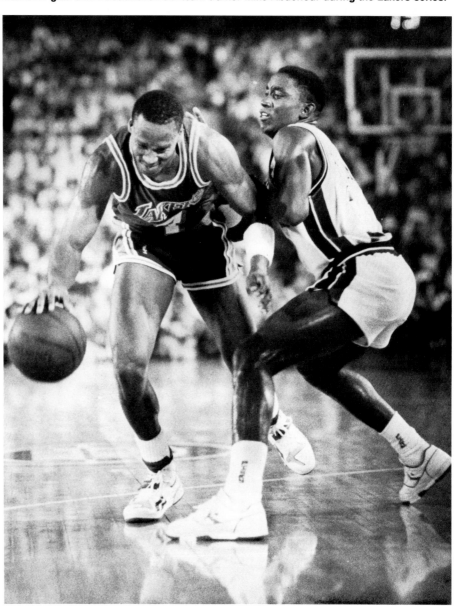

Isiah tightens up on the Lakers' Byron Scott.

"It's forgotten until Thursday," Magic said.

Game Four had been a showcase of Rodman's defensive skills. He wore Johnson down and erased his perpetual smile.

"Jordan is the toughest player I've faced because he's always moving and it's tough to stay with him," Rodman said when asked about playing defense against the league's stars. "Bird is more of a slower tempo player. And Adrian Dantley is the second toughest player I've had to guard. A.D. may be old, but guarding him in practice is tough because he's got so many weapons he can hurt you with.

"Magic is tough because he likes to penetrate. But I try to distract him, and hopefully he won't be able to look up the court and make one of those great passes."

Of the added defensive attention, Magic would only say, "[Rodman] doesn't frustrate me. I don't get frustrated. He creates some problems for me, but not a lot."

The Pistons also aimed their offense at Magic and drove him to the bench early in the second half with foul trouble. "We looked to go inside very strong and try to get fouled. It put Magic on the bench," Salley explained.

Whereas Magic had impressed his coach and teammates by playing despite his illness in games Two and Three, that distinction fell to Thomas for Game Four. He had sustained a lower back bruise trying to block a Mychal Thompson shot in Game Three. Although he spent the hours before Game Four in bed or in a hot tub, there was little doubt where he would be at tipoff.

"He wasn't going to miss a championship game," Salley said later. "I kept whispering in his ear, 'You've never felt better, you've never felt better,' and he said, 'You're right.' "

Although he scored only 10 points on two-of-seven shooting from the floor, Isiah turned in an excellent performance with 12 assists and a game-high nine rebounds. "I think my presence, just my being out on the

court, was really all we needed," he said. "I think I was a threat...the Lakers always had to be conscious of me."

Afterward the Lakers expressed disappointment in his injury. It shifted Thomas from scoring to passing and that caused trouble. He had six assists in the first quarter alone. "I was at home the last two nights and I was looking at the tapes, seeing the kind of defense the Lakers were playing," he said afterward. "I knew we could take advantage of a lot of traps they were using. It was a matter of us handling the ball and getting it in the right position."

Dantley was the major beneficiary of this development. He led the team with 27 points. Vinnie Johnson came off the bench for 16 while James Edwards had another big game in reserve, 14 points and five rebounds.

"He was great offensively in the first half," Daly said of Dantley. "He gave us a big, big game and we've got to

have that kind of game from him to sustain anything in this series."

Mychal Thompson was even more impressed. "A.D. has a great game," he said. "You might be able to hold him down in one game, but he's like nitroglycerin. You can only go so far before it explodes in your face."

With Magic out of the game much of the second half, the Pistons built their substantial lead. During the timeouts, Laimbeer was almost frantic. He kept saying, "No let up! We don't let up!" They didn't, blowing past the defending NBA champions by 25 points.

Daly was probably as pleased as he'd ever been with a Pistons' effort. "It's not just the talent on this team—we've got a lot of pride and determination," he said. "Our guys gave us a big effort. They've been doing it all year when we've had our backs to the wall. Now my only concern is they don't go back to prosperity in the next game."

Vinnie Johnson and Walker Russell during a light moment in practice.

They didn't let up for Game Five either. "The Pistons are like a nagging wife that you're tired of seeing," Mychal Thompson told writers beforehand.

Detroit played well despite the distractions. The final home game in the series would be the last in the Silverdome. After a decade in the indoor football stadium, the Pistons would move to their new home, the Palace of Auburn Hills, for the 1988-89 season.

As a result, the media turned their attention to nostalgia pieces, about the good old days when Pistons teams struggled in the giant arena before tiny crowds. The building had seen the club's transformation from a cellar dweller into a championship contender. Were the Pistons mourning their departure from the dome? reporters asked.

"I don't feel anything," Laimbeer said, "but I'm not a sentimental guy."

Dumars agreed, "I'm more concerned about Game Five."

Still, the coaches paused to pay their respects. They had seen the dome as a competitive edge. "Other teams hate it here," assistant coach Dick Versace said. "The stadium is nowhere—it's out in the country and hard to find. It takes them forever to get here from the airport. They have to hassle over their baggage, drive 55 minutes to their hotel, then drive some more to the stadium...they're irritated before they ever get here. It's been a nice advantage for us."

Daly said that in his own way, he would miss it: "Not the stadium so much but the people around the stadium. You get to know the guards on the door and the ladies who work around the building and that's a nice, comfortable feeling. I know teams don't like playing here— the vastness of it all, the problems they have with the background and the lights. To tell you the truth, I don't especially like giving up the little advantages we have here. I'm not sure we'll have the same edge in Auburn Hills that we have in Pontiac."

The other major distraction would under normal circumstances be considered nothing less than a

The Lakers' A.C. Green struggled to contain Dantley's offense.

**"It seemed to me [the Lakers] were trying to be physical. They made fouls they didn't have to make."
—Adrian Dantley**

bundle of pure joy. On the night before the game, Isiah and Lynn Thomas became parents of a boy, Joshua Isiah. The senior Thomas, however, put off discussions with reporters.

"No," he said when they asked, "why should I talk about it? It's mine and it's got nothing to do with basketball."

Meanwhile, the Lakers approached the game with their characteristic seriousness. They opened with a fury of physical intimidation, scoring the game's first 12 points. But that approach soon stalled, then backfired.

"It seemed to me [the Lakers] were trying to be physical," Dantley said. "They made fouls they didn't have to make. It seemed they were trying to say, 'Hey, we can play physical.' Then they had all their big guys on the bench."

Dantley again played a major role in this reversal, scoring 25 points, 19 of them in the first half, to pace the Pistons to a 59-50 halftime lead. "A.C. [Green] and the guys played him hard, as hard as they could," Magic Johnson said of Dantley. "Give him credit...he made the fallaway jumpers."

"He's really distinguished himself in these playoffs," Daly agreed. "I don't think I've ever seen him play better than in the second quarter. He wants it badly."

Beyond Dantley, Daly turned the full depth of the Pistons' roster on the Lakers early. Vinnie Johnson scored 12 of his 16 points in the first half to keep Detroit moving. "Our bench was paramount to us winning," Daly said. "Vinnie hit some big shots. Jimmy

Magic and Isiah display their affection before tip-off.

Mahorn's back kept him sidelined much of the championship series.

Vinnie struggles for the ball against Los Angeles.

Edwards made some big shots. Rodman and Salley were very big defensively and rebounding."

It was just another example of Detroit relying upon its "Ds"— defense, depth, Dantley, Dumars (19 points on nine of 13 from the floor), and of course, Daly. The depth should get extra emphasis. "They [the Lakers] played great in spots," Vinnie Johnson said, "but we had fresher guys: myself, Salley, Rodman and Edwards. [The Lakers] were playing well. But when you're playing against fresh guys, it's tough to hang in there. I wasn't taking my shot [in Game Three]. I took some advice from a friend and started shooting a little differently, but I came back to my old style [in Game Four]. The Finals aren't the time or place to be changing your shot."

Or your style. The Lakers had gotten away from what they do best— rebounding and running. "We couldn't contain anyone on the boards," Riley said. "We had [two] defensive boards in the fourth quarter and they had 10 offensive boards. You're not going to beat anyone with that."

The 104-94 victory was a perfect sendoff for the Silverdome. "I told Joe Dumars with a minute left in the game to look around and enjoy this because you'll never see anything like it again," Laimbeer said. "Forty-one thousand people waving towels and standing... it was awesome."

Game Six in the Forum is the frustrating part of this story. Still, it's a memory you don't want to erase, not with Isiah Thomas recording 43 points, eight assists and six steals, not with his third quarter, where he left the game with a badly sprained ankle, yet returned moments later to finish an impressive display of grit and talent. He scored 25 points in that critical quarter while painfully hobbled, an NBA Finals record.

"His ankle is pretty swollen," a drained Daly said afterward. "We got a miraculous game from Isiah, as hurt as he was. He literally by himself got us back in the game. On offense, we didn't give him as much support as I would like.

"We were 45 seconds away from

an NBA championship. What can I say?"

The game guaranteed Isiah's place among the stars, if it wasn't guaranteed already. "No one said it would be easy," he told reporters. "I'm not devastated. I want to win this championship. I'm willing to pay whatever it takes. My ankle's hurting, but this game and this series means too much not to be playing. The entire season is down to one game..."

"They said before the series they were going to pound the bleep out of me," he continued. "If I have to take a pounding for us to win it, then I'm willing to take it.... I felt our team really needed a lift. My shot was falling and the guys were working hard to set good screens to get me open."

His effort and their three-point lead going into the final seconds seemed to have assured a Detroit title. "You look up," Rodman said, "and that clock runs r-e-a-l s-l-o-w. I was tasting it. I was going to come in here to the locker room, have my championship hat on, everything. I guess I've got to wait until Tuesday."

Safe in the Lakers' locker room, Magic masked his relief in wisdom. "A minute is a long time," he said. "A long time. It's just two scores and two stops and you're ahead."

There were two major questions for Game Seven: "Would Isiah Thomas play with his ballooned ankle?"

And: "Could he play?"

He answered the first with relative ease: "I'm playing–period," he declared.

The second question only time could answer. Unfortunately, it poses the only real "what if" of the entire Pistons' season. What if Thomas had been full speed in the fourth quarter

Magic takes a shot from Dantley.

Salley stuffs Mychal Thompson.

canned a trey, the score was 106-105 with six seconds showing. Green completed the scoring with a layup, and although the Pistons got the ball to Isiah at midcourt with a second remaining, he fell without getting off a shot.

"We just said, 'Don't give up.' We've come back before," Laimbeer said. "This team has a lot of confidence and pride and we didn't want to lose by 20 points in the seventh game of the NBA Finals."

The furious close made it hard for Daly, even in all his disappointment, not to feel good. "I love the way we fought back," he said. "Obviously. Storm back from 15 down against the world champions? You have to love it. You have to love them. I can't say enough about my club. I had doubts, but this team just wouldn't quit. And they had every reason to quit."

Rodman was obviously despondent about taking and missing the jump shot with 39 seconds left. "I don't know why," he said. "I'm not a jump shooter. I don't know what clicked in me. Why couldn't I have just taken it to the rim and torn it down?"

Riley could only give thanks. "It was a nightmare to the very end," he said. "I kept saying, 'Please don't let this end in a nightmare.' We were a great team trying to hold on.

"Hey, they just put on one of the greatest comebacks in the history of this game and they have nothing to be ashamed of. We're a great team and they had us hanging on at the end. We were able to do it because of who we are, but they gave us all we could handle."

It's hard to have a season end here, at this moment of disappointment. But all those before ended so much worse, it's damned hard not to be pleased. So let's close the eyes a minute and dream. Roll it back to the Eastern Championship over Boston. With that one firmly fixed in reality, it's not so hard to fast forward things a bit to the 1989 NBA Finals, where Isiah is running on good wheels, where it just might be possible to dream that good sweet dream after all.

Isiah sipped champagne after the Game Seven loss to the Lakers in recognition of Detroit's effort.

The Thomas form.

THERE'S NO DOUBTING THOMAS

For the first time since he entered the NBA seven years ago, Isiah Thomas is approaching a basketball season without the baggage of doubt.

In his early years, he was said to be too young, too inexperienced, and playing on a team too thin in talent.

Once he gained experience, it was pointed out that he lacked focus and concentration.

So he focused his efforts and in 1987 took the Detroit Pistons to the Eastern Conference Finals. But once there, he failed in the clutch, throwing a thoughtless pass that led to the Pistons' defeat.

He didn't end his frustration until Game Six of the 1988 NBA Finals against the Los Angeles Lakers. Even then, he didn't lead his team to a championship. Yet when that pivotal game was over, all questions about the professional basketball character of 27 year-old Isiah Lord Thomas II had been answered.

In the legacy of both teams, it will be remembered as one of those "classic" games. The Pistons were down, 56-48, early in the second half, when Thomas scored the next 14 points in trancelike fashion—two free throws after a drive in the lane, then a five-footer off an offensive rebound, followed by four jumpers, a bank shot and a layup

With a little more than four minutes to go in the period, he landed on the foot of the Lakers' Michael Cooper and had to be helped from the floor. Despite a

As a result of his performance in the 1988 playoffs, Isiah now finds himself in a rare league with Bird. They are what you might call the strange and unusual superstars of the NBA.

severely aprained ankle, Thomas returned 35 seconds later and continued the offensive assault. By the end of the quarter, he had hit 11 of 13 shots from the floor for 25 points, setting an NBA Finals record for points in a quarter. Better yet, he had driven

his team to an 81-79 lead.

The Lakers battled back to stop him, and Thomas finished the game with a jammed left pinkie, poked eye, scratched face, ballooned ankle, 43 points, eight assists, six steals and enough respect to last a lifetime.

"What Isiah Thomas did in the second half was just incredible," Lakers' Coach Pat Riley said after his team escaped 103-102.

Magic Johnson, the Lakers' point guard and Thomas's buddy, was even more impressed: "I think he was just unconscious," Johnson said. "I think he said, 'Okay, I'm going to take this game over.' I've seen him do that before. He was in his rhythm. When he starts skipping and hopping, that means he's in his rhythm. That means he's ready."

It was just the kind of praise that in the past had been reserved for the likes of Boston's Larry Bird. But finally, after seven years in the league, Thomas and the Pistons replaced Bird and Boston in the NBA Finals. As a result of his performance in the 1988 playoffs, Isiah now finds himself in a rare league with Bird. They are what you might call the strange and unusual superstars of the NBA.

Both Thomas and Bird are anomalies. In a game dominated by tall, black men, Bird is white and tall, and Isiah is short and black. Through some mysterious forces, both overcome different deficiencies to enforce their own sort of domination. Bird, of course, has been considered a Wunderkind for some time. Isiah,

Isiah delivers the ball to Dantley.

on the other hand, has suffered the frustration that most people just don't realize how impossible it is for a six-footer to dominate an NBA game.

"It's flattering," Isiah says cautiously when asked how it feels to be compared with Boston's star forward. "It makes for good reading."

There remains a bit of uneasiness between the two since Thomas made his comment after the 1987 playoffs that Bird was overrated because he is white. While the media made much of that statement, Bird played it down in public, although there is little question that it bothered him. Isiah said he was grateful that Bird came to his rescue during the incident, something that many of his other basketball friends didn't do.

Still, Thomas and Bird aren't especially close. "We talk when we see each other at games," Thomas says. "But do we call each other up on the phone? No. We've had some good talks, though."

Strange as it may seem, however, their backgrounds reinforce their common bond. Both Bird and Thomas rose from houses of Midwestern poverty using hoops as the escape ladder.

Both were early departures from Bobby Knight's University of Indiana program. Bird left after a few weeks, Thomas after two years. Not surprisingly, both are guarded in their comments on Knight. (Asked if he sees Knight's influence in his play as a Piston, Thomas says, "Yeah, but sometimes the way I play he wouldn't appreciate. There's a lot of Indiana in my game. There has to be. I learned a lot of good things there.")

Both Isiah and Bird pride themselves on work ethic. They usually arrive at the arena on game nights hours ahead of schedule to conduct a pre-game practice ritual alone. (Sometimes Thomas runs through his routine at home on his personal court.)

And both of these guys have relatively heavenly images. Isiah, the eternal cherub, and Bird, the golden angel.

Yet as interesting as these similarities are, there is only one that

The smile.

Thomas fires another burner.

really matters: They have Magic Johnson as a common foe. The Lakers guard is the basketball force that prevents Larry Bird and Isiah Thomas from realizing all the glory and gold they hope to achieve.

It's an old burning feeling for Bird. For a decade, he and Magic seemed

"It doesn't irritate me. Yet it's interesting. What we're trying to establish in Detroit is something they've done in Boston since the '50s and '60s, in terms of tradition, in terms of pride, in terms of style of play."
—Isiah Thomas

locked in a personal one-on-one contest for the NBA throne. Magic and the Lakers have won five NBA titles, Bird and the Celtics three. But the rise of Isiah has changed all that now. Thomas has turned the competition into a game of 21.

If there are those who doubt the Thomas factor, consider that after the 1988 Finals, Magic said he had never faced a tougher challenge. Not even from the Celtics.

Of course, there are many striking differences between Thomas and Bird, none greater than where they play. Bird labors in tradition-laden Boston, on the hallowed Garden parquet floor, beneath the 16 NBA championship banners earned by Bill Russell, Bob Cousy, John Havlicek and all the other greats developed by Red Auerbach.

Thomas, meanwhile, works in Detroit, which is really Pontiac, which is really Auburn Hills, which is really next to nothing in terms of basketball tradition. The Pistons have never won an NBA title.

So where Bird has been the player to renovate a tradition, Thomas has faced the task of building one from scratch. There is no better example of

Airborne against the Bullets.

this than each club's reaction to a loss in the finals. In Boston, a loss to the Lakers is considered a mortal shame. It means the Celtics will do some soul searching in the offseason to determine what went wrong.

The Pistons, meanwhile, are still celebrating reaching the finals for the first time in 30 years. As Detroit Coach Chuck Daly said, "It's as if we won the championship."

Isiah has spent much of the

offseason pondering that disparity in expectations. He wants to build a Bostonlike tradition in Pistonsland.

"It doesn't irritate me," he says. "Yet it's interesting. What we're trying to establish in Detroit is something they've done in Boston since the '50s and '60s, in terms of tradition, in terms of pride, in terms of style of play."

For example, he says, when a journeyman player from the New York

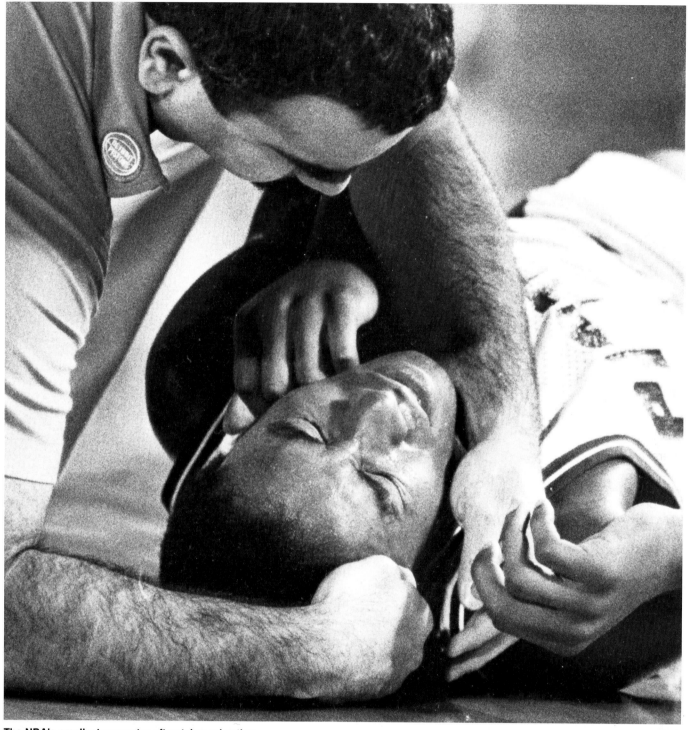

The NBA's smallest superstar often takes a beating.

Knicks is traded to Boston, that player suddenly changes his whole style of play to suit the tradition and team mentality.

"There's no other place in the NBA like that, except maybe Los Angeles," Thomas says. "The tradition creates the pressure for you to succeed. I hope our tradition will create a pressure for the next generation of Pistons to succeed. Whenever the Celtics step on the floor in Boston, they have a level of play they have to meet every night. It's demanded by the fans, by the players themselves.

"That's something we have to establish here in Detroit. We can't just win 45 games anymore in Detroit. In Boston, if you win 45 games, you're considered a failure."

Thomas has aimed at building that tradition since the Pistons made him the second selection of the 1981 draft. He had just left one great tradition, the University of Indiana Hoosiers, after leading Knight's team to the NCAA championship and earning Final Four MVP honors. The confidence he gained in his success at Indiana led him to believe he could succeed in Detroit, despite the fact the Pistons had won only 16 games in 1980.

The new contract, the Pistons' trip to the NBA Finals and the birth of Isiah's first child, son Joshua, last spring, make the opening of the 1988-89 season seem worlds away from the previous year.

It also charged the organization with confidence in him. "I understand the position this franchise is in," he said as he started his first season. "As far as feeling the pressure, I know people are expecting quite a bit from me, but I don't allow myself to feel any. I have expectations myself to win, to win as many games as we possibly can. I'm here to try to help the team attain its goals."

Rod Thorn, then the Chicago Bull's general manager, said Thomas "has a charisma, an ability to inspire confidence in his teammates that only a few players have, like a Larry Bird, Magic Johnson or Julius Erving."

Pistons General Manager Jack McCloskey, the architect of Detroit's renovation, was just as impressed with his first-round pick. "Just in what I've seen, the people on the club respect his ability," McCloskey told reporters at the time. "He has the humility not to overpower anyone with leadership. I think that's most important. He is a good person, one who will help give this club a good chemistry."

Seven years later, Thomas has delivered on his promise. "I knew there would be a challenge," he says now. "I kind of liked it. We had to educate the community about the game of basketball. Now, the people in the stands even know our plays. They call them out for us."

Having played a major role in the turnaround, he throws a similar challenge back to the team's management to reach for an even higher level of competitiveness.

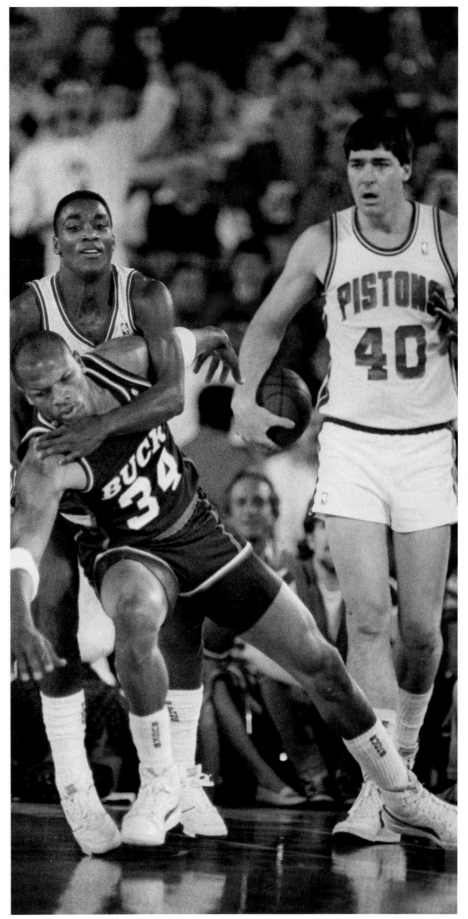

In early March, Thomas turned his thinking to the playoffs.

Point guard supreme.

Whether the Pistons find their tradition or become known as a flash in the pan will depend largely upon management, Thomas says. "Do we want to be successful for the next nine or 10 years? If so, we've got to pay the price financially and organizationally."

The Celtics were built around the unique personality of Red Auerbach, Thomas says. "What Red has that is totally different from a lot of other team management is that he understands athletes' emotions. The game requires energy, and athletes get their energy from their emotions. That's why they talk about Red as if he is a god. Red is a god."

Because he understood players, Auerbach could still afford to be a tough business manager making tough business decisions, Thomas says, adding that when it became time to trade a player like Paul Westphal, Auerbach could tell him face-to-face that he no longer fit in the team's plans.

"And that," Thomas says, "is why Westphal could tell Auerbach, 'Thanks, Red. That's okay. I'm still a Celtic, and you're a hell of a man for telling me.' "

Even more important, Auerbach had a disdain for statistics, Thomas points out. "What Red has that is totally different from a lot of other management is that in Boston they reward you for winning. They don't reward you for points scored or minutes played. If we in Detroit are going to win basketball games, we can't be statistically oriented.

"The entire NBA is kind of tainted because across the league players are rewarded for statistics. Hey, Kevin McHale played behind Cedric Maxwell for four or five years, and Boston won two championships. McHale was rewarded for being the sixth man. Their thinking was simple: 'We win games, and everybody gets rewarded.' "

An even better example, Thomas says, was role player M.L. Carr, "who was not a $500,000 ball player. But his contributions to the team's frame of mind were worth that."

Pistons' management doesn't need to duplicate Auerbach, but it does need to focus on communication and team chemistry, Thomas says. "Keep the players happy. Let them know you appreciate

Thomas talks to the press at the NBA Finals.

49

The Thomas defense is underrated.

It seems that over the past 18 months the boy marvel has become a man.

"I've grown up a lot," Isiah admits.

The first half of 1987-88 was not a happy time for Isiah.

them. A pat on the back and a simple thank-you go a long way."

Thomas got his pat on the back just before the opening of the Pistons' 1988-89 camp, when the team announced it had renegotiated his contract, which had paid him roughly $750,000 per season, to a new deal that pays $16 million over the next eight seasons. Now that he compares to Bird as a player, he's also getting paid at the same level.

The new contract, the Pistons' trip to the NBA Finals and the birth of Isiah's first child, son Joshua, last spring, make the opening of the 1988-89 season seem worlds away from the previous year.

The humiliation of his bone-headed play in the 1987 playoffs had been bad enough, but the media criticism over his Bird comments left him reeling throughout the summer before the 87-88 season.

Frustrated in the locker room after the Pistons Game Seven loss, Detroit forward Dennis Rodman had told reporters Bird was overrated. Asked if he agreed, Thomas replied, "I think Larry is a very, very good basketball player, an exceptional talent. But I'd have to agree with Rodman. If he was black, he'd be just another good guy."

Later, after those comments caused a furor, Thomas offered this explanation to Ira Berkow of the *New York Times*: "What I was referring to was not so much Larry Bird but the perpetuation of stereotypes about blacks. When Bird makes a great play, [paraphrasing the stereotype] it's due to his thinking and his work habits....It's not the case for blacks. All we do is run and jump. We never

practice or give a thought to how we play. It's like I came dribbling out of my mother's womb."

The Bird incident hurt, Thomas told Berkow. "People tried to label me a racist, and in America people would rather go to jail for murder than be labeled a racist. The way I've lived my life, I was upset by that. I guess what I found out was where people stood, and not a lot of people came to bat for me. I could understand people in Boston feeling that 'Isiah doesn't

like whites,' but I couldn't understand how people in Detroit couldn't know me."

Then, just before training camp opened that fall, his father died, adding heartache to his frustration. He buried his father one day and started training camp the next. "My father's death," he says, "was coupled with the fact that many people in sports media didn't particularly care for me because of the whole Larry Bird situation."

The media he could deal with, but his father's death left his emotions a wreck, he says. "When people look at me they see this happy guy who has no problems. Everybody said, 'We don't have time for emotions right now. We gotta play basketball.'" Because Thomas is a player who draws his strength from his emotions, he struggled through the first half of last season while his energies were divided between grieving and basketball.

"There's no comparison between this year and last year," Thomas says. "It's like night and day. Last year I experienced a whole range of emotions from the highest to the lowest, not only through basketball, but through life.

"My father's dying was the lowest point in my life. Then in the same year, my son being born was the greatest thrill I have ever experienced. Add to that our going to the NBA Finals and being 14 or 15 seconds from a championship in Game Six. Then losing and going to a seventh game, and when you lose, the game still isn't over. In one year, I experienced all the highs and lows."

The trademark Isiah Thomas smile confirms all of this. It still breaks easily across his face, curling his cheeks up to his eyes to reveal a million-dollar mouthful of brightness. But where his smile used to light up his entire face, it often stops just short of his eyes these days. A wiser Isiah seems to be holding something back, not giving himself so readily to the joy of the moment.

It seems that over the past 18 months the boy marvel has become a man.

"I've grown up a lot," he admits.

Which brings us to another major difference between Isiah Thomas and Larry Bird. The Boston forward aspires only to be a great basketball player. Nothing more. Nothing less. Isiah, on the other hand, wants to be much, much more. For example, he's currently working to develop as a businessman and television personality.

Whatever Thomas does or doesn't accomplish, he doesn't shy away from risk-taking. It's risky to take an occasional confrontational tone with the team's management, just as it's risky to push for a renegotiated contract so soon after inking a similar long-term deal in 1984. At $750,000

Salley and Thomas trade congrats after defeating the Bulls in the playoffs.

per year, he was one of the best bargains in pro basketball. At $2 million per year, he is asking for the pressure to produce a championship, and eternal criticism if he fails.

"You just try to do what's right," he says of these risks. "You try to be honest, you try to do things right. In terms of the consequences, that's part of the responsibility of being a leader. You have to be strong enough mentally to take the good and the bad."

None of his off-court endeavors has been more ambitious than the 1986 No Crime Day he created to draw awareness to Detroit's inner city problems. His hopes were to encourage people across the city to refrain from crime for just one day. "People keep saying I'm an idealist," he told reporters when the idea was announced. "I'm not pretending we can stop it all, but is it too much to ask for one day? If just one less child has to die and one less mother has to cry because of this, I'd say it was a success.

"The biggest problem we have here in Detroit is the murders. Kids are killing kids. It's terrible. I grew up a street kid, with what they call 'game.' You learn to play the game on the streets, you learn to sell drugs, you learn to hustle. When I was growing up, if someone gave you some game, you had to pay for that knowledge, with money or something. You couldn't just get the knowledge and of how to hustle in the streets.

"There used to be a time when people wouldn't sell drugs to an 11-year-old kid. It was like, okay, I'm dirty. This is what I do. But you're 11 years old, this ain't for you. What has hapened is, some guy decided that, hey, instead of me going to jail, I'm going to get 11- and 12-year-olds to sell my stuff. If they get caught, nothing happens to them and nothing happens to me. So he's giving 11-, 12-, 13-year-olds free game. They have the knowledge, they have the power, but they've paid absolutely no price for it. They know the language but they don't know the rules. So they're just killing each other. For gym shoes. For shirts. You name it."

Thomas shares a laugh with the coaching staff.

The Pistons' point guard doesn't play "little."

To undertake such an idealistic program was another major risk for Thomas. It could have backfired and left him looking naive and foolish. To promote the event, He toured several of the city's roughest neighborhoods and spoke with residents about drug and crime problems there. When No Crime Day arrived on September 26, 1987, Magic Johnson came to Detroit to show his support, school children made posters, and 15,000 people attended a rally at Heart Plaza downtown. Afterward, city authorities said they could find no appreciable decline in crime statistics.

That didn't matter, Thomas said later. "I think we increased people's awareness."

If nothing else, the effort was his attempt to strike back at the poverty that marked his own childhood in a Chicago ghetto. "I know what it's like to grow up poor. And scared," he said when reporters asked why he was attempting No Crime Day.

He recalled the day he saw someone shot over an argument at a neighborhood basketball court. "I was about 10 or 11," he said, "and we were playing a game of basketball. A guy got mad because he said he had next game and another guy said he didn't. The first guy said, 'Wait right here, I'll be back.' He left and came back with a pistol. He started shooting. Everybody ran.

"I jumped under the back of some car. I remember just lying there—I had crawled under the back end— with my hands over my head. And then I heard this guy fall in front of me near the rear bumper. I had seen a lot of people's feet running by and I figured he just fell trying to get away. So I raised my head and saw he was bleeding. It was just...God, nasty, sickening.

"I mean, his chest was hit and blood was coming out, just gushing out. I couldn't drag him anywhere because I couldn't stand up. And I couldn't run away because I thought I'd get shot. So I just laid there. And I watched his face twist up from the pain."

Basketball took him away from this seedy world, away from the

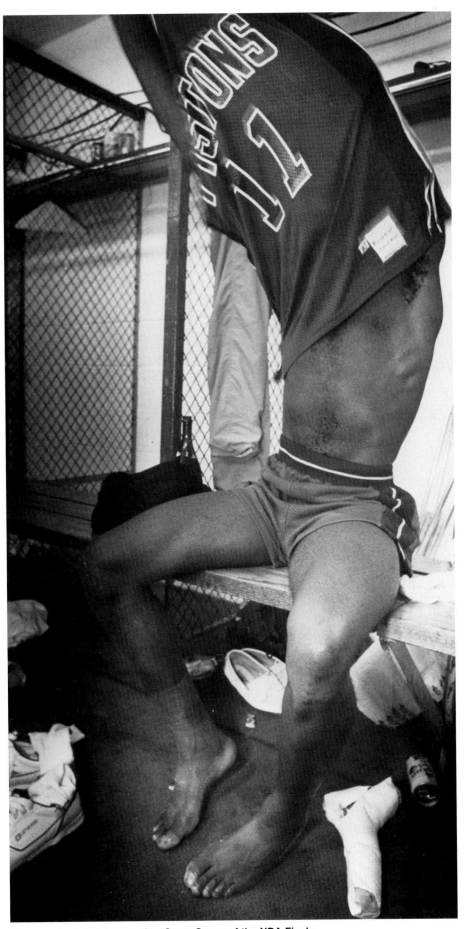

Thomas sheds his jersey after Game Seven of the NBA Finals.

55

The good buddies met in the playoffs.

environment that had snared his older brothers in drug use and vice. Isiah says he doesn't want to forget where he has come from. If nothing else, his No Crime Day was another reminder.

Not every one of his battles against his past is a grand public gesture. Pistons' assistant coach Dick Versace tells of coming into the team's New York hotel at 2 a.m. during a road trip last winter only to find Isiah exiting with a large, steaming pizza on his way to feed the street people out in the cold near Grand Central Station.

Yet, for all his larger hopes, basketball is the vehicle that has carried him away from the ghetto. And the game remains the core of his success. "It's as if God placed his hand on Isiah and said, 'You shall play basketball, and you shall play it

great,' " Bulls guard Rory Sparrow once said of Thomas.

No one is more aware than Thomas of basketball's power over him, of the influence it has had on his life. "It's a beautiful game," he says. "During the season, basketball is like a love for me, like a passion. It controls my emotions. It's like being in love with a woman and she is the only one who can make you happy or upset. Basketball can have me happy, mad, it can have me sad— every range of emotion, this game does to me. And I don't like it. I don't like the game having that much control.

"But when I'm on the court between those four lines and two goals, I don't have a care in the world. I feel so safe and secure on court. It definitely feels like I'm at a

different pace than anyone else. It's like it's my world, I'm in charge of it and I create whatever happens out there. If I want it to go slow, I can make it go slow. If I want it to go fast, I can make it go fast.

"I call it The Feeling. When I'm going right it's like a tingling. That's when everything is flowing, everything is working, every time you shoot you know its going to be two points. It's like there ain't nobody else there. Just me and this ball and this rim."

The only new element for Isiah Thomas in 1988-89 will be the pressure. He's got the good reputation and the good money. Now, he's got to find the good road up to the next level of the game. For himself and his team.

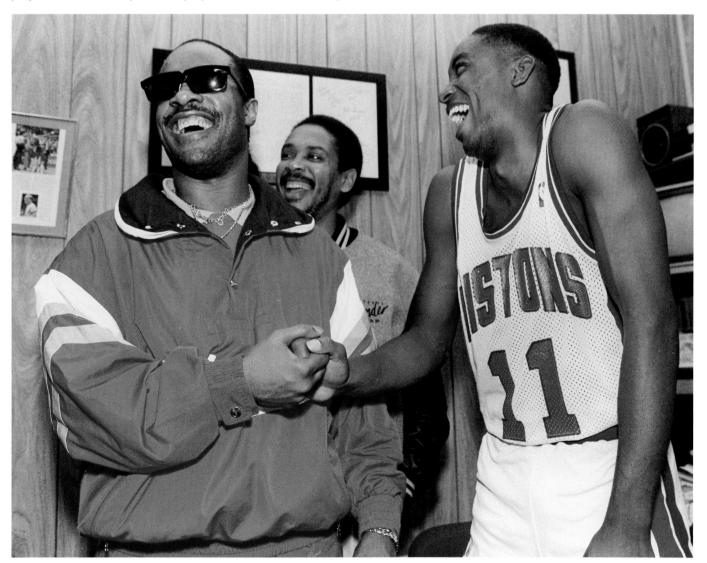

Stevie Wonder congratulates Isiah on the Pistons Eastern Conference championship.

The Pistons' bench did a lot of twisting and shouting during the '88 playoffs.

DADDY RICH'S SLEEK MACHINE

In Detroit, Chuck Daly is "Daddy Rich" because of his wardrobe of $600 suits. But around the NBA, when other coaches cast an envious eye on Daly's wealth, they're looking at the depth of the Pistons' lineup, which ran just about as rich as Daddy could ask in last year's playoffs. All of this brings to mind old sayings about one man's trash being another's treasure. Which, when you get right down to it, is the real reason Daddy is rich anyway.

Maybe it's not exactly right to speak of treasures such as Rick Mahorn and James Edwards and Dennis Rodman in the same breath as trash. But it is kind of interesting to look around the league this fall and see other coaches frantically sifting through their rubbish looking for rubies.

Nowhere is this process more pronounced than in Boston, where new Coach Jimmy Rodgers is an unabashed admirer of Daly. Rodgers recalls that both Rodman and John Salley weren't exactly impressive as rookies in 1986, yet Daly had the patience "to play them through their rough spots." In other words, he gave them the floor time to gain confidence and develop as legitimate big-time players. Rodgers has announced a similar course in developing the Celtics' much-maligned bench.

While Daddy just missed his first NBA title last year, his coaching job was so impressive that he qualifies as the league's 1988-89 trendsetter. Come to think of it, he won the award last year, too, for his sartorial displays. *USA Today* named him the league's best-dressed coach. In his heart of hearts, Daly might admit he takes immense pride in being the ultimate dandy in a profession of

"I learned that at the collegiate level," Daly says of using eight and nine players. "There's no such thing as rookies or freshmen. And with the length of the pro season, team depth is even more important. Its's a player's game, not a coach's game."

dandies. But the trend that really matters is his development of the nine-man rotation.

The caution here is not to speak of a nine-man rotation as if it's some sort of high-tech breakthrough. Just about everybody knows the deep bench has been a much-desired object among basketball coaches for years. It's just that so few of them have the juggling skills to really develop one, to pay it more than lip service. Besides, it's a risky business. The more complicated one makes the equation for a team chemistry, the less likely he'll get it to work.

Talk, however, is a by-product of success. And when you get a difficult old idea to work, as Daly did, people begin talking about it as if it's new. As you might expect, Daly is ready for this talk with an aw shucks. "I learned that at the collegiate level," he says of using eight and nine players. "There's no such thing as rookies or freshmen. And with the length of the pro season, team depth is even more important. It's a player's game, not a coach's game. The players are the ones who win. They've got to be on the floor to play. They've got to train perfectly to keep in shape."

Daly acknowledges that maintaining depth is as much a headache as is building it. "One of the problems for this year," he says, "is finding the minutes for Rodman. He's awfully good." Daly has used the forward as a second guard, which works fine defensively, but the problem there is that it changes the whole team offensively.

"Rodman was just renegotiated," the coach says. "He'll be happy. There isn't a player alive worth his salt who doesn't want more minutes, more shots. They come at me constantly asking for more."

That, as much as anything, indicates the open air around the team. He has created an atmosphere where players can actually breathe. "Chuck sees people, not Xs and Os," Isiah Thomas said last season. "When I'm out there on the court, I'm not his point guard. I'm Isiah. And there's certain things he lets me do because he knows it's me. Same

Daddy Rich and Zeke.

thing when Vinnie Johnson comes in. He's not X2, he's Vinnie. And when Bill Laimbeer comes in, he's not X3, he's Bill. I think that's the greatest gift Chuck has."

With that sensitivity, he mixes just the right amount of toughness. "I told them," Daly says, "at a team meeting [just before the opening of camp this October], 'Don't come to me in January saying you want more minutes and shots. Prove it now. We'll see what training camp brings."

The obvious question for this 58-year-old coach goes to his concerns about how he'll put it all together again for the coming season. "It's hard to project how a team is going to react, coming off that kind of year, as long as it was, as successful as it was," he says.

The team will move into its new home, The Palace of Auburn Hills, the ultimate basketball facility. Left behind is the Silverdome that altered every visitor's game. "It's a nice place to play," Daly says of The Palace, "but the kind of building where visiting teams like to play. We'll have to get used to that. We had a unique home-court advantage in the Silverdome. The lighting, the spacing, the vastness made it difficult to shoot. But we'll overcome the move to a new arena."

Thomas is amused by Daddy Rich's concern. "I look at the Palace probably a little different than the rest of the players," he says. "If I was gonna build an arena, this is how I would build it. For shooting, it's really good," he says and begins chuckling. "I don't think Larry Bird is gonna have too many off nights in The Palace.

"Our crowd has to be the difference. People can't come at the beginning of the second quarter and leave at the end of the third. We have no advantage if that happens."

More worrisome than the new home is the road, where the Pistons will spend much of the first few weeks of the season. "We'll have six or seven days to prepare for our first exhibition game," Daly says. "Then we'll be on the road for nine exhibition games. Then into our regular season, the first 12 out of 16 will be on the

Daly's light touch with players has taken him to the top.

Daly break dancing by the bench.

road. There's no way to put the frosting on that cake."

Thomas, however, cites the team's good road record during the playoffs last year and says that will carry through for 1988-89. "I look at it as kind of a plus for us," he says of the road schedule. "Everywhere we go, everyone is gonna want to kick our butts and beat us bad. The good thing is we're an experienced team. Other teams are not going to be quite together early in the year. Every game we played last year during the playoffs was like a fever-pitched atmosphere.

"The recall, the memory of those games will be fresh. We'll know how hard we have to play."

THE MACHINE

It's not too hard to hear the pride in Daly's voice when he discusses the team that came within seconds of defeating the Lakers for the title. "Our club is kind of a diverse club," he says. "There are no big post-up players. Dantley is a back-to-the-basket player at 6-5. I've never quite figured out how he does it."

Three years ago, Pistons management figured the team had reached a plateau after winning 46 games, 46 games, and 49 games over the three previous seasons. They looked at a front line of Kent Benson, Bill Laimbeer and Kelly Tripucka, Daly says. "We knew we needed to make a change."

That change was the acquisition of Dantley from Utah in a trade for Tripucka and Benson. "Dantley has worked out beautifully," Daly says. "His ability to get to the basket helps stop the transition game against us."

Asked if Dantley had expressed displeasure at being kept on the bench during the fourth quarter of Game Seven with the Lakers while the team made a comeback, Daly said, "There's no real fallout from

"And we can't forget Isiah's and Bill's leadership," Daly says of Thomas and Laimbeer. "They're the guys everybody else on the team relates to the most, talks to the most. Both are great competitors. And Joe Dumars is quietly the best defensive player, always taking on the toughest assignment every night. He could be a larger offensive factor, if we needed it."

that. When you go down by 15, you need to pressure and run. I don't really know if he was upset. I'm not too concerned. We almost

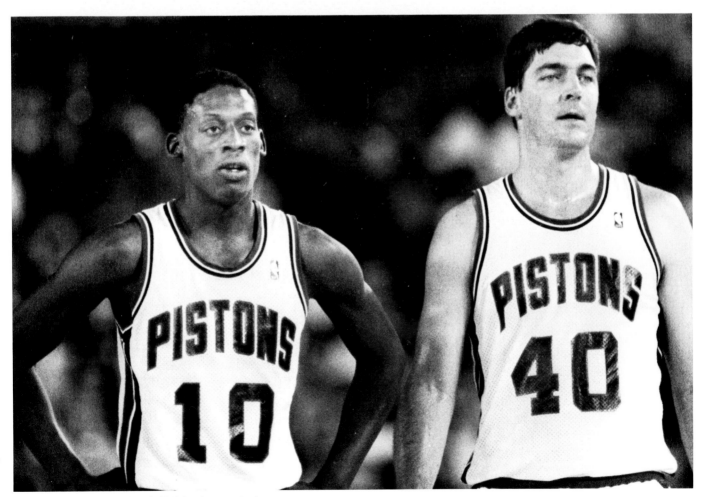

Finding room for the talent is Daly's pleasant task.

The Palace. (Photo by Allen Einstein)

accomplished what we set out to do."

If Dantley's offense puts the brakes on the transition games of other teams, Salley and Rodman have developed into Motown accelerators. "They give us the speed and the shot-blocking," the coach says. "Neither is oriented to the offense. They look to pass first. They think pass."

The pride in his voice rises another notch when he mentions "the resurgence of Rick Mahorn, which gave us another move up the ladder." Mahorn came from the Bullets in 1985 at a time when his career was thought to be on the downslide. He was considered a brute but not much of a player in Washington. But in Detroit, Mahorn has flourished after losing 30 pounds.

"I'd run through a wall if he told me," Mahorn says of Daly. "He helped me out with a new attitude."

There were times during the regular season last year when Mahorn might have been the best

player on the team, Daly says. But disc problems kept the big forward sidelined much of the playoffs. And he probably would have been relegated to backup center duty against Los Angeles as the Pistons tried to counter the Lakers' flexibility with more speed.

Mahorn had surgery in the offseason, and by October seemed to be fine. In preparation for the season, he was playing every day, Daly said.

Reserve center James Edwards helped out nicely during the playoffs with Mahorn's minutes limited by his back. And Daly expects him to provide more offense off the bench this season. Vinnie Johnson, however, remains a question. His age may mean limited playing time.

"And we can't forget Isiah's and Bill's leadership," Daly says of Thomas and Laimbeer. "They're the guys everybody else on the team relates to the most, talks to the most. Both are great competitors. And Joe Dumars is quietly the best defensive

player, always taking on the toughest assignment every night. He could be a larger offensive factor, if we needed it."

Reserve center William Bedford is reported to be returning from drug rehabilitation in excellent shape, and Daly says both draft picks, Fennis Dembo from Wyoming and Michael Williams of Baylor, have potential. "I just don't know where we'll find the time for them," he says.

A NEW CONTRACT

After finishing the playoffs without a contract, Daly signed a new three-year deal in the offseason. The smallest trace of an edge creeps into his voice when you mention his age (58) and ask how long he plans to keep at his crazy profession.

"At the end of this contract, I'll see how I feel physically," he says. "We have our own plane and that cuts down on the wear and tear of the

Mahorn is one of Daly's favorites.

Daly likes Laimbeer's competitiveness.

road. Maybe I'll coach another 10 to 15 years. I might become the oldest coach in the history of mankind."

Asked if age increases his disappointment over the close loss in the Finals, Daly says with a tightness, "I don't live in the past with basketball games. It was almost as if around the country, especially in the Detroit area, we won it, even though we didn't win it."

He already had 30 years of varied experience as a head coach in high school and college and as an assistant in the pros when he came to the Pistons in 1983. Even at Punxsutawney High in Pennsylvania, where he began his coaching career, he was a slick-dressing Daddy Rich.

Vic Bubas had one of the best college programs in the country at Duke in 1963, when he hired Daly as his freshman coach. As a Blue Devils assistant, Daly made three trips to the Final Four before taking the head coaching job at Boston College in

1969. Two years later he moved to Penn and won four Ivy League titles over the next six seasons.

He was preparing for a seventh season in 1977 when Billy Cunningham, the newly named coach of the Philadelphia 76ers, asked him to join the staff. "It was kind of interesting," he says. "I had not been involved in the pro game, as a player or a coach. Billy had not coached, but he had been a player and was very bright. It was a very good marriage, my coaching experience and his NBA background.

"I learned a lot about the handling of the players and what it took to win. The bench decorum in the pro game is entirely different."

He racked up a lot of good will in Philadelphia, staying with the 76ers through the 1980-81 season. ("Chuck Daly is a natural," Julius Erving once told a reporter.) With Philly's resurgence, Daly had numerous job offers. "I was at the point in my career

where I looked around and got choosy," he says. Suddenly all the coaching vacancies were filled, so in late 1981 he took a midseason job with the Cleveland Cavaliers, then owned by mercurial Ted Stepien. Daly was fired after three months with a 9-32 record.

That learning experience didn't taint his resume, however. The Pistons hired him in 1983, and the arrangement has been great for all concerned.

There was brief talk that he might return to Philadelphia when his talks with the Pistons dragged at the end of last season. But Daly really didn't consider going elsewhere.

"I've had a lot of fun coaching here," he says, "as much fun or more than anywhere I've been. We could go through some rough times. But we've got good people. We'll see what the season brings."

PISTONS PROFILES

WILLIAM BEDFORD

Position: Center
Height: 7'1"
Weight: 252 Pounds
College: Memphis State '87 (Criminal Justice Major)
High School: Melrose, Memphis, TN
Birthdate: 12/14/63
Birthplace: Memphis, TN
When Drafted: First Round (6th Overall) Phoenix, 1986
How Acquired: From Phoenix for the Pistons' Number-One Draft Pick in 1988,

Last Season: Played in just 38 games during his first season with the Pistons and averaged 2.7 points per game and 1.7 rebounds per contest...He admitted to a drug dependency problem on March 30 and was admitted to the Adult Substance Abuse Program in Van Nuys, California under the direction of Dr. Rex Fine...Did not rejoin the team for the remainder of the regular season or any of the playoffs...Rejoined the Pistons during the off-season and played in the Central Division Summer League and in the California Summer Pro League...

As A Pro: Acquired by the Pistons on June 21, 1987 from the Phoenix Suns for Detroit's number-one draft pick in the 1988 NBA draft...Had a very slow start with the Suns, then suffered torn knee ligaments and had arthroscopic surgery in October of 1986...Has played in just 88 regular-season games in his first two years in the league...Entered the NBA after his junior season...

As A Collegian: Named Third Team All-American by the Associated Press and was First Team All-Metro Conference in 1986...Finished second behind Keith Lee with 234 career blocked shots at Memphis State...In 1986, he led the Tigers in scoring (17.3), rebounding (8.5), fieldgoal percentage (.584) and blocked shots (86)...Enjoyed career highs of 30 points and 18 rebounds versus Middle Tennessee State in 1986...Sports Illustrated rated him the number one true center in the 1986 NBA College Draft...Memphis State qualified for the NCAA Tournament all three seasons he was there, including one trip to the Final Four...Memphis State was 85-17 during his three-year career...

Personal: Married just prior to the start of the 1987-88 Pistons season to the former Pamela Hicks...Born December 14, 1963 in Memphis, Tennessee...Has three sisters...At Memphis State, he majored in Criminal Justice and was a member of the Phi Beta Sigma Fraternity...Needs one year to complete his degree requirements..

NBA CAREER RECORD

TEAM-YR	GP	MINS	AVE	FGM	FGA	PCT	FTM	FTA	PCT	OFF	DEF	REBS	AVE.	AST	PF-DQ	STE	BLO	PTS.	AVE	HI
PHO.'87	50	979	19.6	142	358	.397	50	86	.581	79	167	246	4.9	57	125-1	18	37	334	6.7	17
DET.'88	38	298	7.8	44	101	.436	13	23	.565	27	38	65	1.7	4	47-0	8	17	101	2.7	14
TOTALS	88	1277	14.5	186	459	.405	63	109	.578	106	205	311	3.5	61	172-1	26	54	435	4.9	17

NBA HIGHS

		MINS		FGM	FGA		FTM	FTA		OFF	DEF	REBS		AST		STE	BLO	PTS.	
		34		6	16		6	8		6	8	12		3		3	4	17	

3-POINT FIELD GOALS: 1986-87, 0-1 (.000).

ADRIAN DANTLEY

Position: Forward
Height: 6'5"
Weight: 210 Pounds
College: Notre Dame (B.A. in Business) '77
High School: DeMatha, Hyattsville, MD
Birthdate: 02-28-56
Birthplace: Washington D.C.
When Drafted: First Round (6th Overall) Buffalo, 1976 As A Hardship Case
How Acquired: From Utah Along With Two Second-Round Draft Choices (1987 and 1990) In Exchange For Kelly Tripucka And Kent Benson, August 21, 1986
Pro Experience: Twelve Years
Nickname: A.D.
Married: Dinitri
Children: Cameron and Adria Kalani
Residence: Washington, D.C.

Last Season: For the second straight regular season, he led the Pistons in scoring...Although he topped the Pistons with his 20.0 points per game average, that represented his second lowest scoring average of his career...Moved into 11th place in the all time NBA scoring list, now having scored 21,058 through his first 12 NBA seasons...Scored his 20,000th point versus the Portland Trailblazers on December 8, 1987...Played in 69 games with the Pistons during the campaign, starting 50 of those contests...Missed 10 straight games during February due to a sprained right ankle, then came off the bench for 19 straight games...For the 12th straight season, he shot better than 50 percent from the field...For the second straight season, he was one of the few NBA players to score more FTs than FGs...Scored his Pistons' high of 45 points versus the Chicago Bulls on November 21...

As A Pro: Enters his 13th NBA season as the 11th leading scorer in NBA history...Should move into 10th place on the list during the 1988-89 season, surpassing Hal Greer (21,586)...Prior to joining the Pistons, he had recorded seven straight seasons of better than 26 points per game, before averaging 20.8 points per game in his first two seasons with the Pistons...He became a Detroit Piston on August 21, 1986, arriving from the Utah Jazz in exchange for Kelly Tripucka and Kent Benson...Has won two NBA scoring titles in 1980-81 and 1983-84...While his scoring average has dropped in his first two years with the Pistons, for the first time in his 12-year NBA career, he was a member of a team that reached the Conference Finals (1987 and 1988) and the NBA Finals (1988)...Among the all-time NBA field goal leaders, connecting on nearly 55 percent of his attempts during his career...Has played in six NBA All-Star Games, all with the Jazz...Named the NBA Rookie of the Year in 1976-77 while a member of the Buffalo Braves...He is now a member of his fifth NBA club...Signed a contract extension with the Pistons prior to the start of the 1987-88 season...Traded three times in little more than two years before playing seven seasons with the Jazz...Tied Wilt Chamberlain's NBA record by sinking 28 (of 29) free throws versus Houston at Las Vegas on January 4, 1984...1983-84 NBA Comeback Player of the Year...

As A Collegian: Left Notre Dame under the old "hardship rule" after junior season, his second All-American year...Drafted by the Buffalo Braves (now the Los Angeles Clippers)...Led USA Gold Medal Olympic Team in scoring in 1976 at Montreal...Had ND averages of 18.3 points and 9.1 rebounds as a freshman, 30.4 and 10.2 as a sophomore and 28.6 and 10.1 as a junior...

Personal: Returned to Notre Dame and received his degree in Economics...Married to the former Dinitri McGhee, who gave birth to the couple's second child on July 21, 1988 (Adria Kalani)...Runs annual basketball camps in both Salt Lake City and Washington, D.C....Has done national ads for Canon AE 1...

NBA CAREER RECORD

TEAM-YR	GP	MINS	AVE.	FGM	FGA	PCT.	FTM	FTA	PCT.	OFF	DEF	REBS	AVE.	AST	PF-DQ	STE	BLO	PTS	AVE.
BUF.'77	77	2816	36.5	544	1046	.520	476	582	.818	251	336	587	7.6	144	215-2	91	15	1564	20.3
IND.'78	79	2933	37.1	578	1128	.512	541	680	.796	265	355	620	7.8	253	233-2	118	24	1697	21.5
L.A.'79	60	1775	19.5	374	733	.510	292	342	.854	131	211	342	5.7	138	162-0	63	12	1040	17.3
UTAH'80	68	2674	39.3	730	1267	.576	443	526	.842	183	333	516	7.6	191	211-2	96	14	1903	28.0
UTAH'81	80	3417	42.7	909	1627	.559	632	784	.806	192	317	509	6.4	322	245-1	109	18	2452	30.7
UTAH'82	81	3222	39.7	904	1586	.570	648	818	.792	231	283	514	6.3	324	252-1	95	14	2457	30.3
UTAH'83	22	887	40.3	233	402	.580	210	248	.847	58	82	140	6.4	105	62-2	20	0	676	30.7
UTAH'84	79	2984	37.7	802	1438	.558	813	946	.859	179	269	448	5.7	310	201-0	61	4	2418	30.6
UTAH'85	55	1971	35.8	512	964	.531	438	545	.804	148	175	323	5.9	186	133-0	57	8	1462	26.6
UTAH'86	76	2744	36.1	818	1453	.563	630	796	.791	178	217	395	5.2	264	206-2	64	4	2267	29.8
DET.'87	81	2736	33.7	601	1126	.534	539	664	.811	104	228	332	4.1	162	193-1	63	7	1742	21.5
DET.'88	69	2144	31.1	444	863	.514	492	572	.860	84	143	227	3.3	171	144-0	39	10	1380	20.0
TOTALS	70	2496	36.6	7449	13633	.546	6154	7503	.820	2004	2949	4953	6.0	2570	2257-13	876	130	21058	25.5

NBA HIGHS

51		24	36	28	31			19	11	7	3	55

3-POINT FIELD GOALS: 1979-80, 0-2; 1980-81, 2-7 (.286); 1981-82, 1-3 (.333); 1983-84, 1-4 (.250); 1985-86, 1-11 (.091); 1986-87, 1-6 (.167); 1987-88, 0-2 (.000). CAREER: 6-35 (.171)

NBA PLAYOFF RECORD

TEAM-YR	GP	MIN	AVE.	FGM	FGA	PCT.	FTM	FTA	PCT.	OFF	DEF	REB	AVE.	AST	PF-DQ	ST	BL	PTS.	AVE.
L.A.'78	3	104	34.6	30	35	.571	11	17	.647	9	16	25	8.3	11	9-0	5	3	51	17.0
L.A.'79	8	236	29.5	50	89	.562	41	52	.788	10	23	33	4.1	11	24-0	6	1	141	17.5
UT.'84	11	454	41.2	117	232	.504	120	139	.863	37	46	83	7.5	46	30-0	10	1	352	32.2
UT.'85	10	398	39.8	79	151	.523	95	122	.779	25	50	75	7.5	20	39-1	16	0	253	15.3
DET.'87	15	500	33.3	111	206	.539	86	111	.775	29	39	68	4.5	35	36-0	13	0	308	20.5
DET.'88	23	804	35.0	153	292	.524	140	178	.787	37	70	107	4.6	46	50-0	19	1	446	19.4
TOTALS	70	2496	35.6	530	1005	.527	493	619	.796	147	244	391	5.6	169	188-1	69	6	1553	22.2

3-POINT FIELD GOALS: 1984-85, 0-1 (.000); 1987-88, 0-1 (.000). CAREER: 0-2 (.000).

NBA ALL-STAR RECORD

TEAM-YR	GP	MIN	FGM	FGA	PCT.	FTM	FTA	PCT.	OFF	DEF	REB	AST	PF-DQ	ST	BL	PTS	AVE.
UTAH'80	1	30	15	8	.533	8	7	.875	4	1	5	2	1-0	2	0	23	23.0
UTAH'81	1	21	9	3	.333	2	2	1.000	2	3	5	0	1-0	1	0	8	8.0
UTAH'82	1	21	8	6	.750	1	0	.000	1	1	2	0	2-0	0	0	12	12.0
UTAH'84	1	18	8	1	.125	0	0	.000	0	2	2	1	4-0	1	0	2	2.0
UTAH'85	1	23	6	2	.333	6	6	1.000	0	2	2	1	4-0	1	0	10	10.0
UTAH'86	1	17	8	3	.375	2	2	1.000	1	6	7	3	1-0	1	0	8	8.0
TOTALS	6	130	54	23	.426	19	17	.895	8	15	23	7	13-0	6	0	63	10.5

JOE DUMARS

Position: Guard
Height: 6'3"
Weight: 195 Pounds
College: McNeese State '85 (Business Management Major)
High School: Natchitoches-Central (LA)
Birthdate: 5/24/63
Birthplace: Natchitoches, LA
When Drafted: First Round (18th Overall) Detroit, 1985
How Acquired: College Draft
Pro Experience: Three Years
Marital Status: Single
Residence: Natchitoches, LA

Last Season: Had his best season as a pro, finishing by averaging 14.1 points per game...For the third straight season, he increased his scoring average...Averaged 9.4 points per game as a rookie and 11.8 points per game in his second season...Over the last three regular seasons, with him as a starter, the Pistons are 129-71 (64-percent winning ratio)...Joined Laimbeer as the only Pistons to start every game during the season...Had a very consistent campaign, scoring better than double figures in 67 of 82 games...Had his best FT shooting campaign of his career, connecting on better than 81 percent of his attempts...

As A Pro: After being inserted into the starting lineup during the middle of his rookie season, he has remained the team's starting off-guard since ..Named to the NBA All-Rookie First Team in 1985-86...Has missed just three games in his NBA career...Has recorded his top two scoring efforts of his career during the Eastern Conference Finals in each of the last two post seasons...Scored 35 points versus Boston in Game 7 of the 1987 Eastern Conference Finals and had 29 points during the 1988 Eastern Conference Finals...His regular-season career high is 25 points...

As A Collegian: Four-time All-Southland Conference selection...Southland Conference leading scorer in 1982, 1984 and 1985...Ranked sixth in the nation in scoring in 1984, averaging 26.4 points per game...All-time McNeese State scoring leader...Holds virtually every McNeese State scoring record...Finished his collegiate career with a 22.3 scoring average...Played in the 1984 U.S. Olympic Trials...Second-leading All-time Southland Conference scoring leader behind Dwight Lamar...Ranked among the nation's top 15 all-time leading scorers...

Personal: Older brother David played pro football in the now defunct United States Football League...Comes from a football-oriented family...Has five brothers and one sister...In the 1984-85 McNeese State Media Guide, he listed his favorite athlete as the Pistons' Isiah Thomas...

NBA CAREER RECORD

TEAM-YR	GP	MIN	AVE.	FGM	FGA	PCT.	FTM	FTA	PCT.	OFF	DEF	REBS	AVE.	AST	PF-DQ	ST	BL	PTS.	AVE.	HI
DET.'86	82	1957	23.8	287	597	.481	190	238	.798	60	59	119	1.4	390	200-1	66	11	769	9.4	22
DET.'87	79	2439	30.8	369	749	.493	184	246	.748	50	117	167	2.1	352	194-1	83	5	931	11.8	24
DET.'88	82	2732	33.3	453	960	.472	251	308	.815	63	137	200	2.4	387	155-1	87	15	1161	14.1	25
TOTALS	243	7128	29.3	1109	2306	.481	625	792	.789	173	313	486	2.0	1129	549-3	236	31	2861	11.8	25

NBA HIGHS

53	11	24			10	12		5	6	8			14		5	2	25		

3-POINT FIELD GOALS: 1985-86, 5-16 (.313); 1986-87, 9-22 (.409); 1987-88, 4-19 (.210).
CAREER: 14-38 (.368)

NBA PLAYOFF RECORD

TEAM-YR	GP	MIN	AVE.	FGM	FGA	PCT.	FTM	FTA	PCT.	OFF	DEF	REB	AVE.	AST	PF-DQ	ST	BL	PTS	AVE.	HI
DET.'86	4	147	36.8	25	41	.610	10	15	.667	6	7	13	3.3	25	16-0	4	0	60	15.0	18
DET.'87	15	473	31.5	78	145	.538	32	41	.780	8	11	19	1.3	72	26-0	12	1	190	12.7	35
DET.'88	23	804	35.0	113	247	.457	56	63	.889	18	32	50	2.2	112	50-1	13	2	284	12.3	29
TOTALS	42	1424	33.9	216	433	.499	98	119	.823	32	50	82	1.9	209	92-1	29	3	534	12.7	35

3-POINT FIELD GOALS: 1986-87, 2-3 (.667); 1987-88, 2-6 (.333).
CAREER: 4-9 (.444).

JAMES EDWARDS

Position: Center
Height: 7'1"
Weight: 263 Pounds
College: Washington, '77
High School: Roosevelt, Seattle, WA
Birthdate: 11/22/55
Birthplace: Seattle, WA
When Drafted: Third Round (46th pick) Los Angeles, 1977
How Acquired: From Phoenix Suns in exchange for Ron Moore and Detroit's Second-Round Draft Choice in 1991
Pro Experience: 11 Years
Marital Status: Single
Residence: Phoenix, AZ

Last Season: Acquired from the Phoenix Suns on February 24 in exchange for Ron Moore and a second round draft choice...Made key contributions during the playoffs for the Pistons...Played in 26 regular-season games with the Pistons, starting two of those contests...With the Pistons, he averaged 5.4 points and 3.0 rebounds per game...In 43 games with the Suns, he averaged 15.5 points and 7.8 rebounds per game.

As A Pro: Was a member of the Cleveland Cavaliers in 1981-82 when Chuck Daly was the coach...Ironically, at that time, Edwards was the starting center, while Bill Laimbeer was the backup...Has averaged better than double figures in each of his NBA seasons and has a career scoring average of 15.0 points per game...Eclipsed the 10,000 career point total during the 1987-88 campaign...Originally drafted by the Los Angeles Lakers in the third round of the 1977 NBA Draft.

As A Collegian: An All-Pac 8 performer at the University of Washington, finished as the school's second-leading all-time scorer with 1,548 points...Scored a collegiate high of 37 points in his junior year against Oregon State...Averaged 20.9 points and 10.4 rebounds as a senior.

Personal: Makes his year-round home in Phoenix...Became heavily involved with several charities while in Phoenix and expects to do the same here in Detroit.

NBA CAREER RECORD

TEAM-YR	GP	MINS	FGM	FGA	PCT.	FTM	FTA	PCT.	OFF	DEF	REBS	AVE.	AST	PF-DQ	STE	BLO	PTS.	AVE.
LA-IN.'78	83	2405	495	1093	.453	272	421	.646	197	418	615	7.4	85	322-12	53	78	1262	15.2
IND.'79	82	2546	534	1065	.501	298	441	.676	179	514	693	8.5	92	363-16	60	109	1366	16.7
IND.'80	82	2314	528	1032	.512	231	339	.681	179	399	578	7.0	127	324-12	55	104	1287	15.7
IND.'81	81	2375	511	1004	.509	244	347	.703	191	380	571	7.0	212	304-7	32	128	1266	15.6
CLV.'82	77	2539	528	1033	.511	232	339	.684	189	392	581	7.5	123	347-17	24	117	1288	16.7
CL-PH.'83	31	667	128	263	.487	69	108	.639	56	99	155	5.0	40	110-5	12	19	325	10.5
PHO.'84	72	1897	438	817	.536	183	254	.720	108	240	348	4.8	184	254-3	23	30	1059	14.7
PHO.'85	70	1787	384	766	.501	276	370	.746	95	292	387	5.5	153	237-5	26	52	1044	14.9
PHO.'86	52	1314	318	587	.542	212	302	.702	79	222	301	5.8	74	200-5	23	29	848	16.3
PHO.'87	14	304	57	110	.518	54	70	.771	20	40	60	4.3	19	42-1	6	7	168	12.0
TOTALS	713	19853	4223	8413	.502	2281	3312	.689	1412	3289	4701	6.6	1109	2719-85	330	710	10727	15.0

NBA HIGHS

TEAM-YR	GP	MINS	FGM	FGA	PCT.	FTM	FTA	PCT.	OFF	DEF	REBS	AVE.	AST	PF-DQ	STE	BLO	PTS.	AVE.
	16	29	18	19							18		7			7	39	

3-POINT FIELD GOALS: 1979-80, 0-1 (.000); 1980-81, 0-3 (.000); 1981-82, 0-4 (.000); 1983-84, 0-1 (.000); 1984-85, 0-3 (.000); 1987-88, 0-1 (.000). CAREER: 0-13 (.000).

NBA PLAYOFF RECORD

TEAM-YR	GP	MIN	AVE.	FGM	FGA	PCT.	FTM	FTA	PCT.	OFF	DEF.	REB	AVE.	AST	PF-DQ	ST	BL	PTS.	AVE.
IND.'81	2	56	28.0	7	24	.292	0	0	.000	4	10	14	7.0	5	8-0	1	1	14	7.0
PHO.'83	3	7	18.0	11	26	.423	6	6	1.000	6	12	18	6.0	4	7-0	1	1	28	9.3
PHO.'84	17	463	27.2	93	189	.492	48	68	.706	22	69	91	5.3	27	62-3	4	11	234	13.8
DET.'88	22	308	14.0	56	110	.509	27	41	.659	23	45	68	3.1	11	55-0	2	10	139	6.3
TOTALS	44	881	20.0	167	349	.478	81	115	.704	55	136	191	4.3	47	132-3	8	23	415	9.4

3-POINT FIELD GOALS: 1987-88, 0-1 (.000).

VINNIE JOHNSON

Position: Guard
Height: 6'2"
Weight: 200 Pounds
College: Baylor '79 (Education Major)
High School: Brooklyn (NY) F.D. Roosevelt
Birthdate: 9/1/56
Birthplace: Brooklyn, NY
When Drafted: First Round (7th Overall) Seattle, 1979
How Acquired: In Exchange for Greg Kelser, Nov. 21, 1981
Pro Experience: Nine Years
Nickname: V.J.
Marital Status: Single
Residence: Southfield, MI

Last Season: Finished the season by averaging 12.2 points per game, which represented his lowest scoring output in his six full seasons with the Pistons...Started the season by averaging 18 points per game in the first 15 games before steadily dropping...His 12.2 scoring average dropped after he enjoyed one of his best seasons as a pro in the previous year (15.7 points per game)...His 44 percent FG shooting was his second lowest of his career...Again was Coach Chuck Daly's first guard off the bench in the team's three-guard rotation..

As A Pro: Had probably his best season as a pro during the 1986-87 when he was runner-up in the balloting for the NBA's Sixth Man Award...For most of the past three seasons, he has joined Dumars and Thomas in Coach Chuck Daly's three-guard rotation...Acquired by the Pistons on November 21, 1981 from the Seattle Supersonics in exchange for Gregory Kelser...Had one strong season in Seattle in 1980-81 when he started 63 games as Gus Williams sat the year out...Was the NBA's top offensive rebounder in that season, averaging 2.4 offensive boards per game.

As A Collegian: Played at Baylor after transferring from McLennon Junior College in Waco, Texas after his sophomore season...Was the Southwest Conference leading scorer his senior season, averaging 25.2 points per game...During his two-year stay at Baylor, he was named to the Associated Press' All-American Second Team twice and became the school's second all-time leading scorer.

Personal: Vinnie is the middle child of four brothers and three sisters...His younger brother, Eric, is in his senior season at Nebraska after transferring out of Baylor...Makes his year-round home in Southfield.

NBA CAREER RECORD

TEAM-YR	GP	MINS	AVE.	FGM	FGA	PCT.	FTM	FTA	PCT.	OFF	DEF	REBS	AVE.	AST	PF-DQ	STE	BLO	PTS.	AVE.	HI
SEA.'80	38	325	8.5	45	115	.391	31	39	.795	19	36	55	1.4	54	40-0	19	4	121	3.2	12
SEA.'81	81	2311	28.5	419	785	.534	214	270	.793	193	173	366	4.5	341	198-0	78	20	1053	13.0	31
SE-D'82	74	1295	17.5	217	444	.489	107	142	.754	82	77	159	2.1	171	101-0	56	25	544	7.4	20
DET.'83	82	2511	30.6	520	1013	.513	245	315	.778	167	186	353	4.3	301	263-2	93	49	1296	15.8	33
DET.'84	82	1909	23.2	426	901	.473	207	275	.753	130	107	237	2.9	271	196-1	44	19	1063	13.0	28
DET.'85	82	2093	25.5	428	942	.454	190	247	.769	134	118	252	3.1	325	205-2	71	20	1051	12.8	28
DET.'86	79	1978	25.0	465	996	.467	165	214	.771	119	107	226	2.9	269	180-2	80	23	1097	13.9	35
DET.'87	78	2166	27.7	533	1154	.462	158	201	.786	123	134	257	3.3	300	159-0	92	16	1228	15.7	30
DET.'88	82	1935	23.6	425	959	.443	147	217	.677	90	141	231	2.8	267	164-0	58	18	1002	12.2	28
TOTALS	678	16523	24.4	3478	7309	.475	1472	1920	.767	1057	1079	2136	3.1	2299	1506-7	591	194	8455	12.5	38

NBA HIGHS

46	16	25	11	12	8	6	12	15		5	3	35	

3-POINT FIELD GOALS: 1979-80, 0-1 (.000); 1980-81, 1-5 (.200); 1981-82, 3-12 (.250); 1982-83, 11-40 (.275); 1983-84, 4-19 (.211); 1984-85, 5-27 (.185); 1985-86, 2-14 (.143); 1986-87, 4-14 (.286); 1987-88, 5-24 (.208).
CAREER: 35-156 (.224).

NBA PLAYOFF RECORD

TEAM-YR	GP	MIN	AVE.	FGM	FGA	PCT.	FTM	FTA	PCT.	OFF	DEF	REB	AVE.	AST	PF-DQ	ST	BL	PTS.	AVE.
SEA.'80	5	12	2.4	1	3	.333	0	0	.—	0	2	2	0.4	2	1-0	1	0	2	0.4
DET.'84	5	132	26.4	17	46	.370	17	19	.895	5	9	14	2.8	12	9-0	1	1	51	10.2
DET.'85	9	235	26.1	53	103	.515	22	28	.786	15	12	27	3.0	29	24-0	6	1	128	14.2
DET.'86	4	85	21.3	22	49	.449	7	13	.538	8	9	17	4.3	11	9-0	3	0	51	12.8
DET.'87	15	388	25.9	95	207	.459	31	36	.861	20	24	44	2.9	62	33-0	9	4	221	14.7
DET.'88	23	477	20.7	101	239	.423	33	50	.660	35	40	75	3.3	43	48-0	17	4	236	10.3
TOTALS	61	1329	21.8	289	647	.447	110	146	.753	83	96	179	2.9	159	124-0	37	10	689	11.3

3-POINT FIELD GOALS: 1984, 0-1 (.000); 1984-85, 0-3 (.000); 1985-86, 0-1 (.000); 1986-87, 0-2 (.000); 1987-88, 1-7 (.142).
CAREER: 1-14 (.071).

BILL LAIMBEER

Position: Center
Height: 6'11"
Weight: 245 Pounds
College: Notre Dame (Degree in Economics)
High School: Palos Verdes, CA:
Birthdate: 5/19/57
Birthplace: Boston, MA
When Drafted: Third Round (65th Overall) Cleveland, 1979
How Acquired: From Cleveland with Kenny Carr for Phil Hubbard, Paul Mokeski, 1982 First Round Draft Choice, 1982 Second Round Draft Choice
Pro Experience: Eight Years
Nickname: Lambs
Married: Chris (1979)
Children: Eric William and Keriann
Residence: Orchard Lake, MI

Last Season: Continued his Iron Man streak by playing in all 82 regular-season games...Has now played in 646 straight regular-season games, while starting 522 straight, both the league's current longest streaks...His 10.1 rebounds per game represented his lowest average since joining the Pistons...But, he had plenty of help on the boards from both Rick Mahorn and Dennis Rodman, who averaged better than 8 rebounds per game each...Completed his 6th straight full season with the Pistons...Among the league leaders in FT percentage connecting on .874 from the charity stripe...Was over the 90 percent mark for much of the season...Shot a career low .493 from the field...For the sixth straight season, he logged more than 2,800 minutes...

As A Pro: Needs to play in just 61 straight games and he will move into 3rd place on the NBA all-time consecutive games played list...Has played in 646 straight and with 61 straight games played will surpass Dolph Schayes (706 straight games played)...Came to the Pistons from Cleveland along with Kenny Carr in a deal that was made 9 minutes prior to the NBA trading deadline on Feb. 16, 1982...Started his first game with the Pistons and every one since...After not scoring 1,000 points in either of his first two NBA seasons, he's now surpassed 1,000 points in each of his last six seasons...Spent the 1979-80 in Italy (22 points per game) after being drafted by Cleveland in the third round of the 1979 NBA draft...Has been named to the NBA All-Star Team four times...Won the NBA rebounding title in 1985-86 when he averaged a career best 13.1 rebounds per game...

As A Collegian: College teammate of former Piston Kelly Tripucka when the two were at Notre Dame...Made one appearance in the Final Four...As a senior at Notre Dame, his team was eliminated by eventual NCAA Champion Michigan State...

Personal: High School All-American and two-time All-State pick in California...Played baseball and football in high school...In golf, has a one handicap and was the winner of the Cleveland Chapter of the NFL Alumni Association Golf Outing in 1982...Has organized the Bill Laimbeer/Isiah Thomas 7-Eleven Muscular Dystrophy Golf Tournament each of the last five summers...Last summer, the event raised nearly $50,000 for MDA...Would love to play tournament golf when his basketball playing days are complete...In June, 1984, he signed a contract that will keep him in Detroit through the 1990 season...He and his wife Chris are the parents of two children, Eric and Keriann.

NBA CAREER RECORD

TEAM-YR	GP	MINS	AVE.	FGM	FGA	PCT.	FTM	FTA	PCT.	OFF	DEF	REBS	AVE.	AST	PF-DQ	STE	BLO	PTS.	AVE.	HI
CLE.'81	81	2460	30.3	337	670	.503	117	153	.765	266	427	693	8.6	216	332-1	456	78	791	9.8	26
CL-D'82	80	1829	22.8	265	36	.494	184	232	.793	234	383	617	7.7	100	296-5	39	64	718	9.0	30
DET.'83	82	2871	35.0	436	877	.497	245	310	.790	282	711	993	12.1	263	320-9	51	118	1119	13.6	30
DET.'84	82	2864	35.0	553	1044	.530	316	365	.866	329	674	1003	12.2	149	273-4	49	84	1422	17.3	33
DET.'85	82	2892	35.2	595	1177	.506	244	306	.797	295	718	1013	12.4	154	308-4	69	71	1438	17.5	35
DET.'86	82	2891	35.2	545	1107	.492	266	319	.834	305	770	1075	13.1	146	291-4	59	65	1360	16.6	29
DET.'87	82	2854	34.8	506	1010	.501	245	274	.894	243	712	955	11.6	151	283-4	72	69	1263	15.4	30
DET.'88	82	2897	35.3	455	923	.493	187	214	.874	165	667	832	10.1	199	284-6	66	78	1110	13.5	30
TOTALS	653	21558	33.0	3692	7344	.503	1804	2173	.830	2119	5062	7181	11.0	1378	2388-50	460	627	9221	14.1	35

NBA HIGHS

	51		16	27		12	13		12	20	24		11			5	6	35	

3-POINT FIELD GOALS: 1980-81, 0-0 (.—); 1981-82, 4-13 (.308); 1982-83, 2-13 (.154); 1983-84, 0-11 (.000); 1984-85, 4-18 (.222); 1985-86, 4-14 (.286); 1986-87, 6-21 (.286); 1987-88, 13-39 (.333). CAREER: 33-129 (.255).

NBA PLAYOFF RECORD

TEAM-YR	GP	MINS	AVE.	FGM	FGA	PCT.	FTM	FTA	PCT.	OFF	DEF	REB	AVE.	AST	PF-DQ	ST	BL	PTS	AVE.	HI
DET.'84	5	165	33.0	29	51	.569	18	20	.900	14	48	62	12.4	12	23-2	4	3	76	15.2	31
DET.'85	9	325	36.1	48	107	.449	36	51	.706	36	60	96	10.7	15	32-1	7	7	132	14.7	27
DET.'86	4	168	42.0	34	68	.500	21	23	.913	20	36	56	14.0	1	19-1	2	3	90	22.5	27
DET.'87	15	543	36.2	84	163	.515	15	24	.625	30	126	156	10.4	37	53-2	15	12	184	12.3	20
DET.'88	23	779	33.9	114	250	.456	40	45	.889	43	178	221	9.6	44	77-2	18	19	273	11.9	29
TOTALS	56	1980	35.3	309	639	.483	130	163	.797	143	448	591	10.5	109	204-8	46	44	755	13.4	31

3-POINT FIELD GOALS: 1984-85, 0-2 (.000); 1985-86, 1-1 (1.000); 1986-87, 1-5 (.200); 1987-88, 5- 17 (.294). CAREER: 7-25 (.280).

NBA ALL-STAR RECORD

TEAM-YR	GP	MINS	AVE.	FGM	FGA	PCT.	FTM	FTA	PCT.	OFF	DEF	REB	AVE.	AST	PF-DQ	ST	BL	PTS	AVE.
DET.'83	1	6	6.0	1	1	1.000	0	0	.—	1	0	1	1.0	0	1-0	0	0	2	2.0
DET.'84	1	17	17.0	6	8	.750	1	1	1.000	1	4	5	5.0	0	3-0	1	2	13	13.0
DET.'85	1	11	11.0	2	4	.500	1	2	.500	1	2	3	3.0	1	1-0	0	0	5	5.0
DET.'87	1	11	11.0	4	7	.571	0	0	.—	0	2	2	2.0	1	1-2	1	0	8	8.0
TOTALS	4	45	11.3	13	20	.650	2	3	.667	3	8	11	2.8	2	7-0	2	2	28	7.0

RICK MAHORN

Position: Forward/Center
Height: 6'10"
Weight: 255 Pounds
College: Hampton Institute '80 (Business Administration Degree)
High School: Weaver (CT)
Birthdate: 09-21-58
Birthplace: Hartford, CT
When Drafted: Second Round By Washington, 1980
How Acquired: From Washington With Mike Gibson In Exchange for Dan Roundfield, June 17, 1985
Pro Experience: Eight Years
Marital Status: Single
Residence: Camp Springs, MD

Last Season: Had his finest regular-season as a pro when he averaged 10.7 points and 8.4 rebounds per game while setting a club record with .574 field-goal shooting...However, he was seriously hampered during the playoffs due to a lower back strain and saw very limited playing time...During the off-season he had a disc in his lower back removed to alleviate the pain...Missed 15 games during the 1987-88 campaign due to his lower back problems...Had never shot better than .507 from the field before shooting .574 last season...Scored a career high of 34 points versus the New Jersey Nets on February 26...Played an average of 29.3 minutes last season compared to his first two years with the club when he played an average of just 19.0 minutes per game...Had probably his best overall game as a pro versus Portland on December 8 when he scored 20 points and grabbed 20 rebounds...

As A Pro: Began his career with the Washington Bullets as a back-up to all-time Bullets great Wes Unseld, that club's current head coach...Was Washington's starting center for three seasons...Was acquired by the Pistons on June 17, 1985 in exchange for Dan Roundfield and Mike Gibson...The first small college player (Hampton Institute) taken the 1980 NBA draft (35th overall)...After not shooting better than 68 percent from the free-throw line in any of his first six seasons, he has now shot better than 75 percent from the charity stripe in each of his last two campaigns.

As A Collegian: A three-time NAIA All-American at Hampton Institute...The leading rebounder (15.8) and fifth leading scorer (27.6) in NCAA Division II during his senior year...Holds 18 Hampton school records...Played in four post-season All-Star Games and was only the third small college player ever to be invited to the Aloha Classic.

Personal: Active in numerous charities...Was an excellent high school football player who had more scholarship offers in that sport than basketball...Earned his Bachelor's Degree in Business while at Hampton.

NBA CAREER RECORD

TEAM-YR	GP	MIN.	AVE.	FGM	FGA	PCT.	FTM	FTA	PCT.	OFF	DEF	REBS	AVE.	AST	PF-DQ	STE	BLO	PTS.	AVE.
WAS.'81	52	696	11.4	111	219	.507	27	40	.675	67	148	215	4.1	25	134-3	21	44	249	4.8
WAS.'82	80	2664	33.3	414	816	.507	148	234	.633	149	555	704	8.8	150	349-12	57	138	976	12.2
WAS.'83	82	3023	36.9	376	768	.490	146	254	.575	71	608	779	9.5	115	335-13	86	148	898	11.0
WAS.'84	82	2701	32.9	307	605	.507	125	192	.651	169	569	738	9.0	131	358-14	62	123	739	9.0
WAS.'85	77	2072	26.9	206	413	.499	71	104	.683	150	458	608	7.9	121	308-11	59	104	483	6.3
DET.'86	80	1442	18.0	157	345	.455	81	119	.681	121	291	412	5.2	64	261-4	40	61	395	4.9
DET.'87	63	1278	20.3	144	322	.447	96	117	.829	93	282	375	5.9	38	221-4	32	50	384	6.1
DET.'88	67	1978	29.3	276	481	.574	164	217	.756	159	406	565	8.4	60	262-4	43	42	717	10.7
TOTALS	583	15839	27.2	1991	3969	.502	858	1277	.672	1079	3317	4396	7.5	704	2206-65	400	710	4841	8.3

NBA HIGHS

			12	23		14	15				20		7		5	8	34	

3-POINT FIELD GOALS: 1981-82, 0-3 (.000); 1982-83, 0-3 (.000); 1985-86, 0-1 (.000); 1987-88, 1-2 (.500); CAREER: 1-9 (.111).

NBA PLAYOFF RECORD

TEAM-YR	GP	MIN	AVE.	FGM	FGA	PCT.	FTM	FTA	PCT.	OFF	DEF	REB	AVE.	AST	PF-DQ	ST	BL	PTS	AVE.
WAS.'82	7	242	34.6	32	73	.438	10	14	.714	14	47	61	8.7	13	30-1	0	10	5	10.6
WAS.'84	4	154	38.5	15	25	.600	8	10	.800	7	36	43	10.8	7	20-0	1	6	38	9.5
WAS.'85	4	41	10.3	4	8	.500	4	4	1.000	2	5	7	1.8	0	9-0	0	3	12	3.0
DET.'86	4	61	15.3	5	13	.385	2	2	1.000	3	9	12	3.0	0	14-0	1	0	12	3.0
DET.'87	15	483	32.2	59	109	.541	28	35	.800	42	100	142	9.5	5	60-1	6	11	146	9.7
DET.'88	23	409	17.8	31	90	.344	13	19	.684	19	70	89	3.9	13	64-2	5	10	75	3.3
TOTALS	57	1390	24.4	146	318	.459	65	84	.774	87	267	354	6.2	38	197-4	13	23	35	35.7

3-POINTS FIELD GOALS: 1983-84, 0-1, (.000).

DENNIS RODMAN

Position: Forward
Height: 6'8"
Weight: 210 Pounds
College: Southeastern Oklahoma State '86
High School: South Oak Cliff HS (TX)
Birthdate: 05/13/61
Birthplace: Dallas, TX
When Drafted: Second Round (27th Overall) Detroit, 1986
How Acquired: College Draft
Pro Experience: Two Years
Nickname: Worm
Marital Status: Single
Residence: Dallas, TX

Last Season: Had an outstanding second season with the Pistons, nearly doubling both his rebounding and scoring averages from his rookie campaign...Finished his second season with averages of 11.6 points and 8.7 rebounds per game...Replaced Dantley in the starting lineup during mid-season for a stretch of 29 games...In his first 26 games as a starter, he averaged 16.0 points and 10.8 rebounds per game...During his first 24 games as a starter, the Pistons were 20-4...Among the league leaders in offensive rebounding and was one of the few NBA players to grab more than 300 offensive boards in 1987-88...Shot 56 percent from the field, but just 54 percent from the free-throw line...Had his best game as a pro versus Portland on January 24 when he scored a career high of 30 points and grabbed 18 rebounds...

As A Pro: Entered the NBA from little-known Southeastern Oklahoma State and made an impact with the Pistons immediately...One of the NBA's most effective offensive rebounders, he also is a standout defensive player...Has been used at both forward positions, and in his second season saw more action at big guard...Has shot better than 54 percent from the field in each of his first two campaigns with the Pistons...While he has shot just 55 percent from the free-throw line during his first two campaigns in the NBA, he used this past off-season to work with a shooting instructor to improve his shooting form...For the third straight off- season, he played on the Pistons Summer League Team...Nicknamed Worm, he suddenly became a Pistons fan favorite during his first year with the club...

As A Collegian: First Team NAIA All-American for three consecutive seasons...Did not play high school basketball and stood only 5'11" after his senior year...After graduation from high school, he grew 7 inches...Played one semester at Cooke County Junior College before transferring...Had 24 points and 19 rebounds in his first collegiate game, then followed with 40 points in his second game...As a sophomore, he scored 42 points and grabbed 24 rebounds in the semi-finals of the District Nine playoffs...Scored a career high of 51 points against Bethany Nazarene in the playoffs...

Personal: His two sisters, Debra and Kim, were High School All- Americans and led South Oak Cliff to two state titles...Debra, 6'3", went on to Louisiana Tech, played on a national championship team and was a three-time All-American...Kim was an All-American at Stephen F. Austin...Needless to say, his two sisters influenced him tremendously...An outstanding pinball player...

NBA CAREER RECORD

TEAM-YR	GP	MINS	AVE.	FGM	FGA	PCT.	FTM	FTA	PCT.	OFF	DEF	REBS	AVE.	AST	PF-DQ	ST	BL	PTS.	AVE.	HI
DET.'87	77	1155	15.0	213	391	.545	74	126	.587	163	169	332	4.3	56	166-1	38	48	500	6.5	21
DET.'88	82	2147	26.2	398	709	.561	152	284	.535	318	397	715	8.7	110	273-5	75	45	953	11.6	30
TOTALS	159	3302	20.8	611	1100	.555	226	410	.551	481	566	1047	6.6	166	439-6	113	93	1453	9.1	30

NBA HIGHS

		42		13	17		8	11		10	13	19		5		4	4	30		

3-POINT FIELD GOALS: 1986-87, 0-1 (.000); 1987-88, 5-17 (.294).
CAREER: 5-18 (.278).

PLAYOFF RECORD

TEAM-YR	GP	MINS	AVE.	FGM	FGA	PCT.	FTM	FTA	PCT.	OFF	DEF	REBS	AVE.	AST	PF-DQ	ST	BL	PTS.	AVE.	HI
DET.'87	15	245	16.3	40	74	.541	18	32	.563	32	39	71	4.7	3	48-0	6	17	98	6.5	14
DET.'88	23	474	20.6	71	136	.522	22	54	.407	51	85	136	5.9	21	87-1	14	14	164	7.1	23
TOTALS	38	719	18.9	111	210	.528	40	86	.465	83	124	207	5.4	24	135-1	20	31	262	6.9	23

3-POINT FIELD GOALS: 1987-88, 0-2 (.000).

WALKER RUSSELL

Position: Guard
Height: 6'5"
Weight: 195 Pounds
College: Western Michigan University '82
High School: Central, Pontiac, MI
Birthdate: 11/26/60
Birthplace: Pontiac, MI
When Drafted: Fourth Round (78th Overall) Detroit, 1982
How Acquired: Signed as a free agent, April 24, 1988
Pro Experience: Six Years
Marital Status: Single
Residence: Pontiac, MI

Last Season: Signed by the Pistons on the final day of the regular season and was a member of the Pistons during the 1988 NBA playoffs...Played in the final game of the regular season...Played in the CBA with the Savannah Spirits and averaged 16.6 points, 6.9 assists and 4.2 rebounds in 49 games during 1987-88.

As A Pro: His appearance with the Pistons in the final game of the 1987-88 regular season marked his fourth stint with Detroit. Has also played with the Atlanta Hawks and the Indiana Pacers during his six-year NBA career...Prior to joining the Pistons, he played in 48 games with the Indiana Pacers during the 1986-87 season and averaged 3.3 points per game.

As A Collegian: Started his collegiate career at nearby Oakland Community College where he averaged 20.4 points per game in 1978-79...Went on to play one season at the University of Houston before playing his final two college seasons at Western Michigan University...In his two campaigns with the Broncos, he averaged 18.4 points per game and was an All Mid-American Conference selection...Original fourth round draft pick of the Pistons in 1982...

Personal: Makes his year-round home in Pontiac...Attended Pontiac Central High School...Brother of former NBA players Frank and Campy Russell.

NBA CAREER RECORD

TEAM-YR	GP	MIN	FGM	FGA	PCT.	FTM	FTA	PCT.	OFF	DEF	REB	AVE.	AST	PF-DQ	STE	BLO	PTS.	AVE.
DET.'83	68	757	67	184	.364	47	58	.810	19	54	73	1.1	131	71-0	16	1	183	2.7
DET.'84	16	119	14	42	.333	12	13	.923	6	13	19	1.1	22	25-0	4	0	41	2.6
ATL.'85	21	377	34	63	.540	14	17	.824	8	32	40	1.9	66	37-1	17	4	83	4.0
DET.'86	1	2	0	1	.000	0	0	.000	0	0	?	0.0	1	0-0	0	0	0	0.0
IND.'87	48	511	64	165	.388	27	37	.730	18	37	55	1.2	129	62-0	20	5	157	3.3
DET.'88	1	1	0	1	.000	0	0	.000	0	0	0	0.0	1	0-0	0	0	0	0.0
TOTALS	155	1767	179	456	.393	100	125	.800	51	136	187	1.2	350	195-1	57	10	464	3.0

NBA HIGHS

		8	12		6	6					10		10			16	

3-POINT FIELD GOALS: 1982-83, 2-18 (.111); 1983-84, 1-2 (.500); 1984-85, 1-1 (1.000); 1986- 87, 2-16 (.125); 1987-88, 0-1 (.000). CAREER: 6-38 (.158)

NBA PLAYOFF RECORD

TEAM-YR	GP	MIN	AVE.	FGM	FGA	PCT.	FTM	FTA	PCT.	OFF	DEF.	REB	AVE.	AST	PF-DQ	ST	BL	PTS.	AVE.
DET.'88	7	10	1.4	2	5	.400	2	2	1.000	0	0	0	0.0	1	1-	0	1-0	6	0.9

JOHN SALLEY

Position: Forward/Center
Height: 6'11"
Weight: 231 Pounds
College: Georgia Tech '86 (Degree in Communications)
High School: Canarsie HS, Brooklyn, NY
Birthdate: 05/16/64
Birthplace: Brooklyn NY
When Drafted: First Round (11th Overall) Detroit, 1986
How Acquired: College Draft
Pro Experience: Two Years
Nickname: Spider
Marital Status: Single
Residence: Brooklyn, NY

Last Season: For the second straight season, he played in all 82 regular-season games...Started 16 games during his second season with the Pistons, replacing an injured Rick Mahorn...Averaged 8.5 points per game during his second season, compared to 5.3 points per game during his rookie season...For the second straight season, he shot better than 56 percent from the field...The only Pistons' player to block more than 100 shots in any of the last five seasons...Recorded 137 rejections during his second season with the Pistons...Increased his FT shooting to 71 percent during his second season, compared to 61 percent in his rookie campaign...Played nearly 7.0 minutes more per game during his second season, compared to his rookie campaign...

As A Pro: Has not missed a game in his professional career, playing in all 164 regular-season games and all 38 playoff games...Started slowly in his rookie campaign, but has proved to be very consistent since that time...Has already recorded 362 blocked shots in his first two campaigns, which ranks him fourth on the all-time Pistons' blocked shots list...Had his best game as a pro during his rookie season when he scored 28 points, adding 10 rebounds and 5 blocked shots versus the Milwaukee Bucks on April 5, 1987...Set an all-time Pistons' playoff record with 10 offensive rebounds versus the Washington Bullets in the first round of the 1988 playoffs...

As A Collegian: Finished fourth on the all-time Georgia Tech scoring list with 1,587 points (12.7 points per game), third in all-time FG percentage (.587) and is the school's all-time shotblocker (243)...Started 27 games as a freshman and averaged 11.5 points and 5.7 rebounds per game...Had a career high of 28 points against Monmouth on January 17, 1985...Set a school record in his junior season when he connected on .627 of his field goal attempts...

Personal: One of the most outgoing and personable players on the Pistons roster...Makes numerous personal appearances on behalf of the club throughout the year...Entered Georgia Tech as a 6-9, 185-pound forward and continued to add both size and strength...His nickname is Spider because of his long arms...Strengths are quickness, passing and shotblocking...For the second straight Summer, he returned to Georgia Tech to work toward completion of his degree...

NBA CAREER RECORD

TEAM-YR	GP	MIN	AVE.	FGM	FGA	PCT.	FTM	FTA	PCT.	OFF	DEF	REB	AVE.	AST	PF-DQ	ST	BL	PTS.	AVE.	HI
DET.'87	82	1463	17.7	163	290	.562	105	171	.614	108	188	296	3.6	54	256-5	44	125	431	5.3	28
DET.'88	82	2003	24.4	258	456	.566	185	261	.709	166	241	402	4.9	113	294-4	53	137	701	8.5	19
TOTALS	164	3466	21.1	421	746	.564	290	432	.671	274	429	698	4.3	167	550-9	97	362	1132	6.9	28

3-POINT FIELD GOALS: 1986-87, 0-1 (.000).

NBA HIGHS

		43		10	15		8	10		7	8	11		4		3	5	28		

NBA PLAYOFF RECORD

TEAM-YR	GP	MIN	AVE.	FGM	FGA	PCT.	FTM	FTA	PCT.	OFF	DEF	REB	AVE.	AST	PF-DQ	ST	BL	PTS.	AVE.	HI
DET.'87	15	311	20.7	33	66	.500	27	42	.643	30	42	72	4.8	11	60-1	3	17	93	6.2	15
DET.'88	23	623	27.1	56	104	.538	49	69	.710	64	91	155	6.7	21	88-2	15	37	161	7.0	17
TOTALS	38	934	24.6	89	170	.523	76	111	.685	94	133	227	6.0	32	148-3	18	54	254	6.7	17

3-POINT FIELD GOALS: 1987-88, 0-1 (.000).

ISIAH THOMAS

Position: Guard
Height: 6'1"
Weight: 185 Pounds
College: Indiana University '83 (Criminal Justice Degree)
High School: Westchester, IL, St. Joseph
Birthdate: 4/30/61
Birthplace: Chicago, IL
When Drafted: First Round (2nd Overall) Detroit, 1981
How Acquired: College Draft
Pro Experience: Seven Years
Married: Lynn
Children: Joshua:
Residence: Bloomfield Hills, MI

Last Season: Had another All-Star season...Named to his 7th straight NBA All-Star Game, his sixth as a starter...Finished the regular season by averaging 19.5 points and 8.4 assists per game...Improved his shooting percentage to 46 percent after starting the season at 43 percent...Had another eventful playoff campaign leading the Pistons in scoring...Scored a playoff career high of 43 points in Game 6 of the NBA Finals versus the Lakers despite spraining his ankle early in the match. Was very limited in the decisive Game 7 and played very little in the final half of the final game due to the sprained right ankle...He averaged less than 20 points per game during the regular season.for only the second time in his career...For only the third time in his seven NBA seasons, he played less than 3,000 minutes...For the sixth straight season, he passed for more than 600 assists...Missed just one game during the 1987- 88 campaign, and remains one of the league's most durable guards, missing just nine games over the last six seasons...

As A Pro: Has been named to the NBA All-Star Team in each of his first seven seasons in the league...Two-time All-Star Game Most Valuable Player, winning the honor in 1984 and 1986...First was MVP in Denver in 1984 when he scored 21 points and added 15 assists...Then in 1986 in Dallas, he scored 30 points, adding

10 assists and 5 steals to gain the honor...All-time Pistons leader in steals and assists, ranks third on the all-time Pistons scoring list...Set the an NBA record for assists in a single season (since broken by John Stockton) when he recorded 1,123 in 1984-85 for an average of 13.9 per game...Owns the Pistons' record for consecutive field goals made with 13...Has had some memorable playoff performances in leading the Pistons to five straight post-season appearances...Scored 25 points in the 3rd quarter of Game 6 versus the Lakers in the 1988 NBA Finals while playing with that sprained ankle, setting a record for points in a quarter in a Finals' game...Had 24 points in the 3rd quarter versus the Atlanta Hawks in the 1987 playoffs...Perhaps his most memorable playoff performance was in 1984 versus the New York Knicks when he scored 16 points in 94 seconds in the fourth quarter of the decisive Game 5 of that series...Was drafted by the Pistons second overall in the 1981 NBA College Draft after leaving Indiana after his sophomore season...

As A Collegian: Helped lead the Indiana Hoosiers to a 47-17 mark and an NCAA Championship (1981) with two Big Ten titles in his two seasons there...Missed only one game during his collegiate career and started all 63 games he played...All Big Ten as a sophomore...Was a consensus All-American after his sophomore season at Indiana...Top college scoring effort was 39 points versus the University of Michigan...Won 1981 NCAA Tournament Most Outstanding Player Award with 91 points in five games (18.2 points per game)...Member of the 1979 Pan-American Games Gold Medal Team, scoring 21 points in the title game, while leading the team in assists...Starter on the 1981 USA Olympic Team which had a 5-1 record against NBA All-Star Teams...

Personal: His wife, the former Lynn Kendall, gave birth to the couple's first child (Joshua Isiah) during the 1988 NBA Finals...Signed a contract on March 12, 1984, which will keep him in Detroit for the remainder of his basketball playing career...Youngest of nine children... One of the league's most vocal players in the fight against drug abuse, has made a 12-minute film entitled "Just Say No"...Received his degree in Criminal Justice in August of 1987.

NBA CAREER RECORD

TEAM-YR	GP	MINS	AVE.	FGM	FGA	PCT.	FTM	FTA	PCT.	OFF	DEF	REBS	AVE.	AST	PF-DQ	STE	BLO	PTS	AVE.	HI
DET.'82	72	2433	33.8	453	1068	.424	302	429	.704	57	152	209	2.9	565	253-2	150	17	1225	17.0	34
DET.'83	81	3093	38.1	725	1537	.472	368	518	.710	105	223	328	4.0	634	318-8	199	29	1854	22.9	46
DET.'84	82	3007	36.6	669	1448	.462	388	529	.733	103	224	327	4.0	914	324-8	204	33	1748	21.3	47
DET.'85	81	3089	38.1	646	1410	.458	399	493	.809	114	247	361	4.5	1123	288-8	187	25	1720	21.2	38
DET.'86	77	2790	36.2	609	1248	.488	365	462	.790	83	194	277	3.6	830	245-9	171	20	1609	20.9	39
DET.'87	81	3013	37.2	626	1353	.463	400	521	.768	82	237	319	3.9	813	251-5	153	20	1671	20.6	36
DET.'88	81	2927	36.3	621	1341	.463	305	394	.774	64	214	278	3.4	678	217-0	141	17	1577	19.5	42
TOTALS	555	20352	36.7	4349	9045	.462	2527	3346	.755	610	1491	2099	3.8	5557	1886-40	1205	161	11404	20.5	47

NBA HIGHS

	52		19	34		16	20		6	11	12		25		7	4	47		

3-POINT FIELD GOALS: 1981-82, 17-59 (.288); 1982-83, 36-125 (.288); 1983-84, 22-65 (.338); 1984-85, 29-113 (.257); 1985-86, 26-84 (.310); 1986-87, 19-98 (.194); 1987-88, 30-97 (.309).
CAREER: 179-641 (.279).

NBA PLAYOFF RECORD

TEAM-YR	GP	MIN	AVE.	FGM	FGA	PCT.	FTM	FTA	PCT.	OFF	DEF	REB	AVE.	AST	PF-DQ	ST	BL	PTS	AVE.	HI
DET.'84	5	198	39.6	39	83	.470	27	35	.771	7	12	19	3.8	55	22-1	13	6	107	21.4	35
DET.'85	9	355	39.4	83	166	.500	47	62	.758	11	36	47	5.2	101	39-2	19	4	219	24.3	37
DET.'86	4	163	40.8	41	91	.451	24	36	.667	8	14	22	5.5	48	17-0	9	3	106	26.5	36
DET.'87	15	562	37.5	134	297	.451	83	110	.755	21	46	67	4.4	130	51-1	39	4	361	24.1	36
DET.'88	23	911	39.6	183	419	.437	125	151	.828	26	81	107	4.6	201	71-2	66	8	504	21.9	43
TOTALS	56	2189	39.1	480	1056	.454	306	394	.776	73	189	262	4.7	535	200-6	146	25	1297	23.2	43

3-POINT FIELD GOALS: 1983-84, 2-6 (.333); 1984-85, 6-15 (.400);1985-86, 0-5 (.000); 1986-87, 10-33 (.303); 1987-88, 13-44 (.296).
CAREER: 31-103 (.301).

NBA ALL-STAR RECORD

TEAM-YR	GP	MIN	AVE.	FGM	FGA	PCT.	FTM	FTA	PCT.	OFF	DEF	REB	AVE.	AST	PF-DQ	ST	BL	PTS	AVE.	HI
DET.'82	1	17	17.0	5	7	.714	2	4	.500	1	0	1	1.0	4	1-0	3	0	12	12.0	12
DET.'83	1	29	29.0	9	14	.643	1	1	1.000	3	1	4	4.0	7	0-0	4	6	19	19.0	19
DET.'84	1	39	39.0	9	17	.529	3	3	1.000	2	3	5	5.0	15	4-0	4	0	21	21.0	21
DET.'85	1	25	25.0	9	14	.643	1	1	1.000	1	1	2	2.0	5	2-0	2	0	22	22.0	22
DET.'86	1	36	36.0	11	19	.579	8	9	.889	0	1	1	1.0	10	2-0	5	0	30	30.0	30
DET.'87	1	24	24.0	4	6	.667	8	9	.889	2	1	3	3.0	9	3-0	0	0	16	16.0	16
DET.'88	1	28	24.0	4	10	.400	0	0	.000	1	1	2	2.0	15	1-0	1	0	8	8.0	8
TOTALS	7	198	28.3	51	87	.586	23	27	.851	10	8	18	2.6	65	13-0	19	0	128	18.3	30

3-POINT FIELD GOALS: 1983-84, 0-2 (.000); 1984-85, 3-4 (.750); 1985-86, 0-1 (.000).
CAREER: 3-7 (.429).

FENNIS DEMBO

Position: Forward-Guard
Height: 6'6"
Weight: 215 Pounds
College: Wyoming '88
High School: Fox Tech High School, San Antonio, TX
Birthdate: 1/24/66
Birthplace: Mobile, Alabama
When Drafted: Second Round (30th Overall) Detroit, 1988
How Acquired: College Draft
Pro Experience: Rookie
Marital Status: Single
Residence: San Antonio, TX

Last Season: Was on the cover of Sports Illustrated in the college basketball preview issue before his senior season...Had his best scoring season when he averaged 20.4 points per game...Ranked among the Western Athletic Conference leaders in virtually every department while leading Wyoming into the NCAA tournament...Was a consensus pre-season All-American before his senior campaign.

As A Collegian: Finished his career as Wyoming's all-time leading scorer (2,311) and rebounder (954), while he was second in assists (405)...Enjoyed an outstanding freshman campaign, averaging 13.5 points and 7.3 rebounds...Became one of the Western Athletic Conference's top players in his sophomore campaign posting averages of 17 points and 6.7 rebounds per game...In his sophomore season he helped lead Wyoming to the National Invitational Tournament Finals and was named to the All-NIT Team...Raised his averages to 20.3 points and 8.3 rebounds per game during his junior season, and was named the WAC Player of the Year...Had an outstanding NCAA Tournament in his junior season when he averaged 27 points per game while leading Wyoming to the field of 16...Played on the United States Pan-American Team in 1987.

Personal: A fierce competitor who is very emotional during the game...Resides in San Antonio.

COLLEGE CAREER RECORD

YEAR	GP	FGM	FGA	PCT.	FTM	FTA	PCT.	REB	AST	PTS.	AVE.
'84	29	152	309	.489	90	130	.692	212	88	392	13.5
'85	34	227	420	.540	123	161	.764	229	120	577	17.0
'86	34	240	469	.512	131	171	.766	282	96	689	20.3
'87	32	205	430	.477	178	216	.824	231	101	653	20.4
TOTALS	129	824	1628	.506	522	678	.770	954	405	2311	17.9

MICHAEL WILLLIAMS

Position: Guard
Height: 6'3"
Weight: 175 Pounds
College: Baylor '88
High School: Carter High School, Dallas, TX
Birthdate: 7/23/66
Birthplace: Dallas, Texas
When Drafted: Second Round (48th Overall)
How Acquired: College Draft
Pro Experience: Rookie
Marital Status: Single
Residence: Dallas, TX

Last Season: Voted the Most Valuable Player of the Southwest Conference post-season tournament...Set the Baylor record for assists in a season (182) and is the school's all-time assist leader (464)...Finished second on the all-time Baylor scoring list with 1,854 points, trailing current NBA player Terry Teagle...Scored his career high with 36 points versus Mississippi Valley State...Two-time All Southwest Conference First Team selection...Played with the Pistons in the Central Division Summer League, where he led the team in scoring with his 20.5 points per game average...Member of the SWC All-Academic First Team...Voted the Baylor Outstanding Senior Award...

As A Collegian: Shattered many of the Baylor all-time basketball records and is the school's all-time leader in assists and steals, while he ranks second on the school's all-time scoring list...Set a single-season mark with 93 steals during his junior campaign...Finished his career ranked eighth on the all-time Southwest Conference scoring list.

Personal: Michael's father Roosevelt is a Baptist Minister...A Business Major, he is expecting to graduate this year.

COLLEGE CAREER RECORD

YEAR	GP	FGM	FGA	PCT.	FTM	FTA	PCT.	REB	AST	PTS.	AVE.
'84	28	149	306	.487	111	140	.793	66	66	410	14.6
'85	22	104	225	.462	68	84	.810	63	59	285	13.0
'86	31	188	396	.475	137	192	.714	94	157	534	17.2
'87	34	216	428	.505	161	231	.697	108	182	625	18.5
TOTALS	115	657	1355	.485	488	661	.738	331	464	1854	16.1

WILLIAM DAVIDSON

MANAGING PARTNER

The success of the Detroit Pistons over the last few seasons can be directly attributed to Managing Partner William Davidson, the club's majority owner since 1974. Under Davidson's direction, the Pistons are now considered one of the top franchises in the National Basketball Association.

Never in the history of the franchise has the future looked brighter for the Detroit Pistons. In 1988-89, the Pistons begin play in the Palace of Auburn Hills, a state-of-the-art arena built with Davidson's financial support. The Pistons are coming off the two most successful seasons in the history of the franchise. In 1988, the club advanced to the NBA Finals for the first time. Also, the Pistons won the Central Division, marking the first divisional title for the club in its 31 years in Detroit.

Davidson acquired the Detroit Pistons in 1974 from the late Fred Zollner, the man who founded the team in Fort Wayne in the 1940s, and moved the franchise to Detroit in 1957. In the past two seasons, no Pistons' team has enjoyed more success. Interested in a wide variety of sports, Davidson is one of the most knowledgeable heads of an NBA franchise. He has studied the talents and abilities of players and coaches in the league and has some very astute observations.

The Pistons' majority owner likes success and has known it in his business interests. That's why the success of the Detroit Pistons comes as no surprise to those who are aware of Davidson's ability to manage people.

Educated in business and law, Davidson received a Bachelor's Degree in Business Administration from the University of Michigan and earned a Juris Doctor's Degree from Wayne State University.

After three years, Davidson gave up his law practice to take over a wholesale drug company. He rescued it from bankruptcy and turned it around in three years. Then he took over a surgical supply company on the verge of bankruptcy and saved it as well. The next step was to take the Guardian Glass Company, the family business. He turned it around in two years, paying off all debts and heading it on a profitable growth path. Guardian Industries remains the flagship of his business interests.

Davidson expects his track record to help pave the way for the Pistons and the Palace. The success he has enjoyed has come from a proven talent for hiring competent managers and placing the responsibility with them. That is the same formula he has used with the Detroit Pistons for the past 14 years. He now expects to do the same with an arena he believes will be one of the best in the world.

The athletic interests of Davidson date back many years and have continued alongside his business career. He was a high school and college trackman and played football in college and in the Navy during World War II. Davidson was an initial inductee into the Jewish Sports Hall of Fame.

Davidson's management talents are continually on display in NBA circles, where he is active on the player relations and finance committees. He was a member of the committee which selected former NBA Commissioner Lawrence O'Brien in 1975. Davidson, who can be found sitting courtside at most Pistons' home games, is active in numerous community and charitable affairs.

The Detroit Pistons ownership group includes Legal Counsel Oscar Feldman, and Advisory Board Members Warren Coville, Ted Ewald, Milt Dresner, Bud Gerson, Dorothy Gerson, David Mondry, Eugene Mondry, Ann Newman, Herb Tyner and William Wetsman.

JACK McCLOSKEY
GENERAL MANAGER

Jack McCloskey enters his 10th season as the General Manager of the Detroit Pistons, and the success the club has enjoyed over the past five seasons is a direct result of his endless hours of hard work. Through the NBA draft and many shrewd trades, McCloskey has built the Pistons into one of the elite franchises in the National Basketball Association.

Throughout the NBA, McCloskey has acquired the nickname "Trader Jack" because of his ability to swing a deal and then have the acquired player make an immediate impact upon the Piston team.

When the Pistons needed an astute basketball mind to direct the on-court fortunes of the club, Managing Partner William Davidson appointed NBA veteran McCloskey as General Manager on December 11, 1979. Over those past nine years, McCloskey's trades have often been the talk of the league due to the success of the Pistons on the court.

At the time of the annnouncement of McCloskey as the team's General Manager, Davidson called the addition "a positive step in the building of our franchise to an NBA championship level." In 1988, the Pistons reached that level, advancing to the NBA Finals for the first time in the history of the franchise. In each of the last two post-seasons, the Pistons have moved to the Eastern Conference Finals. Indeed, the Pistons have arrived as a championship-level basketball team.

In each of the last two seasons, McCloskey has been mentioned among the top executives in the NBA, due to his ability to not only select top-notch collegiate talent through the NBA draft, but also to make trades that keep the Pistons at the top of the NBA. In 1981-82, McCloskey was recognized by his peers as one of the league's top General Managers when he was voted runnerup in the Sporting News' Executive of the Year balloting. In each succeeding season, McCloskey has been considered for the award.

McCloskey's duties include authority over all basketball-playing aspects of the Pistons organization including coaching, player personnel, scouting and trades.

A native of Mahanoy City, Pennsylvania, McCloskey came to the Pistons from the Indiana Pacers where he served as an assistant to Head Coach Bob Leonard during the 1979-80 season. Previously, he assisted Jerry West, now the General Manager of the Los Angeles Lakers, for three seasons.

Upon joining the Pistons, McCloskey, a 1948 graduate of the University of Pennsylvania, had 23 years of coaching experience behind him. During his playing days, he was an acknowledged all-around athlete, playing basketball and football at Penn, plus eight years in the American and Eastern basketball leagues. His career as a player also includes a brief stint in the NBA and four years of professional baseball for the Philadelphia A's. McCloskey and diminutive guard Charlie Criss rank as the

Eastern League's only two-time MVP's. His Eastern League teammates included current Pistons' Director of Scouting Stan Novak and Indiana Pacers' Head Coach Jack Ramsay.

It was after a highly successful high school coaching career that McCloskey returned to Penn in 1956, inheriting a team that went from 7-19, then 13-12 and 12-14, before recording seven straight winning seasons with Ivy League first-division finishes. In his final season, McCloskey led the 1965-66 Penn team to a 19-6 campaign, the most wins since 1954-55. His team captured the Ivy League title that year. His teams were 87-53 in Ivy League play and won the Philadelphia Big Five title in 1963. His record was146-105 in 10 seasons.

McCloskey's next stop was Wake Forest, where he transformed the lowly Deacons into an Atlantic Coast Conference contender. After a 14-39 mark in his first two years, he followed with four successful seasons in the rugged ACC while compiling a 56-50 slate. His assistants were Billy Packer and the late Neil Johnston, former NBA scoring ace of the old Warriors.

His next chore was to take over the expansion Portland Trailblazers in 1972-73 for two painful building seasons. The Pacific Division team was an eventual NBA Champion. In his tenure with the Lakers, he served as the offensive coordinator for two seasons and defensive coordinator for a year. The Lakers bounced back from two losing seasons with three winning campaigns.

Jack and wife Leslie make their home in West Bloomfield. One of the top senior tennis players in the state, Jack was a 1981 inductee into the Jerry Wolman Chapter of the Pennsylvania Sports Hall of Fame.

THOMAS S. WILSON

CHIEF EXECUTIVE OFFICER

Over the last five seasons, the Detroit Pistons have been one of the most successfully marketed franchises in the National Basketball Association. Not only has that been proven through five league-leading attendance marks, but also by the current all-time high interest in the club. One of the major factors behind the financial success of the Detroit Pistons is Chief Executive Officer Thomas S. Wilson.

Over the last 10 years with the Pistons, Wilson's duties and responsibilities have continued to increase dramatically. As the Pistons' chief executive officer, Wilson oversees all the administrative, marketing, broadcasting and promotional efforts of the organization.

Now his workload has dramatically increased with the opening of the Palace of Auburn Hills. New home of the Detroit Pistons, the Palace has been designed largely around Wilson's input. The Pistons have been able to customize the new facility to provide the finest sightlines and comfort level for basketball of any arena in the country. Wilson has taken on the responsibility of staffing the arena and of developing the philosophies that will present all of the arena's events in the finest manner possible.

Wilson spent much of the past three years traveling around the United States and Canada studying all aspects of the various arenas and incorporating the best features of each into the Pistons' new home.

"The success of the Detroit Pistons has been very rewarding to the organization, to me personally. But the challenge of designing the finest facility ever built for basketball and other events has been the most exciting project I have been involved with.

"We began with the Pistons in their final season at Cobo, lived through the down season and shared the success of the current era. I know our staff anxiously awaits the opportunity as we move into the brightest time in our history."

Wilson joined the Pistons in 1978 and watched the team linger through several poor seasons. After a 16-66 season, the Pistons' attendance figures dropped below 6,000 per game. But, when the team drafted Isiah Thomas in 1981 and made several other key acquisitions through trades and subsequent drafts, the future began to look much brighter.

Under Wilson's leadership, the Pistons have now led the NBA in attendance in each of the last five seasons. The Pistons set the all-time NBA record for attendance in 1987-88, becoming the first NBA franchise to attract one million fans during the regular season. By averaging 26,012 fans per game, the Pistons have established an NBA record that truly may never be broken. The Pistons' outstanding success in broadcasting is also headed by Wilson. When the Pistons moved both the television and radio broadcast in-house he was responsible for overseeing all aspects.

He continues to be involved with broadcasting as he serves in his role as the color commentator for all Pistons' games on Pro-Am Sports Systems (PASS). As he has for the last four seasons, Wilson will again team-up with Channel 2's Fred McLeod to telecast the games on cable.

A native Detroiter, Wilson received his Bachelor's of Business Administration from Wayne State University. Prior to joining the Pistons, he worked for both the Los Angeles Lakers and the Los Angeles Kings, and the Forum. He also worked in films and television in California, appearing in over 40 television programs.

An inveterate runner, he has participated in two Detroit Free Press Marathons. Tom and his wife Linda reside in Rochester Hills with daughters Kasey and Brooke.

CHUCK DALY

HEAD COACH

In just five seasons, Chuck Daly has become the most successful (and most popular) coach in the history of the Detroit Pistons, directing the club to its best years.

During this past off-season, Daly signed a contract extension keeping him on the Pistons' bench for the next three campaigns.

With Daly directing the club from the sidelines, the Pistons have recorded five straight winning seasons and made five straight playoff appearances. Before his arrival, the club had never recorded back-to-back winning campaigns. Last season, Daly directed the Pistons to the most successful year in the history of the franchise.

The Pistons won the NBA's Central Division, marking the first divisional title in the club's 31 years in Detroit. In doing so, the team set the club record for wins with a 54-28 mark, winning the Central Division by four games.

Then, the Pistons advanced to the NBA Finals for the first time in the history of the franchise. In each of the last two seasons, the Pistons have gone to the Eastern Conference Finals, and have now been established as one of the top teams in the NBA.

Daly's five-year coaching record now stands at 265-178, easily making him the winningest coach in the history of the franchise. His five-year playoff coaching record is 32-24 (57 percent), trailing only Pat Riley among active NBA coaches in playoff winning percentage.

In his first season with the Pistons in 1983-84, Daly improved the club by 12 games, as the Pistons finished with a 49-33 record. Then in the next two campaigns, the Pistons finished with 46-36 marks and postseason appearances. The Pistons enjoyed the most successful seasons in the history of the franchise in Daly's fourth and fifth seasons with the club.

Daly was named the head coach of the Pistons on May 17, 1983. His more than 30 years of success at all levels of coaching easily carried over with the Pistons.

Prior to joining the Pistons, Daly spent four-plus seasons as an assistant to Billy Cunningham and the Philadelphia 76ers. The Sixers were 236-104 in regular-season play during those years, winning two division titles and finishing second twice. The Sixers also logged a 32-21 playoff record in the four seasons before he departed for the Cleveland Cavaliers' head coaching position. Daly was regarded by the Sixers as especially adept at setting up offenses and defenses for various opponents.

In Daly's six seasons (1971-77) as the head coach of the University of Pennsylvania, his teams won four Ivy League titles and were runners-up twice. Penn won three Big Five Championships outright and tied for another under Daly's guidance, while compiling an overall record of 125-38 (74.4

percent) and won 20 of 25 Big Five games (80 percent). In his first season as the Penn head coach, he led the Quakers to a 25-3 record, a No. 3 ranking nationally and first place in the Eastern Collegiate Athletic Conference (ECAC). Daly led Penn to more NCAA berths and Big Five titles than any other head coach at Penn.

Daly was the head coach at Boston College for two seasons (1969-71) with a 26-26 record. He had served as an assistant at Duke for seven years (1963-69), first as freshman coach and then four years as the varsity assistant coach.

A graduate of Bloomsburg (Pennsylvania) State, after starting his collegiate career at St. Bonaventure, Daly earned a Master's Degree at Penn State and began his coaching career at Punxsutawney High School.

Daly, a native of Kane, Pennsylvania, has become a very popular speaker on the banquet circuit, and has numerous endorsements with sponsors. He is the host of the very popular television show Chuck Daly's One on One.

Chuck, his wife Terry and daughter Cydney, a Penn State graduate, reside in West Bloomfield.

WILL ROBINSON

ADMINISTRATIVE ASSISTANT TO THE GENERAL MANAGER

Will Robinson has dedicated his life to basketball. Recently, the game has been returning the favor as the Robinson legacy continues.

In the spring of 1982, Will was inducted into the Michigan Sports Hall of Fame, the supreme honor in the state where he enjoyed most of his coaching success. That success has continued during his years with the Pistons where he currently is the team's director of community relations and the administrative assistant to General Manager Jack McCloskey. His duties include scouting, special assignments and working the Pistons' training camp.

The list of names of the athletes who played for Robinson reads like a Who's Who in sports. His teams were usually tagged with the title "Champion."

Robinson's Detroit Miller High School team, paced by the great Sammy Gee, won the city championship over St. Joseph's High School in 1947, drawing 16,249 to Olympia Stadium. The game turnout set a Michigan attendance mark that stood until the Pistons moved to the Pontiac Silverdome in 1978.

When Robinson moved to Detroit Pershing High School, the name changed but the results were the same as his teams continued rolling up championships, winning at an 85 percent clip.

In 1963, Pershing and the PSL returned to state tournament play, and the team went to the final four of the state tournament led by Mel Daniels (former ABA center), Ted Sizemore (major league baseball player) and Willie Iverson (ABL Miami Floridians.)

One of the strongest high school basketball teams ever asembled played for Robinson in 1967. The five all later played in professional sports. Spencer Haywood and Ralph Simpson (both NBA and ABA), Glen Doughty and Paul Seals (pro football) and Marvin Lane (major league baseball) won the state championship.

The Robinson name had been recognized nationally, and Illinois State Athletic Director Milt Weisbecker gave the coach a chance at the big-time collegiate game. Robinson became the first black coach to direct a major college team and recorded five consecutive winning seasons. Among his standouts were All-Pro guard Doug Collins, one of the many Olympians Robinsons produced, and Bubbles Hawkins, who later played guard with the New Jersey Nets.

There have been other standouts: Wayne State all-time great Charlie Primas, Baltimore Colt All-Pro Big Daddy

Lipscomb, Wayne State VP Noah Brown, Olympians Lorenzo Wright and Charley Fonville and political advisor Ofield Dukes. The athletic field was not the only place where Robinson was developing outstanding individuals. He is just as proud of the 25 Detroit police officers who played for him, the college grads with PhD's attached to their names and the sons of his players who are now headline-makers.

Robinson's induction into the Michigan Sports Hall of Fame marked the fifth such honor for him. He was previously tapped for the Michigan High School Coaches' Hall of Fame, the West Virginia State Hall of Fame, the Illinois State Hall of Fame and the Dapper Dan Hall of Fame.

Robinson, who makes his home in Detroit, has one son, William Jr., the coordinator of academic programs at the University of Michigan.

DICK VERSACE

ASSISTANT COACH

Dick Versace begins his third campaign as an assistant coach for the Pistons, but now moves up to the team's top assistant with added duties and responsibilities. Versace will be on the Pistons' bench for every game, his duties now including practice and game coaching as well as scouting. For the previous two seasons, Versace was the Pistons' second assistant and did all of the advanced scouting of Pistons' opponents.

After eight successful seasons as the head coach at Bradley University, Versace was hired by Chuck Daly in August of 1986. In Versace's last year at the school, his Bradley Braves recorded a 32-3 record, including a record 22 consecutive wins, Versace was named the National Coach of the Year by the United States Basketball Writer's Association in 1986.

In his eight seasons at Bradley, Versace recorded a 156-88 mark (.639). He finished fourth on the all-time Bradley win list and third in winning percentage. His Bradley teams advanced to post-season play on four occasions (1980 NCAA, 1982 NIT, 1985 NIT, 1986 NCAA) and won the National Invitational Tournament in 1982. Versace, who was MVC and District V Coach of the Year in 1980, finished second nationally in both the UPI and the National Association of Basketball Coaches poll that year.

Versace is no stranger to Michigan, where he has spent part of his coaching career. After spending a season as an

assistant at St. Louis University, he coached two seasons as an assistant at Michigan State University. In 1976, Versace became the head coach at Jackson Community College. In two seasons at that school, his teams recorded a 47-13 mark and gained national prominence.

A 1964 graduate of the University of Wisconsin, Versace immediately began his coaching career—in football—at the high school level. After a year, he moved on to coaching basketball. Dick and his wife Joann reside in West Bloomfield.

BRENDAN MALONE

ASSISTANT COACH

Brendan Malone, a 20-year coaching veteran, begins his first season in 1988-89 as an assistant to Head Coach Chuck Daly on the Pistons' staff.

Malone replaces Ron Rothstein, who left the Pistons to become the head coach of the expansion Miami Heat. Malone's duties will include advance scouting all Pistons' opponents, in addition to his game and practice coaching responsibilities.

For the past two seasons, Malone was an assistant coach and scout for the New York Knicks. His duties with the Knicks included scouting college talent and advance scouting NBA opponents in addition to his bench coaching duties.

Malone joined the Knickerbockers in 1986, following a two-year stint as the head coach at the University of Rhode Island.

Prior to coaching at Rhode Island, Brendan was an assistant coach under Jim Boeheim at Syracuse University for six seasons. From 1978 through 1984, the Orangemen posted a record of 134-52 (72 percent), including three NCAA Tournament appearances. Malone was an assistant coach at Fordham University in 1976-77 and at Yale University in 1977-78.

He began his coaching career at Power Memorial Academy in New York City, where he remained for 10 successful

seasons. In Malone's final six seasons at Power Memorial, his teams won a pair of city championships, and he was a three-time New York City "Coach of the Year."

Malone played high school basketball at Rice High School in New York City, and earned his Bachelor's Degree at Iona College in New Rochelle. He earned his Master's Degree in Physical Education at New York University. Brendan and his wife Maureen have six children and plan to make their home in metro Detroit.

RECORDS

PISTONS ALL-TIME RECORDS AGAINST NBA OPPONENTS 1957-1988

TEAM	57–58	58–59	59–60	60–61	61–62	62–63	63–64	64–65	65–66	66–67	67–68
ATL*	6–6	4–8	5–8	3–10	7–5	4–8	2–10	3–7	2–8	2–7	4–3
BOS	1–8	1–8	0–9	2–8	3–5	0–8	1–7	0–10	4–6	3–6	2–6
CHI	---	---	---	---	---	---	---	---	---	5–4	4–3
CLE	---	---	---	---	---	---	---	---	---	---	---
DAL	---	---	---	---	---	---	---	---	---	---	---
DEN	---	---	---	---	---	---	---	---	---	---	---
GS#	5–4	5–4	2–7	5–5	1–7	7–5	3–9	8–2	2–8	2–7	4–3
HOU	---	---	---	---	---	---	---	---	---	---	5–2
IND	---	---	---	---	---	---	---	---	---	---	---
LAC!	---	---	---	---	---	---	---	---	---	---	---
LAL%	6–6	4–8	7–6	4–9	4–8	1–11	5–7	3–7	2–8	5–4	2–5
MIL	---	---	---	---	---	---	---	---	---	---	---
NJ	---	---	---	---	---	---	---	---	---	---	---
NY	4–5	3–6	4–5	5–5	5–4	8–1	4–5	5–5	2–8	4–5	4–4
PHIL+	5–4	2–7	4–5	4–6	4–5	3–6	3–5	4–6	3–7	0–9	1–7
PHOE	---	---	---	---	---	---	---	---	---	---	---
PORT	---	---	---	---	---	---	---	---	---	---	---
SAC$	6–6	9–3	8–5	11–2	6–6	4–4	2–7	4–6	2–8	2–7	4–4
SA	---	---	---	---	---	---	---	---	---	---	---
SEA	---	---	---	---	---	---	---	---	---	---	6–1
UTAH@	---	---	---	---	---	---	---	---	---	---	---
WASH=	---	---	---	---	7–3	7–3	3–7	4–6	5–5	7–2	4–4
TOTAL	33–39	28–44	30–45	34–45	37–43	34–46	23–57	31–49	22–58	30–51	40–42

TEAM	68–69	69–70	70–71	71–72	72–73	73–74	74–75	75–76	76–77	77–78	78–79
ATL*	0–6	3–3	5–0	2–3	2–2	4–0	2–2	3–1	4–0	2–2	1–3
BOS	1–5	3–4	3–2	0–5	1–3	1–3	1–3	0–4	2–2	3–1	2–2
CHI	3–3	3–3	3–3	1–5	4–3	2–5	5–4	4–3	2–2	2–2	2–2
CLE	---	---	2–2	3–1	3–1	2–2	2–2	2–2	3–1	2–2	3–1
DAL	---	---	---	---	---	---	---	---	---	---	---
DEN	---	---	---	---	---	---	---	---	1–3	2–2	2–2
GS#	2–4	3–3	1–4	0–5	2–4	5–1	1–3	0–5	3–1	2–2	1–3
HOU	3–3	3–3	4–2	3–3	1–3	3–1	2–2	2–2	2–2	3–1	2–2
IND	---	---	---	---	---	---	---	---	2–2	1–3	2–2
LAC!	---	---	5–1	4–2	3–1	3–1	2–2	3–1	1–3	3–1	2–2
LAL%	3–3	3–3	2–3	1–4	1–5	4–2	3–1	1–4	1–3	2–2	2–2
MIL	2–4	1–6	1–5	1–5	2–5	3–4	3–6	3–4	3–1	2–2	3–1
NJ	---	---	---	---	---	---	---	---	3–1	3–1	0–4
NY	3–4	1–6	2–3	1–4	1–3	1–3	2–2	3–1	1–2	0–3	1–3
PHIL+	3–4	1–5	2–3	1–4	3–1	2–2	3–1	1–3	2–2	0–4	1–3
PHOE	4–2	3–3	2–4	2–4	4–2	6–0	2–2	1–4	2–2	2–2	0–4
PORT	---	---	3–1	2–2	6–0	5–1	3–1	2–3	2–2	1–3	1–3
SAC$	4–3	2–4	4–1	3–2	3–3	4–2	2–6	5–2	4–0	1–3	2–2
SA	---	---	---	---	---	---	---	---	1–2	1–2	1–3
SEA	4–2	3–3	3–1	0–4	2–4	5–1	2–2	3–2	1–3	1–3	0–3
UTAH@	---	---	---	---	---	---	4–0	1–3	3–1	3–1	2–2
WASH=	0–7	2–5	3–2	2–3	2–2	2–2	1–3	2–2	1–3	2–2	1–3
TOTAL	32–50	31–51	45–37	26–56	40–42	52–30	40–42	36–46	44–38	38–44	30–52

*St. Louis 1957-68   &San Diego 1967-71 $Cincinnati 1957-72, Kansas City 1972-85
%Minneapolis 1957-60   +Syracuse 1957-63   !Buffalo 1970-78, San Diego 1979-84
@New Orleans 1974-79   =Chicago 1961-63, Baltimore 1963-74
#Philadelphia 1957-62, San Francisco 1962-79.

PISTONS ALL-TIME RECORDS AGAINST NBA OPPONENTS 1957-1988

TEAM	79-80	80-81	81-82	82-83	83-84	84-85	85-86	86-87	87-88	TOTAL	HOME	ROAD	NEUTRAL
ATL*	0-6	2-4	4-2	3-3	4-2	5-1	2-4	3-3	4-2	97-129	52-49	34-66	11-14
BOS	0-6	1-4	0-6	3-3	3-3	2-4	1-4	2-3	3-3	48-152	27-66	16-61	5-25
CHI	1-1	1-5	6-0	4-2	5-1	3-3	4-2	3-3	4-2	71-61	45-19	24-40	2-2
CLE	0-6	3-3	5-1	5-1	5-1	4-1	5-1	5-1	5-1	59-30	33-14	26-16	---
DAL	---	2-0	1-1	0-2	2-0	2-0	2-0	1-1	1-1	11-5	6-2	5-3	---
DEN	1-1	0-2	1-1	0-2	1-1	2-0	1-1	2-0	1-1	14-16	8-7	6-9	---
GS#	1-1	0-2	2-0	2-0	1-1	2-0	1-1	1-1	2-0	76-102	46-32	23-50	7-20
HOU	1-5	1-1	2-0	2-0	1-1	1-1	1-1	1-1	1-1	44-37	28-10	12-26	4-1
IND	1-5	2-4	2-4	4-2	4-2	6-0	5-1	3-3	3-3	35-31	24-9	11-22	---
LAC!	0-2	1-1	2-0	1-1	2-0	1-1	2-0	2-0	1-1	38-20	22-7	16-13	---
LAL%	0-2	0-2	0-2	0-2	1-1	1-1	1-1	1-1	0-2	70-125	31-52	24-61	15-12
MIL	1-1	1-5	2-4	3-3	3-2	3-3	2-4	3-3	4-2	45-70	31-26	14-42	0-2
NJ	2-4	3-3	2-4	3-2	1-4	1-5	4-2	5-1	5-1	32-32	18-14	14-18	---
NY	2-4	1-5	3-3	1-5	4-2	3-2	4-1	6-0	4-2	92-111	50-42	30-57	12-12
PHIL+	1-5	1-4	2-3	0-6	3-3	1-5	2-4	5-0	4-1	71-129	43-44	15-66	13-20
PHOE	0-2	0-2	0-2	1-1	2-0	2-0	0-2	1-1	2-0	36-38	22-16	13-23	1-0
PORT	0-2	0-2	0-2	1-1	1-1	1-1	1-1	0-2	1-1	30-29	21-9	10-19	---
SAC$	0-2	1-1	2-0	0-2	1-1	1-1	0-2	1-1	2-0	100-96	59-21	25-51	16-24
SA	2-4	0-2	0-2	1-1	1-1	1-1	1-1	1-1	1-1	11-21	5-11	6-10	---
SEA	0-2	0-2	1-1	0-2	1-1	1-1	2-0	2-0	1-1	38-39	23-14	10-25	5-0
UTAH@	1-1	0-2	1-1	0-2	1-1	0-2	1-1	1-1	2-0	20-18	13-6	7-12	---
WASH=	2-4	1-5	2-0	3-2	3-3	3-3	4-2	3-3	3-2	78-92	43-29	21-54	14-9
TOTAL	16-66	21-61	39-43	37-45	49-33	46-36	46-36	52-30	54-28	1116-1383	650-499	362-744	105-141

*St. Louis 1957-68   &San Diego 1967-71 $Cincinnati 1957-72, Kansas City 1972-85
%Minneapolis 1957-60   +Syracuse 1957-63   !Buffalo 1970-78, San Diego 1979-84
@New Orleans 1974-79   =Chicago 1961-63, Baltimore 1963-74
#Philadelphia 1957-62, San Francisco 1962-79.

Pistons Honor Roll Performances

40 or More Points
56 Kelly Tripucka, Chicago, 1-29-83
54 Dave Bing, Chicago, 2-21-71
52 George Yardley, Syracuse, 2-4-58
51 George Yardley, Boston, 1-15-58
49 Goerge Yardley, Minneapolis, 3-6-58
49 Dave Bing, Phoenix, 3-9-71
49 Kelly Tripucka, Golden St., 3-12-82
48 George Yardley, St. Louis, 12-26-57
48 George Yardley, Syracuse, 2-18-58
48 Bob Lanier, Portland, 11-28-72
47 Dave Bing, Baltimore, 3-8-67
47 Isiah Thomas, Denver, 12-13-83
46 Isiah Thomas, San Antonio, 2-8-83
45 George Yardley, Syracuse
45 Gene Shue, Boston, 11-9-58
45 Dave Bing, Los Angeles, 3-17-68
45 Bob Lanier, Buffalo, 2-15-74
45 Bob Lanier, Buffalo, 11-10-74
45 Kelly Tripucka, Philadelphia, 11-14-84
45 Adrian Dantley, Chicago, 11-21-87
44 George Yardley, Minneapolis, 1-23-58
44 George Yardley, St. Louis, 2-25-58
44 Dave Bing, Baltimore, 12-6-70
44 Bob Lanier, Portland, 10-19-71
44 Jimmy Walker, Portland, 12-7-71
44 Kelly Tripucka, Cleveland, 1-14-84
43 George Yardley, Minneapolis, 2-19-58
43 Bailey Howell, Los Angeles, 11-25-60
43 Don Ohl, Los Angeles, 1-23-63
43 Dave Bing, New York, 12-13-67
43 Bob Lanier, Atlanta, 1-11-75
42 Bailey Howell, Philadelphia, 2-26-64
42 Dave Bing, Baltimore, 11-3-67
42 Dave Bing, Milwaukee, 3-6-70
42 Bob Lanier, Los Angles, 1-11-72
42 Bob Lanier, New York, 2-1-72
42 Bob Lanier, Phoenix, 3-7-72
42 Bob Lanier, Houston, 11-4-72
42 Dave Bing, Philadelphia, 2-16-73
42 Bob Lanier, Houston, 2-25-73
42 Isiah Thomas, LA Clippers, 2-21-88
41 Dave DeBusschere
41 George Yardley, Minneapolis, 2-27-58

41 Dave Bing, Baltimore, 1-31-68
41 Bob Lanier, Portland, 11-14-73
41 Bob Lanier, Cleveland, 10-31-74
41 Bob Lanier, Los Angles, 10-29-75
41 Bob Lanier, New Orleans, 2-11-78
41 John Long, Washington, 12-29-81
41 John Long, Denver, 12-13-83
41 Kelly Tripucka, Chicago, 2-24-86
41 Adrian Dantley, Boston, 11-15-86
40 Dave Bing, Los Angeles, 2-4-70
40 Dave Bing, Buffalo, 2-26-71
40 Bob Lanier, Buffalo, 3-19-71
40 Bob Lanier, Atlanta, 1-30-73
40 Bob Lanier, Milwaukee, 11-13-74
40 Bob Lanier, Boston, 11-20-76
40 Bob Lanier, Portland, 12-29-76
40 Bob Lanier, Denver, 2-4-77
40 John Long, San Antonio, 2-3-81
40 Isiah Thomas, Cleveland, 2-26-84

25 or More Rebounds
33 Bob Lanier, Seattle, 12-22-72
31 Happy Hairston, San Diego, 2-8-69
28 Otto Moore, New York, 3-17-70
27 George Yardley, Minneapolis, 2-27-58
26 Bob Lanier, Phoenix, 12-6-72
26 Bob Lanier, New York, 12-29-72
26 Bob Lanier, Milwaukee, 11-15-75
25 Bill Hewitt, Chicago, 2-19-71
25 Bob Lanier, Portland, 1-23-76
25 Earl Williams, Boston, 1-23-76

20 or More Field Goals
22 Dave Bing, Chicago, 2-21-71
20 Bob Lanier, Buffalo, 11-10-74

20 or More Assists
25 Kevin Porter, Boston, 3-9-79
25 Kevin Porter, Phoenix, 4-1-79
25 Isiah Thomas, Dallas, 2-13-85
25 Isiah Thomas, Washington, 2-7-85
23 Kevin Porter, Houston, 12-27-78
23 Kevin Porter, Los Angeles, 3-30-79
22 Kevin Porter, San Antonio, 12-23-78
22 Kevin Porter, Chicago, 2-6-79
21 Kevin Porter, Houston, 2-6-79
21 Isiah Thomas, Kansas City, 12-22-84

21 Isiah Thomas, Washington, 4-12-85
20 Kevin Porter, Boston, 11-20-76
20 Kevin Porter, Los Angeles, 11-15-78
20 Kevin Porter, Indiana, 3-17-79
20 Isiah Thomas, Atlanta, 2-28-84
20 Isiah Thomas, LA-Lakers, 1-13-85
20 Isiah Thomas, Atlanta, 1-22-85
20 Isiah Thomas, LA-Clippers, 3-11-85
20 Isiah Thomas, Milwaukee, 4-4-85

15 or More Free Throws
20 George Yardley, St. L., 12-26-57 (24)
20 Walter Dukes, LA, 1-19-61 (24)
20 Kelly Tripucka, Chi., 1-29-83 (22)
19 Adrian Dantley, Chi., 11-21-87 (22)
18 Adrian Dantley, Chi., 11-7-87 (20)
17 George Yardley, Cinci., 11-3-57 (24)
17 George Yardley, Bos., 1-15-58 (19)
17 Dave Bing, Balt., 11-23-68 (22)
17 Dave Bing, San Fran., 1-27-71 (21)
17 Dave Bing, Portland, 1-15-73 (22)
17 Kelly Tripucka, Phil., 11-14-84 (18)
16 George Yardley, Syracuse, 2-4-58 (16)
16 George Yardley, Syr., 2-18-58 (19)
16 Jimmy Walker, Cinci., 12-16-71 (20)
16 Bob Lanier, New Jersey, 10-13-78 (24)
16 Isiah Thomas, Chicago, 10-26-85 (20)
16 Isiah Thomas, Atlanta, 2-28-86 (16)
15 George Yardley, Minn., 11-15-57 (16)
15 Harry Gallatin, Boston, 12-3-57 (17)
15 George Yardley, Minn., 12-25-57 (20)
15 Isiah Thomas, San Ant., 3-25-83 (18)
15 Dave Bing, Baltimore, 10-16-68 (15)
15 Jimmy Walker, New York, 3-5-69 (16)
15 Dave Bing, San Fran., 3-14-69 (21)
15 Dave Bing, Cincinnati, 11-3-70 (18)
15 Dave Bing, Phoenix, 3-9-71 (18)
15 Jimmy Walker, Buffalo, 11-20-71 (19)
15 Dave Bing, Cincinnati, 2-5-72 (16)
15 Bob Lanier, Washington, 12-11-74 (16)
15 John Shumate, Chicago, 12-23-77 (18)
15 Isiah Thomas, Cleveland, 1-31-84 (18)

Detroit Pistons Coaching Records

SEASON	COACH	REGULAR	PLAYOFFS	TOTAL
1957-1958	Charles Eckman	9-16		9-16
	Red Rocha	24-23	3-4	27-27
1958-1959	Red Rocha	28-44	1-2	29-46
1959-1960	Red Rocha	13-21		13-21
	Dick McGuire	17-24	0-2	17-26
1960-1961	Dick McGuire	34-45	2-3	36-48
1961-1962	Dick McGuire	37-43	5-5	42-48
1962-1963	Dick McGuire	34-46	1-3	35-49
1963-1964	Charles Wolf	23-57		23-57
1964-1965	Charles Wolf	2-9		2-9
	Dave DeBusschere	29-40		29-40
1965-1966	Dave DeBusschere	22-58		22-58
1966-1967	Dave DeBusschere	28-45		28-45
	Donnis Butcher	2-6		2-6
1967-1968	Donnis Butcher	40-42	2-4	42-46
1968-1969	Donnis Butcher	10-12		10-12
	Paul Seymour	22-38		22-38
1969-1970	Bill van Breda Kolff	31-51		31-51
1970-1971	Bill van Breda Kolff	45-37		45-37
1971-1972	Bill van Breda Kolff	6-4		6-4
	Terry Dischinger	0-2		0-2
	Earl Lloyd	20-50		20-50
1972-1973	Earl Lloyd	2-5		2-5
	Ray Scott	38-37		38-37
1973-1974	Ray Scott	52-30	3-4	55-34
1974-1975	Ray Scott	40-42	1-2	41-44
1975-1976	Ray Scott	17-25		17-25
	Herb Brown	19-21	4-5	23-26
1976-1977	Herb Brown	44-38	1-2	45-40
1977-1978	Herb Brown	9-15		9-15
	Bob Kauffman	29-29		29-29
1978-1979	Dick Vitale	30-52		30-52
1979-1980	Dick Vitale	4-8		4-8
	Richie Adubato	12-58		12-58
1980-1981	Scotty Robertson	21-61		21-61
1981-1982	Scotty Robertson	39-43		39-43
1982-1983	Scotty Robertson	37-45		37-45
1983-1984	Chuck Daly	49-33	2-3	51-36
1984-1985	Chuck Daly	46-36	5-4	51-40
1985-1986	Chuck Daly	46-36	1-3	47-39
1986-1987	Chuck Daly	52-30	10-5	62-35
1987-1988	Chuck Daly	54-28	14-9	68-37

Coaching Totals

	W	L	PCT.
Charles Eckman	9	16	.360
Red Rocha	69	94	.423
Dick McGuire	130	171	.432
Charles Wolf	25	66	.275
Dave DeBusschere	79	143	.356
Donnis Butcher	54	64	.458
Paul Seymour	22	38	.367
Bill van Breda Kolff	82	92	.471
Terry Dischinger	0	2	.000
Earl Lloyd	22	55	.286
Ray Scott	151	140	.519
Herb Brown	77	81	.487
Bob Kauffman	29	29	.500
Dick Vitale	34	60	.362
Richie Adubato	12	58	.171
Scotty Robertson	97	149	.394
Chuck Daly	279	187	.600

All-Time Detroit Pistons Roster

Player and Years with Detroit only	SEASONS	GP	REB	AST	PTS	AVG
Adams, Don (Northwestern), 1972-73 to 74-75	3	195	1111	328	1710	8.8
Alcorn, Gary (Fresno), 1959-60	1	58	279	22	230	4.0
Atha, Dick (Indiana State), 1957-58	1	18	24	19	44	2.4
Austin, Ken (Rice), 1983-84	1	7	3	1	12	1.7
Barnhill, John (Tennessee State), 1965-66	1	45	112	113	337	7.5
Barnes, Marvin (Providence), 1976-78	2	65	344	64	630	9.7
Bedford, William (Memphis State), 1987-88	1	38	65	4	101	2.7
Behagen, Ron (Minnesota), 1978-79	1	1	1	0	0	0.0
Bellamy, Walt (Indiana), 1968-69 to 69-70	2	109	1113	154	1554	14.3
Benson, Kent (Indiana), 1979-80 to 85-86	6	398	2437	784	3810	9.6
Bing, Dave (Syracuse), 1966-67 to 74-75	9	675	2828	4330	15235	22.6
Black, Norman (St. Joseph's-Pa.), 1980-81	1	3	2	2	8	2.7
Bolstorff, Doug (Minnesota), 1957-58	1	3	0	0	4	1.3
Bostic, Jim (New Mexico St.), 1977-78	1	4	16	3	26	6.5
Boyd, Dennis (Detroit), 1978-79	1	5	2	7	6	1.2
Brewer, Jim (Minnesota), 1978-79	1	25	95	13	57	2.3
Britt, Wayman (Michigan), 1977-78	1	7	4	2	9	1.3
Brown, Roger (Kansas), 1975-76 to 76-77	2	72	220	24	132	1.8
Buntin, Bill (Michigan), 1965-66	1	42	252	36	324	7.7
Butcher, Donnis (Pikeville, Ky.), 1963-64 to 65-66	3	138	495	330	967	7.0
Cable, Barney (Bradley), 1958-59	1	32	88	12	109	3.4
Caldwell, Joe (Arizona State), 1964-65 to 65-66	2	99	631	183	1055	10.7
Campbell, Tony (Ohio State), 1984-85 to 86-87	3	178	383	88	1102	6.2
Carr, Ken (N.C. State), 1981-82	1	28	137	23	207	7.4
Carr, M.L. (Guilford), 1976-77 to 78-79	3	241	1777	628	3568	14.8
Carter, George (St. Bonaventure), 1967-68	1	1	0	1	3	3.0
Cash, Cornelius (Bowling Green), 1976-77	1	6	16	1	21	3.5
Chappell, Len (Wake Forest), 1967-68	1	57	346	48	570	10.0
Clark, Archie (Minnesota), 1975-76	1	79	137	218	600	7.6
Clifton, Nat (Xavier, La.), 1957-58	1	68	403	76	525	7.7
Conlin, Eddie (Fordham), 1958-59 to 59-60	2	85	437	143	958	11.3
Crevier, Ron (Boston College), 1985-86	1	2	1	0	0	0.0
Cureton, Earl (Detroit), 1983-84 to 85-86	3	234	1210	256	1376	5.9
Dantley, Adrian (Notre Dame), 1986-87 to 87-88	2	150	559	333	3122	20.8
Davis, Jim (Colorado), 1971-72 to 74-75	4	309	1035	270	1285	4.2
Dawkins, Darryl (No College), 1987-88	1	2	0	1	4	2.0
DeBusschere, Dave (Detroit), 1962-63 to 69-69	7	440	4947	1152	7096	16.1
Dees, Archie (Indiana), 1959-60 to 60-61	2	101	491	70	852	8.4
Dickerson, Henry (Morris Harvey), 1975-76	1	17	3	8	28	1.6
Dischinger, Terry (Purdue), 1964-65; 67-68 to 71-72	6	456	2341	716	5522	12.1
Douglas, Leon (Alabama), 1976-77 to 79-80	4	309	2273	375	2939	9.5
Dove, Sonny (St. John's N.Y.), 1967-68 to 68-69	2	57	114	23	174	3.1
Doyle, Dan (Belmont Abbey), 1962-63	1	4	8	3	16	4.0
Drew, Larry (Missouri), 1980-81	1	76	120	249	504	6.6
Driscoll, Terry (Boston College), 1970-71	1	69	402	54	372	5.4
Duerod, Terry (Detroit), 1979-80	1	67	98	117	624	9.3
Duffy, Bob (Colgate), 1963-64 to 64-65	2	46	58	79	228	5.0
Dukes, Walter (Seton Hall), 1957-58 to 62-63	6	422	4986	515	4580	10.9
Dumars, Joe (McNeese State), 1985-86 to 87-88	3	243	486	1129	2861	11.8
Ebben, Bill (Detroit), 1957-58	1	8	8	4	15	1.9
Eberhard, Al (Missouri), 1974-75 to 77-78	4	220	760	175	1490	6.8
Edwards, James (Washington), 1987-88	1	26	77	5	141	5.4
Egan, John (Providence), 1961-62 to 63-64	3	128	207	332	860	6.7
Evans, Earl (UN-LV), 1979-80	1	36	75	37	157	4.4
Farley, Dick (Indiana), 1958-59	1	70	195	124	491	7.0
Ferry, Bob (St. Louis), 1960-61 to 63-64	4	312	1968	538	3851	12.3
Ford, Chris (Villanova), 1972-73 to 78-79	7	485	1686	1698	4120	8.5
Foster, Fred (Miami, O.), 1972-73	1	63	183	94	547	8.7
Fox, Jim (South Carolina), 1967-68 to 68-69	1	49	274	40	222	4.5
Fuller, Tony (Pepperdine), 1980-81	1	15	42	28	60	4.0
Gallatin, Harry (N.E. Missouri), 1957-58	1	72	749	86	1072	14.9
Gambee, Dave (Oregon State), 1968-69	1	25	78	15	169	6.8
Gerard, Gus (Virginia), 1977-78 to 78-79	2	49	147	44	375	7.7
Gibson, Mike (SC-Spartanburg), 1985-86	1	32	40	5	48	1.5
Green, Ricky (Michigan), 1978-79	1	27	40	63	179	6.6
Green, Sidney (Nevada, Las Vegas), 1986-87	1	80	653	62	631	7.9
Hagan, Glen (St. Bonaventure), 1981-82	1	4	8	7	7	1.8
Harding, Reggie (No College), 1963-64 to 64-65	2	117	1316	231	1357	11.7
Hardy, Alan (Michigan), 1981-82	1	38	34	20	142	3.7
Hairston, Happy (New York U.), 1967-68 to 69-70	3	122	1309	157	2113	17.3
Hairston, Lindsay (Michigan State), 1975-76	1	47	179	21	273	5.8
Hamilton, Roy (UCLA), 1979-80	1	72	107	192	333	4.6
Hawkins, Bubbles (Illinois St.), 1978-79	1	4	6	4	18	4.5
Hayes, Steve (Idaho St.), 1981-82	1	26	100	24	117	4.5
Herron, Keith (Villanova), 1980-81	1	80	211	148	1094	13.7
Hewitt, Bill (S. California), 1969-70 to 71-72	3	175	1037	231	986	5.6
Hightower, Wayne (Kansas), 1966-67	1	29	164	28	248	8.6
Hollins, Lionel (Arizona State), 1983-84	1	32	22	62	59	1.8
Hollis, Essie (St. Bonaventure), 1978-79	1	25	45	6	69	2.8
Hogsett, Bob (Tennessee), 1966-67	1	7	3	1	16	2.3
Holup, Joe (George Washington), 1957-58 to 58-59	2	105	529	96	779	7.4
Howard, Otis (Austin Peay), 1978-79	1	11	34	4	49	4.5
Howell, Bailey (Mississippi State), 1959-60 to 63-64	5	387	4583	882	8182	21.1
Houbregs, Bob (Washington), 1957-58	1	17	65	19	128	7.5
Hubbard, Phil (Michigan), 1979-80 to 81-82	3	196	1178	287	2266	11.6
Imhoff, Darrall (California), 1962-63 to 63-64	1	103	438	84	397	3.9
Johnson, Lee (E. Tenn. St.), 1980-81	1	2	2	0	0	0.0
Johnson, Ron (Minnesota), 1960-61	1	4	14	1	18	4.5
Johnson, Vinnie (Baylor), 1981-82 to 87-88	7	552	1700	1893	7254	13.1
Johnstone, Jim (Wake Forest), 1982-83	1	16	30	10	24	1.5
Jones, Edgar (UN-Reno), 1981-82 to 82-83	2	97	488	109	784	8.1
Jones, Major (Albany State), 1984-85	1	47	128	15	129	2.7
Jones, Wali (Villanova), 1975-76	1	1	0	2	8	8.0
Jones, Willie (Northwestern), 1960-61 to 64-65	5	272	767	545	2016	7.4
Jordan, Phil (Whitworth), 1957-58 to 58-59	2	118	871	115	1442	12.1

All-Time Detroit Pistons Roster (Continued)

Player and Years with Detroit only	SEASONS	GP	REB	AST	PTS	AVG
Judkins, Jeff (Utah), 1981-82	1	30	34	14	79	2.6
Kelser, Gregory (Michigan State), 1979-80 to 81-82	3	86	435	165	1114	13.0
Kelso, Ben (Central Michigan), 1973-74	1	46	31	18	85	1.8
Kenville, Billy (St. Bonaventure), 1957-58 to 58-59	2	60	173	112	385	6.4
Kojis, Don (Marquette), 1964-65 to 65-66	2	125	503	105	862	6.9
Komives, Howard (Bowling Green), 1968-69 to 71-72	4	298	721	1081	2957	9.9
Laimbeer, Bill (Notre Dame), 1981-82 to 87-88	7	522	6211	1117	8095	15.5
Lanier, Bob (St. Bonaventure), 1970-71 to 79-80	10	681	8063	2256	15488	22.7
Lantz, Stu (Nebraska), 1972-73 to 73-74	2	101	285	235	937	9.3
Lawrence, Ed (McNeese St.), 1980-81	1	3	4	1	12	4.0
Lee, George (Michigan), 1960-61 to 61-62	2	149	839	153	1467	9.9
Lee, Ron (Oregon), 1979-80 to 81-82	3	194	465	848	844	4.4
Levingston, Cliff (Wichita St.), 1982-83 to 83-84	2	142	777	161	929	6.5
Lewis, Ralph (LaSalle), 1987-88	1	50	51	14	83	1.7
Ligon, Bill (Vanderbilt), 1974-75	1	38	26	25	126	3.3
Lloyd, Earl (W. Virginia State), 1958-59 to 59-60	2	140	822	179	1207	8.6
Long, John (Detroit), 1978-79 to 85-86	8	559	1814	1103	8878	15.9
Long, Paul (Wake Forest), 1967-68 to 69-70	2	41	26	29	140	3.4
Loughery, Kevin (St. John's NY), 1962-63 to 63-64	2	58	109	106	363	6.3
Lowe, Sidney (N. Carolina State), 1984-85	1	6	1	8	4	0.7
Mahorn, Rick (Hampton Institute), 1985-86 to 87-88	3	210	1352	162	1496	7.1
Malovic, Steve (San Diego St.), 1979-80	1	10	28	15	26	2.6
Marlatt, Harvey (E. Michigan), 1970-71 to 71-72	2	54	85	90	221	4.1
Marshall, Tom (W. Kentucky), 1957-58	1	9	7	3	21	2.3
May, Scott (Indiana), 1982-83	1	9	26	12	59	6.6
McAdoo, Bob (N. Carolina), 1979-80 to 80-81	2	64	508	220	1294	20.2
McElroy, James (C. Michigan), 1979-80	1	36	50	159	422	11.7
McGuire, Dick (St. John's NY), 1957-58 to 59-60	3	208	840	1255	1695	8.1
McLemore, McCoy (Drake), 1968-69 to 69-70	2	123	572	127	851	6.9
McMillon, Shellie (Bradley), 1958-59 to 61-62	4	215	1267	179	1831	8.5
McNeill, Larry (Marquette), 1978-79	1	11	10	3	29	2.6
McQueen, Cozell (N. Carolina State), 1986-87	1	3	8	0	6	2.0
Mengelt, John (Auburn), 1972-73 to 75-76	4	291	671	585	2987	10.3
Miles, Eddie (Seattle), 1963-64 to 69-70	7	497	1673	1094	7419	14.9
Mix, Steve (Toledo), 1969-70 to 71-72	3	61	251	53	446	7.3
Mokeski, Paul (Kansas), 1980-81 to 81-82	2	119	540	159	691	5.8
Money, Eric (Arizona), 1974-75 to 77-78; 79-80	5	350	725	1276	4123	11.8
Moore, Ron (West Virginia St.), 1987-88	1	9	2	1	10	1.1
Moore, Otto (Pan America), 1968-69 to 70-71; 74-75	4	239	2126	261	2274	9.5
Moreland, Jackie (Louisiana Tech), 1960-61 to 64-65	5	348	1779	432	2684	7.7
Mueller, Erwin (San Francisco), 1969-70 to 71-72	3	168	839	369	1250	7.4
Murrey, Dorie (Detroit), 1966-67	1	36	102	12	98	2.8
Nash, Bob (Hawaii), 1972-73 to 73-74	2	71	108	30	149	2.1
Nevitt, Chuck (N. Carolina State), 1985-86 to 86-87	3	83	126	9	132	1.6
Niemann, Rich (St. Louis U.), 1968-69	1	16	41	9	48	3.0
Nimphius, Kurt (Arizona State), 1986-87	1	28	54	7	96	3.4
Noble, Chuck (Louisville), 1957-58 to 61-62	5	285	679	882	2114	7.4
Norwood, Willie (Alcorn A-M), 1971-72 to 74-75; 77-78	5	381	1011	187	2172	5 7
Ohl, Don (Illinois), 1960-61 to 63-64	4	307	942	1059	5137	1C.7
Olsen, Bud (Louisville), 1968-69	1	10	11	7	20	2.0
Owens, Tom (S. Carolina), 1982-83	1	49	186	44	207	4.2
Patterson, George (Toledo), 1967-68	1	59	159	51	120	2.0
Pierce, Ricky (Rice), 1982-83	1	39	35	14	85	2.2
Poquette, Ben (C. Michigan), 1977-78 to 78-79	2	128	481	77	737	5.8
Porter, Howard (Villanova), 1974-75 to 77-78	4	202	986	97	2173	10.8
Porter, Kevin (St. Francis, Pa.), 1975-76 to 78-79	4	190	366	1920	2217	11.7
Price, Jim (Louisville), 1977-78	1	34	101	102	390	11.5
Quick, Bob (Xavier), 1969-70 to 71-72	3	93	344	78	695	7.5
Reed, Hub (Oklahoma City), 1964-65	1	62	206	38	208	3.4
Reed, Ron (Notre Dame), 1965-66 to 66-67	2	118	762	173	951	8.1
Reynolds, George (Houston), 1969-70	1	10	14	12	21	2.1
Robinson, Jackie (UNLV), 1979-80	1	7	5	9	27	3.9
Robinson, Wayne (Virginia Tech), 1980-81	1	81	294	112	643	7.9
Rodman, Dennis (SE Oklahoma State), 1986-87 to 87-88	2	159	1047	166	1453	9.1
Romar, Lorenzo (Washington), 1984-85	1	5	0	10	9	1.8
Roundfield, Dan (C. Michigan), 1984-85	1	56	453	102	611	10.9
Rowe, Curtis (UCLA), 1971-72 to 75-76	5	407	3256	711	5407	13.3
Russell, Walker (W. Michigan), 1982-83 to 83-84; 85-86; 87-88	4	87	92	155	226	2.6
Salley, John (Georgia Tech), 1986-87 to 87-88	2	164	698	167	1132	6.9
Schweitz, John (Richmond), 1986-87	1	3	1	0	0	0.0
Scott, Ray (Portland), 1961-62 to 66-67	6	421	4508	1228	6724	16.0
Sellers, Phil (Rutgers), 1976-77	1	44	41	25	198	4.5
Sheppard, Steve (Maryland), 1978-79	1	20	19	4	32	1.6
Shue, Gene (Maryland), 1957-58 to 61-62	5	368	1783	1693	7247	19.7
Shumate, John (Notre Dame), 1977-78 to 79-80	3	71	624	131	1045	14.7
Simpson, Ralph (Michigan State), 1976-77 to 77-78	2	109	263	267	1190	10.9
Skinner, Al (Massachusetts), 1977-78	1	69	172	113	485	7.0
Smith, Jim (Ohio St.), 1982-83	1	4	5	0	8	2.0
Staverman, Larry (Villa Madonna), 1963-64	1	20	69	12	114	5.7
Steppe, Brook (Georgia Tech), 1984-85	1	54	57	36	253	4.7
Strawder, Joe (Bradley), 1965-66 to 67-68	3	231	2296	245	1977	8.6
Tatum, Earl (Marquette), 1978-79	1	76	121	72	594	7.8
Taylor, Jeff (Texas Tech), 1986-87	1	12	4	3	21	1.8
Teagle, Terry (Baylor), 1984-85	1	2	0	0	2	1.0
Thieben, Bill (Hofstra), 1957-58	1	27	65	7	100	3.7
Thigpen, Justus (Weber St.), 1972-73	1	18	9	8	46	2.6
Thirdkill, David (Bradley), 1983-84 to 84-85	2	56	39	28	106	1.9
Thomas, Isiah (Indiana), 1981-82 to 87-88	7	555	1899	5557	11404	20.5
Thomas, Terry (Detroit), 1975-76	1	28	36	3	77	2.8
Thorn, Rod (W. Virginia), 1964-65 to 65-66	2	101	367	225	1192	11.8
Tolbert, Ray (Indiana), 1982-83 to 83-84	2	77	189	44	293	3.8
Trapp, George (Long Beach), 1973-74 to 76-77	4	242	828	197	2092	8.6
Tresvant, John (Seattle), 1965-66 to 67-68	3	169	1302	264	1792	10.6
Tripucka, Kelly (Notre Dame), 1981-82 to 85-86	5	352	1579	1135	7597	21.6
Tyler, Terry (Detroit), 1978-79 to 84-85	7	574	3583	776	6638	11.6

All-Time Detroit Pistons Roster (Continued)

Player and Years with Detroit only	SEASONS	GP	REB	AST	PTS	AVG
Van Arsdale, Tom (Indiana), 1965-66 to 67-68	3	208	782	477	2128	10.2
Vaughn, Charles (S. Illinois), 1965-66	1	37	63	104	280	7.6
Wakefield, Andre (Loyola, ILL), 1978-79	1	71	76	69	170	2.4
Walker, Jimmy (Providence), 1967-68 to 71-72	5	388	972	1278	6262	16.1
Warlick, Bob (Pepperdine), 1965-66	1	10	16	10	24	2.4
Wilkes, James (UCLA), 1982-83	1	9	19	10	34	3.8
Wilkinson, Dale (Idaho State), 1984-85	1	2	1	0	0	0.0
Williams, Cliff (Bowling Green), 1968-69	1	3	3	2	4	1.3
Williams, Earl (Winston-Salem), 1975-76	1	46	251	18	168	3.7
Wilson, Isaiah (Bunny) (Baltimore U.), 1971-72	1	48	47	41	167	3.5
Windis, Tony (Wyoming), 1959-60	1	9	47	32	36	4.0
Workman, Tom (Seattle), 1969-70	1	2	0	0	0	0.0
Wright, Larry (Grambling), 1980-81 to 81-82	2	46	80	153	335	7.3
Yardley, George (Stanford), 1957-58 to 58-59	2	118	1095	137	2959	25.1
Zoet, Jim (Kent St.), 1982-83	1	7	8	1	2	0.3

Pistons First Round Draft Choices

1958—Choice to New York
in Dick McGuire trade
1959—Bailey Howell
1960—Jackie Moreland
1961—Ray Scott
1962—Dave DeBusschere
1963—Eddie Miles
1964—Joe Caldwell
1965—Bill Buntin
1966—Dave Bing
1967—Jimmy Walker
1968—Otto Moore
1969—Terry Driscoll
1970—Bob Lanier
1971—Curtis Rowe
1972—Bob Nash
1973—Choice to Atlanta
for George Trapp
1974—Al Eberhard
1975—Choice to New York
for Howard Porter

1976—Leon Douglas
1977—Choice to Washington
for Kevin Porter
1978—Choice to Seattle
for Archie Clark
1979—Greg Kelser (4)
Roy Hamilton (10)
Phil Hubbard (15)
1980—Larry Drew (17)
1981—Isiah Thomas (2)
Kelly Tripucka (12)
1982—Cliff Levingston (9)
Ricky Pierce (18)
1983—Antoine Carr (8)
1984—Tony Campbell (20)
1985—Joe Dumars (18)
1986—John Salley (11)
1987—Choice to LA Clippers
for Kurt Nimphius
1988—Choice to Phoenix
for William Bedford

Transactions Involving Detroit Pistons

April 3, 1957	Obtained Harry Gallatin, Dick Atha, Nat Clifton from New York for Mel Hutchins and No. 1, 1957 draft choice; also obtained Dick McGuire from New York for No. 1, 1958 draft choice.
May 14, 1957	Obtained Ed Kalafat from Minneapolis for Walt (Corky) Devlin.
September 12, 1957	Obtained Walter Dukes from Minneapolis for Larry Foust.
December 10, 1957	Obtained Phil Jordon from New York and Tom Marshall from Cincinnati.
December 28, 1957	Obtained Joe Holup from Syracuse.
June 10, 1958	Obtained Earl Lloyd and Dick Farley from Syracuse for cash.
February 7, 1959	Obtained Ed Conlin from Syracuse for George Yardley.
March 31, 1959	Obtained Archie Dees and No. 2, 1959 draft choice from Cincinnati for Phil Jordon.
November 10, 1959	Sold Barney Cable to Syracuse.
April 16, 1960	Obtained Bob Ferry from St. Louis for Ed Conlin: also obtained right to Don Ohl from Philadelphia.
December 1, 1961	Sold Shellie McMillon to St. Louis.
August 28, 1962	Sold George Lee to San Francisco.
August 29, 1962	Obtained Darral Imhoff and cash from New York for Gene Shue.
October 28, 1963	Obtained Larry Staverman from Baltimore for Kevin Loughery.
December 15, 1963	Traded John Egan to New York and Larry Staverman to Cincinnati in exchange for Donnis Butcher, Bob Duffy and Hub Reed.
April 16, 1964	Sold Darrall Imhoff to Los Angeles.
June 16, 1964	Obtained Terry Dischinger, Rod Thorn and Don Kojis from Baltimore for Bailey Howell, Don Ohl, Bob Ferry, Les Hunter and Wally Jones.
May 8, 1965	Obtained right to Bill Chmielewski from Cincinnati.

Transactions Involving Detroit Pistons

December 24, 1965	Obtained Charles Vaughn and John Tresvant from St. Louis for Rod Thorn.
December 28, 1965	Obtained John Barnhill from St. Louis for Joe Caldwell.
January 14, 1967	Traded Ray Scott to Baltimore in three-way deal which was to have brought Rudy LaRusso to Pistons from Los Angeles. When LaRusso didn't report, Detroit was awarded Lakers No. 1 draft pick in 1968.
October 2, 1967	Traded Reggie Harding to Chicago for future draft choice.
November 27, 1967	Obtained Len Chappell from Cincinnati for draft pick.
January 29, 1968	Obtained Happy Hairston and Jim Fox from Cincinnati for John Tresvant and Tom VanArsdale.
December 8, 1968	Acquired Bud Olsen on waivers from Boston.
December 17, 1968	Obtained McCoy McLemore from Phoenix for Jim Fox.
December 19, 1968	Obtained Walt Bellamy and Howard Komives from New York for Dave DeBusschere.
January 1, 1969	Obtained Dave Gambee from Milwaukee for Rich Niemann.
November 3, 1969	Obtained Erwin Mueller from Seattle for second round draft pick.
November 26, 1969	Obtained Bill Hewitt and third round draft choice from Los Angeles for Happy Hairston.
February 1, 1970	Obtained Bob Quick and second round draft choice from Baltimore for Eddie Miles.
February 1, 1970	Obtained John Arthurs from Milwaukee in deal which sent Walt Bellamy to Atlanta.
March 30, 1971	Traded Otto Moore to Phoenix for No. 1 draft choice.
December 10, 1971	Obtained Jim Davis from Houston in exchange for No. 1 draft choice.
July 31, 1972	Obtained Fred Foster in the three-cornered deal from Philadelphia, in which Terry Dischinger went to Portland and Portland sent draft choice to Philadelphia.
August 1, 1972	Obtained Stu Lantz from Houston for Jimmy Walker.
September 30, 1972	Traded Howie Komives to Buffalo for second round draft choice (1973).
October 31, 1972	Obtained Don Adams from Atlanta Hawks in exchange for Pistons No. 2 draft choice (1973).
November 10, 1972	Obtained John Mengelt from Kansas City-Omaha in exchange for Pistons second draft pick obtained from Buffalo in Howie Komives deal.
April 15, 1973	Obtained George Trapp from Atlanta in exchange for Pistons first draft pick (1973).
December 26, 1974	Obtained Howard Porter from New York in exchange for Pistons first round draft choice (1975).
May 28, 1975	Obtained Earl Williams from Phoenix for second round draft choice (1976).
August 28, 1975	Obtained Kevin Porter from Washington Bullets for Dave Bing and Pistons first round draft choice (1977).
September 24, 1975	Obtained Archie Clark from Seattle SuperSonics for first round draft choice (1978).
October 22, 1977	Obtained Ralph Simpson from Denver Nuggets in 3-way deal which sent Curtis Rowe to Boston and Paul Silas to Denver.
November 7, 1977	Obtained Al Skinner and two second round draft choices (1978 and 1979) from New Jersey for Kevin Porter and Howard Porter.
November 23, 1977	Obtained John Shumate and Gus Gerard and Milwaukee's number one draft choice in 1979 or 1980 from Buffalo for Marvin Barnes.
February 1, 1978	Obtained Jim Price and Denver's number one draft choice in 1979 for Ralph Simpson.
September 8, 1978	Obtained Kevin Porter from New Jersey for Eric Money.
October 10, 1978	Obtained Rickey Green from Golden State for a future draft choice.
October 19, 1978	Obtained Earl Tatum from Boston for Chris Ford and a future draft choice.
October 23, 1978	Obtained Otis Howard from Milwaukee for a future draft choice.
February 15, 1979	Obtained Jim Brewer from Cleveland for future considerations.
April 12, 1979	Sent Earl Tatum to Cleveland to complete Brewer trade.
June 25, 1979	Traded No. 5 first-round pick and cash to Milwaukee for No. 4 pick in 1979 draft.
July 12, 1979	Received Washington No. 1 draft picks in 1980 and 1982 in exchange for free agent signing of Kevin Porter.

Transactions Involving Detroit Pistons

August 27, 1979 . . . . Traded Andre Wakefield to Phoenix for future draft pick.

September 6, 1979 . . . . Sent Detroit No. 1 pick in 1980 and Washington No. 1 pick in 1980 to Boston (along with free agent M.L. Carr) for Bob McAdoo.

September 18, 1979 . . . . . Traded Jim Brewer to Portland for future draft pick.

November, 1979 . . . . Sent 1980 2nd round pick and cash to Utah to complete veteran free agent signings of Ben Poquette and James McElroy.

January 24, 1980 . . . . Acquired Ron Lee and 1980 2nd and 3rd round picks from Atlanta for James McElroy.

February 4, 1980 . . . . Acquired Kent Benson and 1980 1st round pick from Milwaukee for Bob Lanier.

October 1, 1980 . . . . Acquired Wayne Robinson from Los Angeles for 1981 2nd round draft pick.

October 7, 1980 . . . . Acquired Paul Mokeski from Houston for 1982 2nd round draft pick.

November 13, 1980 . . . . . . Signed veteran free agent Larry Wright and compensated Washington with 1981 3rd round and 1983 2nd round draft picks.

June 11, 1981 . . . . Acquired Edgar Jones from New Jersey for future considerations.

August 26, 1981 . . . . Traded Larry Drew to Kansas City for 2nd round draft choices in 1982 and 1984.

September 25, 1981 . . . . . . Traded negotiating rights to Brad Branson to Dallas for future draft considerations.

October 1, 1981 . . . . Acquired Jeff Judkins from Utah for 1982 3rd round pick and future considerations.

November 21, 1981 . . . . . . Acquired Vinnie Johnson from Seattle for Greg Kelser.

February 16, 1982 . . . . Acquired Ken Carr, Bill Laimbeer from Cleveland for Phil Hubbard, Paul Mokeski and 1982 1st and 2nd round draft picks.

June 23, 1982 . . . . Traded Ken Carr to Portland for a 1982 1st round pick.

August 2, 1982 . . . . Acquired 3rd round pick in 1983, 1984 or 1985 for waiving right of first refusal in Portland's signing of free agent Jeff Judkins.

September 23, 1982 . . . . . . Acquired Tom Owens from Indiana for future draft pick.

October 6, 1982 . . . . Sent Steve Hayes to Cleveland for future draft pick.

February 10, 1983 . . . . Obtained 1983 2nd and 1984 3rd round picks from San Antonio for Edgar Jones.

February 13, 1983 . . . . Obtained Ray Tolbert from Seattle for 2nd round picks in 1984 and 1985.

August 18, 1983 . . . . Obtained Petur Gudmundsson from Portland in exchange for 3rd round 1984 pick (originally Portland's).

October 17, 1983 . . . . Acquired David Thirdkill from Phoenix Suns in exchange for two second round draft picks (1985 and 1986) acquired from The Clippers in exchange for Ricky Pierce.

November 12, 1983 . . . . . . Signed free agent Earl Cureton and traded two second round draft picks (1989 and 1990) to Philadelphia 76ers for their waving the right of first refusal.

June 18, 1984 . . . . Obtained Dan Roundfield from the Atlanta Hawks in exchange for Cliff Levingston, the rights to Antoine Carr and two second round draft picks (1986 and 1987).

June 17, 1985 . . . . Obtained Rick Mahorn and Mike Gibson from the Washington Bullets in exchange for Dan Roundfield.

August 21, 1986 . . . . Obtained Adrian Dantley and two second-round draft picks (1987 and 1990) from Utah in exchange for Kelly Tripucka and Kent Benson.

August 22, 1986 . . . . Obtained Sidney Green from Chicago in exchange for Earl Cureton and a 1987 second-round draft pick.

January 29, 1987 . . . . Obtained Kurt Nimphius from the LA Clippers in exchange for a first and second-round draft pick in 1987.

June 22, 1987 . . . . Obtained William Bedford from Phoenix for Detroit's 1988 first-round draft pick.

October 28, 1987 . . . . Obtained Ron Moore and a 1988 second-round draft choice from the New York Knicks in exchange for Sidney Green.

November 26, 1987 . . . . . . Acquired Darryl Dawkins from the Utah Jazz in exchange for a second-round draft choice (1988) and an undisclosed amount of cash.

February 24, 1988 . . . . Obtained James Edwards from the Phoenix Suns in exchange for Ron Moore and a second-round draft pick (1991).

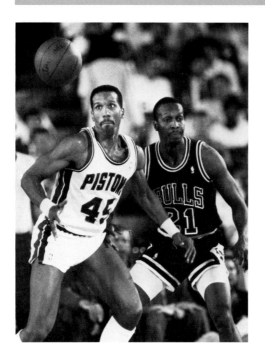

Detroit Pistons Draft History

1957 — 1, Charles Tyra, Louisville; 2, Bob McCoy, Grambling; 3, Bill Ebben, Detroit; 4, Kurt Englebert, St. Joseph's (PA); 5, Ron Kramer, Michigan; 6, Walt Adamushko, St. Francis (NY); 7, Carl Boldt, San Francisco; 8, Doug Bolstorff, Minnesota; 9, Bob Lazor, Pittsburg.

1958 — 1, Mike Farmer, San Francisco; 2, Barney Cable, Bradley; 3, Roy DeWitz, Kansas State; 4, Ralph Crosthwaite, Western Kentucky; 5, Hank Morano, St. Peter's; 6, Shelly McMillon, Bradley; 7, Ed Blair, Western Michigan; 8, Jack Quiggle, Michigan State; 9, Harry Marske, North Dakota State; 10, Pete Gaudin, Loyola (LA); 11, Herb Merritt, Tennessee Tech; 12, Jim Drew, Alabama State.

1959 — ¹, Bailey Howell, Mississippi State; 2, Don Goldstein, Louisville; 3, Gary Alcorn, Fresno State; 4, George Lee, Michigan; 5, Tony Windis, Wyoming; 6, Lou Jordan, Cornell (NY); 7, Doug Smart, Washington; 8, Chuck Curtis, Pacific Lutheran; 9, Doyle Edmiston, Hardin-Simmons; 10, Bruno Boin, Washington; 11, M.C. Burton, Michigan.

1960 — 1, Jack Moreland, Louisiana Tech; 2, Ron Johnson, Minnesota; 3, Frank Case, Dayton; 4, Ken Remley, W.V.-Wesleyan; 5, Willie Jones, Northwestern; 6, Bill Lowry, Christian Brothers; 7, Doug Moe, North Carolina; 8, Mike Yugovich, Youngstown; 9, Martin Holland, Kentucky Wesleyan; 10, Mel Peterson, Wheaton; 11, Don Dobbert, Wheaton; 12, Lee Hopfenspirger, Hamline.

1961 — 1, Ray Scott, Portland; 2, John Egan, Providence; 3, Doug Kistler, Duke; 4, George Finley, Tennessee A & I; 5, Dan Doyle, Belmont Abbey; 5, Lee Patrone, West Virginia; 7, Burt Price, Wittenberg; 8, Walter Ward, Hampton; 9, Peter Baltic, Penn State; 10, Wayne Monson, Northern Michigan; 11, Richard Kraft, Brockport.

1962 — 1, Dave Debusschere, Detroit; 2, Kevin Loughery, St. John's (NY); 3, Harold Hudgens, Texas Tech; 4, Reggie Harding; 5, Lindbergh Moody, South Carolina; 6, Ed Noe, Morehead State; 7, John Bradley, Lawrence Tech; 8, Mike Rice, Duquesne; 9, Bill Nelson, Hamline; 10, Glenn Moore, Oregon.

1963 — 1, Eddie Miles, Seattle; 2, Jerry Smith, Furman; 3, Mike McCoy, Miami; 4, Dave Erickson, Marquette; 5, Bill Small, Illinois; 6, Reggie Harding; 7, Ira Harge, New Mexico; 8, Gary Silc, Northern Michigan; 9, Ernie Dunston, Seattle.

1964 — 1, Joe Caldwell, Arizona State; 2, Les Hunter, Loyola (ILL); 3, Wally Jones, Villanova; 4, Jim Davis, Colorado; 5, Ray Wolford, Toledo; 6, Larry Phillips, Rice; 7, Jerry Jackson, Ohio; 8, Ralph Telken, Rockhurst.

1965 — 1, Bill Buntin, Michigan; 2, Tom Van Arsdale, Indiana; 3, Ron Reed, Notre Dame; 4, Jim King, Oklahoma State; 5, Ted Manning, N. Carolina College; 6, Barry Smith, High Point.

1966 — 1, Dave Bing, Syracuse; 2, Dorrie Murray, Detroit; 3, Oliver Darden, Michigan; 4, Jeff Congdon, Brigham Young; 5, William Pickens, Georgia Southern; 6, Carroll Hooser, Southern Methodist; 7, Ted Manning, N. Carolina College; 8, George McNeil, Southern Illinois.

1967 — 1, Jimmy Walker, Providence; 2, Steve Sullivan, Georgetown (DC); 3, Darrell Hardy, Baylor; 4, Ron Franz, Kansas; 5, Paul Long, Wake Forest; 6, Bob Lloyd, Rutgers; 7, George Carter, St. Bonaventure; 8, George Dalzell, Colgate; 9, Matthew Aitch, Michigan State.

1968 — 1, Otto Moore, Pan American; 2, Manny Leaks, Niagara; 3, Fred Foster, Miami (OHIO); 4, Rich Niemann, St. Louis; 5, Carl Fuller, Bethune-Cookman; 6, Wally Anderzunas, Creighton; 7, Larry Newbold, Long Island U.; 8, Harry Laurie, St. Peter's; 9, Vaughn Harper, Syracuse; 10, Tom Baack, Nebraska.

1969 — 1, Terry Driscoll, Boston College; 2, Willie Norwood, Alcorn A & M; 3, Lamar Green, Morehead State; 4, Ted Wierman, Washington State; 5, Steve Mix, Toledo; 6, Larry Jeffries, Trinity (TX); 7, Steve Vanderberg, Duke; 8, Bob Arnzen, Notre Dame; 9, George Reynolds, Houston; 10, Bill English, Winston-Salem; 11, Rusty Clark, North Carolina.

1970 — 1, Bob Lanier, St. Bonaventure; 2, Jake Ford, Maryland State; 3, Bob St. Pierre, Hanover; 4, Bill Stricker, Pacific (CA); 5, Bill Jankas, Long Beach State; 6, Sevira Brown, DePaul; 7, Marv Copeland, Michigan Lutheran; 8, Dan Issel, Kentucky; 9, Alex Wynn, Dartmouth; 10, Bruce Chapman, Nevada; 11, Rick Anheuser, N. Carolina State; 12, Don Ogletree, Cincinnati; 13, Ernest Hardy, Harvard; 14, Randy Smith, Buffalo State; 15, Dennis Clark, Springfield; 16, Harvey Marlatt, Eastern Michigan.

1971 — 1, Curtis Rowe, UCLA; 2, Bunny Wilson, Baltimore; 3, Marv Roberts, Utah State; 4, Jarrett Durham, Duquesne; 5, Vincent White, Savannah State; 6, Jim Larranga, Providence; 7, Steve Kelly, Brigham Young; 8, Wayne Jones, Niagara; 9, Paul Botts, Central Michigan; 10, Steve Butcher, Pikeville; 11, Larry Saunders, Duke; 12, Bob Horn, Drake; 13, Willie Roberson, Wyoming; 14, Art Davis, Johnson C. Smith; 15, James Fleming, Alcorn A & M; 16, Fred Smiley, Detroit College; 17, Leroy Jenkins, Detroit College; 18, Ike Bundy, Detroit Tech; 19, Ed Jenkins, Shaw College (MI).

1972 — 1, Corky Calhoun, Pennsylvania; 2, Chris Ford, Villanova; 3, Don Buse, Evansville; 4, Ernie Fleming; Jacksonville; 5, Ernest Pettis, Western Michigan; 6, Terry Benton, Wichita State; 7, Bruce Anderson, Arizona; 8, Ben Kelso, Central Michigan; 9, Jessie Mangham, Ferris State; 10, Kent Hollenbeck, Kentucky.

1973 — 1, Dwight Jones, Houston; 2, Tom Inglesby, Villanova; 3, Dwight Lamar, S.W. Louisiana St.; 4, Ken Brady, Michigan; 5, Dennis Johnson, Ferris State (MI); 6, Fred Smiley, Northwood Mich. Inst.; 7, Ben Kelso, Central Michigan; 8, Bill Kilgore, Michigan State; 9, Bob Solomon, Wayne State (MI); 10, Len Paul, Akron; 11, Clarence Carlisle, Ferris State (MI).

1974 — 1, Al Eberhard, Missouri; 2, Eric Money, Arizona; 3, Roland Grant, New Mexico State; 4, Mickey Martin, Pittsburgh; 5, Joe Newman, Temple; 6, Mike Sylvester, Dayton, 7, Sammy High, Tulsa; 8, Greg Newman, Drexel; 9, Gary Deitelhoff, Milliken; 10, Bill Ligon, Vanderbilt.

1975 — 1, Bill Robinzine, DePaul; 2, Walter Luckett, Ohio; 3, Peter Trgovich, UCLA; 4, Lindsey Hairston, Michigan; 5, Cliff Pratt, Shaw College (MI); 6, Allen Spruill, N. Carolina A & T; 7, Ike Williams, Armstrong State; 8, John Kelley, Dillard; 9, Terry Thomas, Detroit; 10, Mickey Fox, St. Mary's (NS).

1976 — 1, Leon Douglas, Alabama; 2, Earl Tatum, Marquette; 3, Phil Sellers, Rutgers; 4, Scott Thompson, Iowa; 5, Jim Hearns, Marymount; 6, Russell Davis, Virginia Tech; 7, Curt Peterson, Puget Sound; 8, Randy Henry, Illinois State; 9, Bill Martin, Hartwick; 10, Bob Johnson, Wisconsin.

1977 — 1, Ben Poquette, Central Michigan; 2, John Irving, Hofstra; 3, Bruce King, Iowa; 4, Jim Kennedy, Missouri; 5, Herb Nobles, Kansas; 6, Robert Lewis, Johnson C. Smith; 7, Tim Appleton, Kenyon.

Detroit Pistons Draft History (Continued)

1978 — 1, Terry Tyler, Detroit; 2, John Long, Detroit; 3, Dave Caligaris, Northeastern; 4, Audie Matthews, Illinois; 5, Herb Entzminger, Johnson C. Smith; 6, Earl Evans, Nevada-Las Vegas; 7, Ulice Payne, Marquette; 8, Dave Grauzer, Central Michigan.

1979 — 1, Gregory Kelser, Michigan State; 2, Roy Hamilton, UCLA; 3, Phil Hubbard, Michigan; 4, Tony Price, Pennsylvania; 5, Terry Duerod, Detroit; 6, Flintie Ray Williams, Nevada-Las Vegas; 7, Truman Claytor, Kentucky; 8, Ken Jones, St. Mary's (CA); 9, Rodney Lee, Memphis State; 10, Val Bracey, Central Michigan; 11, Willie Polk, Grand Canyon.

1980 — 1, Larry Drew, Missouri; 2, Brad Branson, Southern Methodist; 3, Jonathan Moore, Furman; 4, Darwin Cook, Portland; 5, Tony Fuller, Pepperdine; 6, Tony Turner, Alaska-Anchorage; 7, Carl Pierce, Gonzaga; 8, Leroy Loggins, Fairmont State; 9, Terry Dupris, Huron.

1981 — 1, Isiah Thomas, Indiana, 2, Kelly Tripucka, Notre Dame, 3, John May, South Alabama; 4, Donnie Koonce, UNC-Charlotte; 5, George DeVone, UNC-Charlotte; 6, Vince Brookins, Iowa; 7, Greg Nance, West Virginia; 8, Joe Schoen, St. Francis (PA); 9, Ed Baker, Alcorn State; 10, Melvin Maxwell, Western Michigan.

1982 — 1, Cliff Levingston, Wichita St.; 2, Ricky Pierce, Rice; 3, Walker Russell, W. Michigan; 4, John Ebeling, Florida Southern; 5, Gary Holmes, Minnesota; 6, Dean Marquardt, Marquette; 7, Brian Nyenhuis, Marquette; 8, Kevin Smith, Michigan St.; 9, Dave Coulthard, York (Ont.).

1983 — 1, Antoine Carr, Wichita St.; 2, Erich Santifer, Syracuse; 3, Steve Bouchie, Indiana; 4, Ken Austin, Rice; 5, Derek Perry, Michigan St.; 6, Rob Gonzalez, Colorado; 7, George Wenzal, Augustana; 8, Marlow McClain, Eastern Michigan; 9, Isaac Person, Michigan.

1984 — 1, Tony Campbell, Ohio State; 2, Eric Turner, Michigan; 3, Kevin Springman, St. Joseph's; 4, Philip Smith, New Mexico; 5, Rick Doyle, Texas-San Antonio; 6, Rennie Bailey, Louisiana Tech; 7, Barry Francisco, Bloomsburg State (PA); 8, Dale Roberts, Appalachian State; 9, Ben Tower, Michigan State; 10, Dan Pelekoudas, Michigan.

1985 — 1, Joe Dumars, McNeese State; 2, Andre Goode, Northwestern; 3, Rich Johnson, Evansville; 4, Anthony Webb, North Carolina State; 5, Mike Lahm, Murray State; 6, Vincent Giles, Eastern Michigan; 7, Frank James, Nevada-Las Vegas.

1986 — 1, John Salley, Georgia Tech; 2, Dennis Rodman, Southeast Oklahoma State; 3, Chauncey Robinson, Mississippi State; 4, Clarence Hanley, Old Dominion; 5, Greg Grant, Utah State; 6, Larry Polec, Michigan State.

1987 — 1, Freddie Banks, UNLV; 2, Eric White, Pepperdine; 3, Dave Popson, North Carolina; 4, Gerry Wright, Iowa; 5, Antoine Joubert, Michigan; 6, Mark Gottfried, Alabama.

1988 — 1, Fennis Dembo, Wyoming; 2, Michael Williams, Baylor; 3, Lee Johnson, Norfolk State.

All-Time Detroit Pistons Team Records

Team — One Season

Most Points	9725		1967-68
Highest Scoring Average	118.6		1967-68
Lowest Defensive Average	100.3		1974-75
Field Goals	3840		1984-85
Field Goals Attempted	8502		1965-66
Field Goal Percentage	.493		1987-88
Free Throws	2408		1960-61
Free Throws Attempted	3220		1960-61
Free Throw Percentage	788		1984-85
Most Rebounds	5823		1961-62
Offensive Rebounds	1430		1983-84
Defensive Rebounds	2649		1986-87
Assists	2319		1985-86
Personal Fouls	2240		1967-68
Disqualifications	58		1958-59
Steals	877		1976-77
Blocked Shots	572		1982-83
Most Turnovers	1858		1977-78
Most Victories	54		1987-88
Best Winning Percentage	.659	(54-28)	1987-88
Poorest Winning Percentage	.195	(16-66)	1979-80
Most Home Victories	34		1987-88
Fewest Home Victories	9		1963-64
Most Road Victories	23	(of 40)	1973-74
Fewest Road Victories	3	(of 19)	1960-61
	3	(of 41)	1979-80
Most Games Over .500	26	(52-26)	April 16, 1988
		(53-27)	April 21, 1988
		(54-28)	April 24, 1988
Most 100-point Games	78		1983-84; 1985-86
Most Opponent Games Under 100 points	41		1973-74
3-point Field Goals	72		1982-83
3-point Field Goal Attempts	272		1982-83
3-point Field Goal Percentage	.302		1985-86

All-Time Detroit Pistons Team Records

Team — One Game or Portion

Most Points
— Game . . . . **186**   at Denver (NBA Record)   Dec. 13, 1983
— Half (1st) . . . . **83**   vs. Chicago   Mar. 23, 1969
— Half (2nd) . . . . **77**   at Dallas   Nov. 17, 1984
                     77   vs. Golden State   Jan. 24, 1985
— Quarter (1st) . . . . **46**   vs. Chicago   Mar. 23, 1969
— Quarter (2nd) . . . . **43**   vs. San Antonio   Feb. 9, 1977
                     43   vs. Milwaukee   Apr. 2, 1978
— Quarter (3rd) . . . . **44**   vs. Golden State   Jan. 24, 1985
— Quarter (4th) . . . . **46**   at Dallas   Nov. 17, 1984

Most Field Goals
— Game . . . . **74**   vs. Denver   Dec. 13, 1983
— Half . . . . **37**   at Los Angeles   Nov. 24, 1972
                     37   vs. Boston   Mar. 9, 1979
— Quarter . . . . **22**   vs. Chicago (1st Q)   Mar. 23, 1969

Most Field Goals Attempted
— Game . . . . **142**   vs. Boston (2 QT @ U-D)   Nov. 17, 1959
— Half . . . . **65**   vs. Boston (2st H @ U-D)   Nov. 17, 1959
— Quarter . . . . **45**   vs. Los Angeles (4th Q)   Nov. 28, 1965

Most Free Throws
— Game . . . . **48**   vs. Syracuse @ Philadelphia   Jan. 5, 1962
— Half . . . . **34**   vs. New Jersey (2nd + OT)   Feb. 29, 1980
— Quarter . . . . **21**   vs. Cincinnati (4th Q)   Jan. 7, 1972

Most Free Throws Attempted
— Game . . . . **65**   at Seattle   Feb. 16, 1962
— Half . . . . **45**   vs. Baltimore (2nd H)   Jan. 15, 1966
— Quarter . . . . **25**   vs. Cincinnati (4th Q)   Jan. 7, 1972

Most Rebounds
— Game . . . . **107**   vs. Boston @ New York (OT)   Nov. 15, 1960
— Half . . . . **52**   vs Seattle (2 nd H)   Jan 19, 1968
— Quarter . . . . **38**   vs. St. Louis (2nd H @ Olympia)   Dec. 7, 1960

Most Offensive Rebounds
— Game . . . . **36**   at Los Angeles   Dec. 14, 1975
— Half . . . . **19**   vs. Los Angeles (1st H)   Dec. 12, 1973
— Quarter . . . . **14**   at Los Angeles (2nd Q)   Dec. 14, 1975

Most Defensive Rebounds
— Game . . . . **46**   at Cleveland   Jan. 17, 1974
— Half . . . . **27**   vs. Kansas City (1st H)   Nov. 6, 1974
— Quarter . . . . **16**   vs. Seattle (1st Q)   Jan. 26, 1974

Most Assists
— Game . . . . **48**   at Cleveland (OT)   Mar. 28, 1973
— Half . . . . **26**   vs. Chicago (1st H)   Nov. 3, 1982
— Quarter . . . . **16**   vs. Boston (1st Q)   Apr. 13, 1983

Most Personal Fouls
— Game . . . . **44**   at Denver   Dec. 13, 1983
— Half . . . . **23**   vs. St. Louis (1st H)   Jan. 1, 1962
                     23   vs. New Jersey (2nd H)   Oct. 13, 1978
— Quarter . . . . **15**   vs. Milwaukee (4th Q)   Apr. 9, 1982

Most Steals
— Game . . . . **22**   at New Jersey   Nov. 16, 1980
— Half . . . . **14**   vs. Phoenix (2nd H)   Feb. 1, 1978
— Quarter . . . . **9**   at Phoenix (3rd Q)   Jan. 13, 1978

Most Turnovers
— Game . . . . **38**   vs. Atlanta (OT)   Oct. 18, 1980
                     35   at New Jersey   Oct. 13, 1980
— Half . . . . **21**   vs. Atlanta (1st H)   Dec. 29, 1979
                     21   vs. Atlanta (1st H)   Oct. 18, 1980
— Quarter . . . . **13**   at Kansas City (3rd Q)   Dec. 5, 1979

Most Blocked Shots
— Game . . . . **21**   vs. Atlanta   Oct. 18, 1980
— Half . . . . **15**   vs. Washington (2nd H)   Nov. 19, 1981
— Quarter . . . . **10**   vs. Washington (4th Q)   Nov. 19, 1981

Most Three-Point Field Goals Attempted
— Game . . . . **14**   vs. Kansas City   Mar. 3, 1983
— Half . . . . **7**   vs. Houston (2nd H)   Mar. 16, 1980
— Quarter . . . . **5**   vs. Houston (3rd Q)   Mar. 16, 1980

Most Three-Point Field Goals Made
— Game . . . . **6**   vs. Houston   Mar. 16, 1980
— Half . . . . **3**   Several Times
— Quarter . . . . **3**   at Golden State   Dec. 8, 1983

Field Goal Pct.
— Game . . . . **691**   vs. San Diego   Jan. 28, 1979
                       (NBA Record — since broken)

Detroit Pistons All-Time Individual Career Leaders

(Includes records of players who performed both in Fort Wayne and Detroit — regular season games only)

POINTS

		GAMES	PTS.	AVG.
1.	Bob Lanier (ten seasons)	681	15,488	22.7
2.	Dave Bing (nine seasons)	675	15,235	22.6
3.	Isiah Thomas (seven seasons)	555	11,404	20.5
4.	John Long (eight seasons)	559	8,878	15.9
5.	Bailey Howell (five seasons)	387	8,182	21.1
6.	Bill Laimbeer (seven seasons)	522	8,095	15.5
7.	Gene Shue (six seasons)	440	8,034	18.2
8.	Kelly Tripucka (five seasons)	352	7,597	21.6
9.	Eddie Miles (seven seasons)	497	7,419	14.9
10.	George Yardley (six seasons)	384	7,339	19.1

TOP SCORING AVERAGES
(Minimum 100 games)

1.	Bob Lanier (681 games)	22.7
2.	Dave Bing (675 games)	22.6
3.	Kelly Tripucka (352 games)	21.6
4.	Bailey Howell (387 games)	21.1
5.	Adrian Dantley (150 games)	20.8
6.	Isiah Thomas (555 games)	20.5
7.	George Yardley (384 games)	19.1
8.	Gene Shue (440 games)	18.2
9.	Happy Hairston (122 games)	17.3
10.	Don Ohl (307 games)	16.7

FIELD GOALS MADE

1.	Bob Lanier	6276
2.	Dave Bing	5772
3.	Isiah Thomas	4349
4.	John Long	3797
5.	Bill Laimbeer	3236
6.	Eddie Miles	3019
7.	Vinnie Johnson	3005
*8.	Gene Shue	2940
9.	Bailey Howell	2905
10.	Terry Tyler	2854

FREE THROWS MADE

1.	Dave Bing	3691
2.	Bob Lanier	2936
3.	Isiah Thomas	2527
4.	Bailey Howell	2372
5.	George Yardley	2237
*6.	Gene Shue	2154
7.	Kelly Tripucka	1948
8.	Bill Laimbeer	1594
9.	Ray Scott	1590
10.	Dave DeBusschere	1530

REBOUNDS

1.	Bob Lanier	8063
2.	Bill Laimbeer	6211
3.	Walter Dukes	4986
4.	Dave DeBusschere	4947
5.	Bailey Howell	4583
6.	Ray Scott	4508
7.	Terry Tyler	3583
8.	Curtis Rowe	3256
9.	Dave Bing	2828
10.	Kent Benson	2437

STEALS

1.	Isiah Thomas	1205
2.	Chris Ford	785
3.	John Long	640
4.	Terry Tyler	615
5.	M.L. Carr	509
6.	Bob Lanier	504
7.	Vinnie Johnson	488
8.	Eric Money	437
9.	Ron Lee	366
10.	Kelly Tripucka	363

GAMES

1.	Bob Lanier	681
2.	Dave Bing	675
3.	Terry Tyler	574
4.	John Long	559
5.	Isiah Thomas	555
6.	Vinnie Johnson	552
7.	Bill Laimbeer	522
8.	Eddie Miles	497
9.	Chris Ford	485
10.	Terry Dischinger	456

FIELD GOALS ATTEMPTED

1.	Dave Bing	13119
2.	Bob Lanier	12347
3.	Isiah Thomas	9045
4.	John Long	7935
*5.	Gene Shue	7294
6.	Eddie Miles	6804
7.	Dave DeBusschere	6553
8.	Terry Dischinger	6488
9.	Ray Scott	6455
10.	Bill Laimbeer	6421

FREE THROWS ATTEMPTED

1.	Dave Bing	4789
2.	Bob Lanier	3797
3.	Isiah Thomas	3346
4.	Bailey Howell	3063
*5.	George Yardley	2873
*6.	Gene Shue	2595
7.	Kelly Tripucka	2340
8.	Ray Scott	2256
9.	Dave DeBusschere	2222
10.	Walter Dukes	2154

ASSISTS

1.	Isiah Thomas	5557
2.	Dave Bing	4330
3.	Bob Lanier	2256
4.	Gene Shue	1931
5.	Kevin Porter	1920
6.	Vinnie Johnson	1893
7.	Chris Ford	1698
8.	Jimmy Walker	1278
9.	Eric Money	1276
10.	Dick McGuire	1255

BLOCKED SHOTS

1.	Terry Tyler	1070
2.	Bob Lanier	859
3.	Bill Laimbeer	492
4.	John Salley	362
5.	Kent Benson	331
6.	Leon Douglas	246
7.	Vinnie Johnson	168
8.	Isiah Thomas	161
9.	Rick Mahorn	153
10.	Howard Porter	139
10.	John Long	139

*Includes Fort Wayne Totals

Yearly Pistons Departmental Leaders

TOP SCORERS

YEAR	G	PTS	AVG	PLAYER
1957-58	72	2001	27.8	George Yardley*
1958-59	72	1266	17.6	Gene Shue
1959-60	75	1712	22.8	Gene Shue
1960-61	77	1815	23.6	Bailey Howell
1961-62	79	1576	19.9	Bailey Howell
1962-63	79	1793	22.7	Bailey Howell
1963-64	77	1666	21.6	Bailey Howell
1964-65	80	1456	18.2	Terry Dischinger
1965-66	80	1566	19.6	Eddie Miles
1966-67	80	1601	20.0	Dave Bing
1967-68	79	2142	27.1	Dave Bing*
1968-69	77	1800	23.4	Dave Bing
1969-70	70	1604	22.9	Dave Bing
1970-71	82	2213	27.0	Dave Bing
1971-72	80	2056	25.7	Bob Lanier
1972-73	81	1927	23.8	Bob Lanier
1973-74	81	1822	22.5	Bob Lanier
1974-75	76	1823	24.0	Bob Lanier
1975-76	64	1366	21.3	Bob Lanier
1976-77	64	1616	25.3	Bob Lanier
1977-78	63	1542	24.5	Bob Lanier
1978-79	53	1253	23.6	Bob Lanier
1979-80	58	1222	21.1	Bob McAdoo
1980-81	59	1044	17.7	John Long
1981-82	69	1514	21.9	John Long
1982-83	58	1536	26.5	Kelly Tripucka
1983-84	76	1618	21.3	Kelly Tripucka
1983-84	82	1748	21.3	Isiah Thomas
1984-85	81	1720	21.2	Isiah Thomas
1985-86	77	1609	20.9	Isiah Thomas
1986-87	81	1742	21.5	Adrian Dantley
1987-88	69	1380	20.0	Adrian Dantley

BEST FREE THROW SHOOTERS

YEAR	FTM	FTA	AVG	PLAYER
1957-58	276	327	.844	Gene Shue
1958-59	338	421	.803	Gene Shue
1959-60	472	541	.872	Gene Shue
1960-61	465	543	.856	Gene Shue
1961-62	362	447	.810	Gene Shue
1962-63	519	650	.798	Bailey Howell
1963-64	470	581	.809	Bailey Howell
1964-65	320	424	.755	Terry Dischinger
1965-66	323	435	.743	Ray Scott

*Led NBA

1966-67	272	347	.784	Tom Van Arsdale
1967-68	134	175	.766	Jimmy Walker
1968-69	404	553	.731	Happy Hairston
1969-70	119	145	.821	McCoy McLemore
1970-71	344	414	.831	Jimmy Walker
1971-72	397	480	.827	Jimmy Walker
1972-73	456	560	.814	Dave Bing
1973-74	139	164	.848	Stu Lantz
1974-75	211	248	.851	John Mengelt
1975-76	100	116	.862	Archie Clark
1976-77	103	120	.858	Howard Porter
1977-78	84	103	.815	Jim Price
1978-79	157	190	.826	John Long
1979-80	160	194	.825	John Long
1980-81	160	184	.870	John Long
1981-82	238	275	.865	John Long
1982-83	392	465	.843	Kelly Tripucka
1983-84	243	275	.884	John Long
1984-85	255	288	.885	Kelly Tripucka
1985-86	380	444	.856	Kelly Tripucka
1986-87	245	274	.894	Bill Laimbeer
1987-88	187	214	.874	Bill Laimbeer

BEST SHOOTING AVERAGE

YEAR	FGM	FGA	PCT	PLAYER
1957-58	673	1624	.413	George Yardley
1958-59	127	289	.439	Shellie McMillon
1959-60	510	1119	.456	Bailey Howell
1960-61	607	1293	.469	Bailey Howell
1961-62	553	1193	.464	Bailey Howell
1962-63	637	1235	.516	Bailey Howell
1963-64	598	1267	.472	Bailey Howell
1964-65	568	1153	.493	Terry Dischinger
1965-66	634	1418	.447	Eddie Miles
1966	172	382	.450	Reggie Harding
1967-68	255	458	.513	Len Chappell
1968-69	264	513	.515	Terry Dischinger
1969-70	666	1394	.478	Jimmy Walker
1970-71	799	1710	.467	Dave Bing
1971-72	834	1690	.493	Bob Lanier
1972-73	547	1053	.519	Curtis Rowe
1973-74	748	1483	.504	Bob Lanier
1974-75	731	1438	.510	Bob Lanier
1975-76	541	1017	.532	Bob Lanier
1976-77	678	1269	.534	Bob Lanier

Yearly Pistons Departmental Leaders

YEAR	FGM	FGA	PCT	PLAYER
1977-78	622	1159	.537	Bob Lanier
1978-79	489	948	.516	Bob Lanier
1979-80	588	1164	.505	John Long
1980-81	476	895	.532	Terry Tyler
1981-82	336	643	.523	Terry Tyler
1982-83	520	1013	.513	Vinnie Johnson
1983-84	248	451	.550	Kent Benson
1984-85	201	397	.506	Kent Benson
1985-86	285	564	.505	Earl Cureton
1986-87	163	290	.562	John Salley
1987-88	276	481	.574	Rick Mahorn

MOST ASSISTS

YEAR	G	AST	AVG	PLAYER
1957-58	69	454	6.6	Dick McGuire
1958-59	71	443	6.2	Dick McGuire
1959-60	68	358	5.3	Dick McGuire
1960-61	78	530	6.8	Gene Shue
1961-62	80	465	5.8	Gene Shue
1962-63	80	325	5.1	Don Ohl
1963-64	80	244	3.1	Donnis Butcher
1963-64	80	244	3.1	Ray Scott
1964-65	79	253	3.2	Dave DeBusschere
1965-66	79	238	3.0	Ray Scott
1966-67	80	330	4.1	Dave Bing
1967-68	79	509	6.4	Dave Bing
1968-69	77	546	7.1	Dave Bing
1969-70	70	418	6.0	Dave Bing
1970-71	82	408	5.0	Dave Bing
1971-72	45	317	7.1	Dave Bing
1972-73	82	637	7.8	Dave Bing
1973-74	81	555	6.9	Dave Bing
1974-75	79	610	7.7	Dave Bing
1975-76	80	338	4.2	Eric Money
1976-77	81	592	7.3	Kevin Porter
1977-78	82	381	4.6	Chris Ford
1978-79	82	1099	13.4	Kevin Porter*
1979-80	55	238	4.3	Eric Money
1980-81	82	362	4.4	Ron Lee
1981-82	72	565	7.8	Isiah Thomas
1982-83	81	634	7.8	Isiah Thomas
1983-84	82	914	11.1	Isiah Thomas
1984-85	81	1123	13.9	Isiah Thomas*
1985-86	77	830	10.8	Isiah Thomas
1986-87	81	813	10.0	Isiah Thomas
1987-88	81	678	8.4	Isiah Thomas

MOST MINUTES PLAYED

YEAR	G	MIN	AVG	PLAYER
1957-58	72	2843	39.5	George Yardley
1958-59	72	2745	38.1	Gene Shue
1959-60	75	3338	44.5	Gene Shue*
1960-61	78	3361	43.1	Gene Shue
1961-62	80	3143	39.3	Gene Shue
1962-63	79	2971	37.6	Bailey Howell
1963-64	80	2964	37.1	Ray Scott
1964-65	79	2769	35.1	Dave DeBusschere
1965-66	80	2788	34.9	Eddie Miles
1966-67	78	2897	37.1	Dave DeBusschere
1967-68	79	3209	40.6	Dave Bing
1968-69	77	3039	39.5	Dave Bing
1969-70	81	2869	35.4	Jimmy Walker
1970-71	82	3065	37.4	Dave Bing
1971-72	80	3092	38.7	Bob Lanier
1972-73	82	3361	41.0	Dave Bing
1973-74	81	3124	38.6	Dave Bing
1974-75	79	3222	40.8	Dave Bing
1975-76	80	2998	37.5	Curtis Rowe
1976-77	82	2643	32.2	M. L. Carr
1977-78	82	2582	31.5	Chris Ford
1978-79	80	3207	40.1	M. L. Carr
1979-80	82	2670	32.6	Terry Tyler
1980-81	82	2549	31.1	Terry Tyler
1981-82	82	3077	37.5	Kelly Tripucka
1982-83	81	3092	38.1	Isiah Thomas*
1983-84	82	3007	36.7	Isiah Thomas
1984-85	81	3089	38.1	Isiah Thomas
1985-86	82	2891	35.3	Bill Laimbeer
1986-87	81	3013	37.2	Isiah Thomas
1987-88	81	2927	36.1	Isiah Thomas

MOST PERSONAL FOULS

YEAR	G	PF	AVG	PLAYER
1957-58	72	311	4.3	Walter Dukes*
1958-59	72	332	4.6	Walter Dukes*
1959-60	66	310	4.7	Walter Dukes
1960-61	73	313	4.3	Walter Dukes
1961-62	77	327	4.2	Walter Dukes
1962-63	79	301	3.8	Bailey Howell
1963-64	80	296	3.7	Ray Scott
1964-65	78	258	3.3	Reggie Harding
1965-66	79	305	3.9	Joe Strawder
1966-67	79	344	4.4	Joe Strawder*
1967-68	73	312	4.3	Joe Strawder
1968-69	77	256	3.3	Dave Bing
1969-70	82	247	3.0	Howard Komives
1970-71	82	272	3.3	Bob Lanier
1971-72	80	297	3.7	Bob Lanier
1972-73	81	278	3.4	Bob Lanier
1973-74	81	273	3.4	Bob Lanier
1974-75	76	237	3.1	Bob Lanier
1975-76	81	250	3.1	Al Eberhard
1976-77	82	294	3.6	Leon Douglas
1977-78	79	295	3.7	Leon Douglas
1978-79	82	302	3.7	Kevin Porter
1979-80	70	219	3.6	Leon Douglas
1980-81	80	317	4.0	Phil Hubbard
1981-82	72	253	3.5	Isiah Thomas
1982-83	82	320	3.9	Bill Laimbeer
1983-84	82	324	3.9	Isiah Thomas
1984-85	82	308	3.8	Bill Laimbeer
1985-86	82	291	3.6	Bill Laimbeer
1986-87	82	283	3.5	Bill Laimbeer
1987-88	82	294	3.6	John Salley

TOP REBOUNDERS

YEAR	G	RBS	AVG	PLAYER
1957-58	72	954	13.3	Walter Dukes
1958-59	72	958	13.3	Walter Dukes
1959-60	66	883	13.4	Walter Dukes
1960-61	77	1111	14.4	Bailey Howell
1961-62	79	996	12.6	Bailey Howell
1962-63	79	910	11.5	Bailey Howell
1963-64	80	1078	13.5	Ray Scott
1964-65	78	906	11.6	Reggie Harding
1965-66	79	916	11.6	Dave DeBusschere
1966-67	78	924	11.8	Dave DeBusschere
1967-68	80	1081	13.5	Dave DeBusschere
1968-69	81	959	11.8	Happy Hairston
1969-70	81	900	11.2	Otto Moore
1970-71	82	700	8.5	Otto Moore
1971-72	80	1132	14.2	Bob Lanier
1972-73	81	1205	14.9	Bob Lanier
1973-74	81	1074	13.3	Bob Lanier
1974-75	76	914	12.0	Bob Lanier
1975-76	64	746	11.7	Bob Lanier
1976-77	64	745	11.6	Bob Lanier
1977-78	63	715	11.3	Bob Lanier
1978-79	78	664	8.5	Leon Douglas
1979-80	82	627	7.6	Terry Tyler
1980-81	80	586	7.3	Phil Hubbard
1981-82	75	653	8.7	Kent Benson
1982-83	82	993	12.1	Bill Laimbeer
1983-84	82	1003	12.2	Bill Laimbeer
1984-85	82	1013	12.4	Bill Laimbeer
1985-86	82	1075	13.1	Bill Laimbeer*
1986-87	82	955	11.6	Bill Laimbeer
1987-88	82	832	10.1	Bill Laimbeer

MOST STEALS

YEAR	G	STE	AVG	PLAYER
1973-74	82	148	1.8	Chris Ford
1974-75	79	116	1.5	Dave Bing
1975-76	82	178	2.2	Chris Ford
1976-77	82	179	2.2	Chris Ford
1977-78	82	166	2.0	Chris Ford
1978-79	80	197	2.5	M. L. Carr
1979-80	69	129	1.9	John Long
1980-81	82	166	2.0	Ron Lee
1981-82	72	150	2.1	Isiah Thomas
1982-83	81	199	2.5	Isiah Thomas
1983-84	82	204	2.5	Isiah Thomas
1984-85	81	187	2.3	Isiah Thomas
1985-86	77	171	2.2	Isiah Thomas
1986-87	81	153	1.9	Isiah Thomas
1987-88	81	141	1.7	Isiah Thomas

*Led NBA

MOST TURNOVERS

YEAR	G	TRN	AVG	PLAYER
1977-78	76	322	4.2	Eric Money
1978-79	82	340	4.1	Kevin Porter
1979-80	58	238	4.1	Bob McAdoo
1980-81	59	190	3.2	Kent Benson
1981-82	72	299	4.2	Isiah Thomas
1982-83	81	326	4.0	Isiah Thomas
1983-84	82	307	3.7	Isiah Thomas
1984-85	81	302	3.7	Isiah Thomas
1985-86	77	289	3.8	Isiah Thomas
1986-87	81	343	4.2	Isiah Thomas
1987-88	81	273	3.4	Isiah Thomas

MOST BLOCKED SHOTS

YEAR	G	BS	AVG	PLAYER
1973-74	81	247	3.1	Bob Lanier
1974-75	76	172	2.3	Bob Lanier
1975-76	64	86	1.3	Bob Lanier
1976-77	64	126	1.9	Bob Lanier
1977-78	63	93	1.5	Bob Lanier
1978-79	82	201	2.5	Terry Tyler
1979-80	82	220	2.7	Terry Tyler
1980-81	82	180	2.2	Terry Tyler
1981-82	82	160	2.0	Terry Tyler
1982-83	82	160	2.0	Terry Tyler
1983-84	82	84	1.0	Bill Laimbeer
1984-85	82	90	1.1	Terry Tyler
1985-86	82	65	0.8	Bill Laimbeer
1986-87	82	125	1.5	John Salley
1987-88	82	137	1.7	John Salley

MOST DISQUALIFICATIONS

YEAR	G	DQ	PLAYER
1957-58	72	17	Walter Dukes
1958-59	72	22	Walter Dukes
1959-60	66	20	Walter Dukes
1960-61	73	16	Walter Dukes
1961-62	77	20	Walter Dukes
1962-63	79	9	Bailey Howell
1962-63	76	9	Ray Scott
1963-64	77	9	Bailey Howell
1963-64	78	9	Jack Moreland
1964-65	80	5	Terry Dischinger
1964-65	79	5	Dave DeBusschere
1964-65	66	5	Ray Scott
1964-65	78	5	Reggie Harding
1965-66	79	10	Joe Strawder
1966-67	79	19	Joe Strawder
1967-68	73	18	Joe Strawder
1968-69	75	5	Terry Dischinger
1969-70	75	5	Terry Dischinger
1970-71	62	5	Bill Hewitt
1971-72	79	7	Terry Dischinger
1972-73	81	4	Bob Lanier
1973-74	81	7	Bob Lanier
1974-75	66	3	Eric Money
1974-75	79	3	Dave Bing
1975-76	81	5	Al Eberhard
1976-77	82	10	Leon Douglas
1977-78	79	6	Leon Douglas
1978-79	78	13	Leon Douglas
1979-80	70	10	Leon Douglas
1980-81	80	14	Phil Hubbard
1981-82	81	3	Ron Lee
1981-82	48	3	Edgar Jones
1982-83	82	9	Bill Laimbeer
1983-84	82	8	Isiah Thomas
1984-85	81	8	Isiah Thomas
1985-86	77	9	Isiah Thomas
1986-87	81	5	Isiah Thomas
tie	82	5	John Salley
1987-88	82	6	Joe Dumars

Highest/Lowest Scores
Games Involving Pistons

Pistons Highest Scores
— Game	186	@ Denver (3 OT) (NBA Record)	Dec. 13, 1983
— Road Game	186	@ Denver (3 OT)	Dec. 13, 1983
— Half	87	vs. Cincinnati (2nd H)	Jan. 7, 1972
— Quarter	53	vs. Cincinnati (4th Q)	Jan. 7, 1972

Pistons Lowest Scores
— Cobo Home Game	79	vs. Chicago	Dec. 28, 1974
	79	vs. San Francisco	Jan. 15, 1964
— Silverdome Home Game	83	vs. Philadelphia	Jan. 20, 1981
	83	vs. New York	Apr. 15, 1983
— Road Game	75	at Cincinnati	Nov. 19, 1957
	75	at Philadelphia	Mar. 25, 1981
— Half	32	at Phoenix (1st H)	Dec. 17, 1970
— Quarter	9	at New York (2nd Q)	Nov. 19, 1983

Rivals Highest Scores
— Rivals Home Game	184	by Denver @ Denver (3 OT)	Dec. 13, 1983
— Cobo Arena Game	162	by Syracuse @ Detroit	Feb. 8, 1963
— Silverdome Home Game	147	by New Jersey	Apr. 17, 1982
— Half	91	by Boston @ Providence (2nd H)	Feb. 10, 1960
		by Syracuse @ Syracuse (2nd H)	Jan. 13, 1963
— Quarter	52	by Baltimore @ Baltimore (3rd Q)	Dec. 18, 1965

Rivals Lowest Scores
— Rivals Home Game	69	by Cincinnati @ Cincinnati	Jan. 10, 1959
— Cobo Arena Game	69	by Houston @ Cobo Arena	Dec. 4, 1974
— Silverdome Home Game	73	by Dallas	Nov. 8, 1980
		by Indiana	Apr. 2, 1987
— Half	26	by Kansas City-Omaha @ Cobo Arena (1st H)	Jan. 20, 1974
— Quarter	8	by Chicago @ Cobo Arena (2nd Q)	Dec. 19, 1973
		by Phoenix @ Cobo Arena (4th Q)	Feb. 18, 1976
		at Chicago (2nd Q)	Feb. 9, 1988

Combined Scores
— Road High Game	370	Det. (186) Denver (184) @ Denver (3 OT)	Dec. 13, 1984
— Cobo Arena High Game	297	Detroit (135), Syracuse (162)	Feb. 8, 1963
— Silverdome High Game	296	Detroit (152), Chicago (144)	Nov. 3, 1982
— Road Low Game	162	Detroit (85), Chicago (77) @ Chicago	Mar. 26, 1976
— Cobo Arena Low Game	149	Detroit (79), Chicago (70)	Dec. 28, 1974
— Silverdome Low Game	158	Detroit (83), Philadelphia (75)	Jan. 20, 1981

All-Time Detroit Team Records
Consecutives

Game or Portion
Most Consecutive Points	20	at Atlanta (3rd Q)	Nov. 6, 1982
Most Consecutive Free Throws	26	vs. Kansas City	Mar. 23, 1976

Season
Longest Winning Streak	10	Dec. 1-26, 1987
Longest Home Winning Streak	18	Jan. 15-March 22, 1988
Longest Road Winning Streak	6	Oct. 14-28, 1970
Best Start	9-0	Oct. 14-Oct. 28, 1970
Best Finish	5-0	Mar. 21-28, 1973; Apr. 7-14, 1985
Longest Losing Streak	14	Mar. 7-30, 1980
Longest Losing Streak (2 seasons)	21	(Mar. 7-30, 1980 — 14; Oct. 10-22, 1980 — 7)
Longest Home Losing Streak	10	Jan. 23-Feb. 27, 1980
Longest Home Losing Streak (2 seasons)	14	(Last 8 1979-80, First 6 1980-81)
Longest Road Losing Streak	19	Dec. 5, 1980 — Feb. 7, 1981
Poorest Start	0-7	1963-64 season; 1980-81 season
Poorest Finish	0-14	1979-80 season
Winning Margin OT Game	14	Detroit 132, Portland 118 (NBA Record)	Nov. 26, 1982

Where Pistons Have Finished

(Pistons were in Western Division through 1966-67; then in Eastern Division from 1967-70; then assigned to Midwest Division in Western Conference starting with 1970-71 season; Detroit assigned to Eastern Conference's Central Division in 1978-79.)

1957-58—Tied for second (33-39)
1958-59—Third (28-44)
1959-60—Second (30-45)
1960-61—Third (34-45)
1961-62—Third (37-43)
1962-63—Third (34-46)
1963-64—Fifth (23-57)
1964-65—Fourth (31-49)
1965-66—Fifth (22-58)
1966-67—Fifth (30-51)

1967-68—Fourth (40-42)
1968-69—Sixth (32-50)
1969-70—Seventh (31-51)
1970-71—Fourth (45-37)
1971-72—Fourth 26-56)
1972-73—Third (40-42)
1973-74—Third (52-30)
1974-75—Third (40-42)
1975-76—Second (36-46)
1976-77—Tied for second (44-38)

1977-78—Fourth (38-44)
1978-79—Tied for fourth (30-52)
1979-80—Sixth (16-66)
1980-81—Sixth (21-61)
1981-82—Third (39-43)
1982-83—Third (37-45)
1983-84—Second (49-33)
1984-85—Second (46-36)
1985-86—Third (46-36)
1986-87—Second (52-30)

Pistons All-Time
Largest Home Crowds

40,000-Plus Attendance
*61,983 vs. Boston, Jan. 29, '88
52,745 vs. Atlanta, Feb. 21, '87
47,692 vs. Atlanta, Mar. 30, '88
44,180 vs. Philadelphia, Feb. 15, '86
43,816 vs. Philadelphia, Feb. 16, '85
41,732 vs. L.A. Lakers, June 16, '88#
41,311 vs. Philadelphia, Mar. 14, '87
40,369 vs. Chicago, Feb. 13, '88
40,278 vs. L.A. Lakers, Jan. 8, '88

30,000-Plus Attendance

39,188# vs. L.A. Lakers, June 12, '88	34,523 vs. Boston, Dec. 4, '84
38,912# vs. Boston, June 3, '88	34,297# vs. L.A. Lakers, June 12, '88
38,873 vs. Chicago, Feb. 1, '87	33,896# vs. Boston, Mar. 8, '87
37,462 vs. Boston, Feb. 28, '88	33,854 vs. Cleveland, Mar. 12, '88
37,712 vs. Milwaukee, Apr. 5, '87	30,743 vs. San Antonio, Nov. 27, '87
37,279 vs. Boston, Jan. 10, '87	30,281 vs. Chicago, Mar. 4, '87
35,884 vs. Altanta, Feb. 12, '88	30,177 vs. Philadelphia, Nov. 16, '85
35,407 vs. Milwaukee, Mar. 31, '84	30,104 vs. L.A. Lakers, Mar. 4, '84
35,364 vs. San Antonio, Feb. 11, '84	30,091 vs. Boston, Apr. 13, '84

Playoff Games
41,732 vs. L.A. Lakers, June 16, '88
39,188 vs. L.A. Lakers, June 12, '88
38,912 vs. Boston, June 3, '88
34,297 vs. L.A. Lakers, June 14, '88

*All-Time NBA Record
#Playoff Game

Detroit Pistons in the Playoffs

1958—Eliminated Cincinnati, two games to none
　　　Lost to St. Louis, four games to one
1959—Lost to Minneapolis, two games to one
1960—Lost to Minneapolis, two games to none
1961—Lost to Los Angeles, three games to two
1962—Eliminated Cincinnati, three games to one
　　　Lost to Los Angeles, four games to two
1963—Lost to St. Louis, three games to one
1968—Lost to Boston, four games to two
1974—Lost to Chicago, four games to three
1975—Lost to Seattle, two games to one

1976—Eliminated Milwaukee, two games to one
　　　Lost to Golden State, four games to two
1977—Lost to Golden State, two games to one
1984—Lost to New York, three games to two
1985—Eliminated New Jersey, three games
　　　to none
　　　Lost to Boston, four games to two
1986—Lost to Atlanta, three games to one
1987—Eliminated Washington, three games
　　　to none
　　　Eliminated Atlanta, four games to one
　　　Lost to Boston, four games to three

Detroit Pistons in NBA All-Star Games

1958—George Yardley, Gene
　　　Shue, Dick McGuire
1959—George Yardley, Gene
　　　Shue, Dick McGuire
1960—George Yardley, Walter
　　　Dukes, Chuck Noble
1961—Walter Dukes, Gene
　　　Shue, Bailey Howell
1962—Bailey Howell,
　　　Gene Shue
1963—Bailey Howell, Don Ohl
1964—Bailey Howell, Don Ohl
1965—Terry Dischinger

1966—Dave DeBusschere,
　　　Eddie Miles
1967—Dave DeBusschere
1968—Dave Bing,
　　　Dave DeBusschere
1969—Dave Bing
1970—Jimmy Walker
1971—Dave Bing
1972—Bob Lanier,
　　　Jimmy Walker
1973—Dave Bing, Bob Lanier
1974—Dave Bing, Bob Lanier
1975—Dave Bing, Bob Lanier

1976—Curtis Rowe
1977—Bob Lanier
1978—Bob Lanier
1979—Bob Lanier
1982—Isiah Thomas,
　　　Kelly Tripucka
1983—Isiah Thomas,
　　　Bill Laimbeer
1984—Isiah Thomas, Bill
　　　Laimbeer, Kelly Tripucka
1985—Isiah Thomas,
　　　Bill Laimbeer
1986—Isiah Thomas
1987—Isiah Thomas,
　　　Bill Laimbeer

Detroit Pistons on Post-Season
NBA All-Star Teams

1957-58—George Yardley
　　　　(first team)
1959-60—Gene Shue
　　　　(first team)
1960-61—Gene Shue
　　　　(second team)
1962-63—Bailey Howell
　　　　(second team)

1967-68—Dave Bing
　　　　(first team)
1970-71—Dave Bing
　　　　(first team)
1970-71—Dave Bing
　　　　(second team)
1982-83—Isiah Thomas
　　　　(second team)

1983-84—Isiah Thomas
　　　　(first team)
1984-85—Isiah Thomas
　　　　(first team)
1985-86—Isiah Thomas
　　　　(first team)
1986-87—Isiah Thomas
　　　　(second team)

Detroit Pistons NBA Coach of the Year

1973-74—Ray Scott

Detroit Pistons on NBA All-Defense Teams

1978-79—M. L. Carr (second team)

Detroit Pistons on All-Rookie Teams

1964-65—Joe Caldwell (first team)
1965-66—Tom Van Arsdale (first team)
1966-67—Dave Bing (first team)
1970-71—Bob Lanier (first team)
1971-72—Curtis Rowe (honorable mention)
1972-73—Chris Ford (second team)

1976-77—Leon Douglas (honorable mention)
1978-79—Terry Tyler (first team), John Long (second team)
1979-80—George Kelser (second team)
1981-82—Isiah Thomas (first team),
      Kelly Tripucka (first team)
1985-86—Joe Dumars (first team)

Detroit Pistons Attendance

AT OLYMPIA	GAMES	TOTAL	AVERAGE
1957-58	28	134,411	4,789
1958-59	30	119,351	3,978
1959-60	31	178,007	5,742
1960-61	31	164,230	5,298
AT COBO ARENA	**GAMES**	**TOTAL**	**AVERAGE**
1961-62	30	143,081	4,769
1962-63	30	144,150	3,806
1963-64	30	100,386	3,346
1964-65	30	121,239	4,011
1965-66	30	120,013	4,000
1966-67	30	193,782	6,459
1967-68	32	224,164	7,005
1968-69	38	201,433	5,301
1969-70	38	167,648	4,412
1970-71	41	283,913	6,925
1971-72	41	188,763	4,604
1972-73	41	212,094	5,190
1973-74	41	300,565	7,331
1974-75	41	307,180	7,492
1975-76	41	251,352	6,130
1976-77	41	303,792	7,410
1977-78	41	223,382	5,448
AT PONTIAC SILVERDOME	**GAMES**	**TOTAL**	**AVERAGE**
1978-79	41	389,936	9,510
1979-80	41	333,233	8,128
1980-81	41	228,349	5,569
1981-82	41	406,317	9,910
1982-83	41	522,063	12,733
1983-84 (Led NBA)	41	652,865	15,923
1984-85 (Led NBA)	41	691,540	16,867
1985-86 (Led NBA)	41	695,239	16,957
1986-87 (Led NBA)	41	908,240	22,152
1987-88 (Led NBA)	41	1,066,505	26,012*

*NBA All-Time Record

Top Crowds In Detroit

AT PONTIAC SILVERDOME:
Regular Season — *61,983, Boston, January 29, 1988
All-Star Game — 31,745, Feb. 4, 1979.
Playoffs — *41,732, vs. LA Lakers, June 16, 1988

AT COBO ARENA:
Regular Season (single game) — 11,468, Pistons vs. Milwaukee, Feb. 9, 1971.
Regular Season (doubleheader) — 11,028, Pistons vs. San Francisco, Boston
    vs. Los Angeles, Feb. 12, 1963.
Playoffs — 11,499, Pistons vs. Chicago, April 1, 1974.

AT OLYMPIA:
Regular Season — 13,121, Pistons vs. Minneapolis, Philadelphia vs. St. Louis,
    Dec. 4, 1959.
All-Star Game — 10,541, Jan. 23, 1959.

AT JOE LOUIS ARENA:
Regular Season — 22,136, Pistons vs. Boston, March 31, 1985.
Playoffs — 21,208, Pistons vs. New York, April 27, 1984.

BIGGEST ROAD OR NEUTRAL FLOOR CROWD PISTONS EVER HAVE PLAYED BEFORE:
41,163 in doubleheader at Astrodome in Houston, Texas, Feb. 4, 1969.
    Detroit played Cincinnati while Boston opposed San Diego in
    doubleheader.

BIGGEST PISTONS CROWD FOR GAME IN ROAD CITY:
21,639 at Seattle (Kingdome), March 31, 1979.

BIGGEST PRE-SEASON CROWDS:
14,175 vs. Los Angeles at Silverdome, Oct. 12, 1982.
13,433 vs. New York at Ann Arbor, Sept. 24, 1970.
12,147 vs. Los Angeles at Detroit (JLA), Oct. 17, 1981.

BIGGEST OPENING NIGHT CROWD:
27,563 vs. Boston, October 26, 1984.

*NBA All-Time Record.

All-Time Detroit Individual Records

Individual — One Season

Most Points	2213	Dave Bing, 1970-71
Highest Scoring Average	27.8	George Yardley, 1957-58
Field Goals	836	Dave Bing, 1967-68
Field Goals Attempted	1903	Dave Bing, 1967-68
Field Goal Percentage	.574	Rick Mahorn, 1987-88
Free Throws	655	George Yardley, 1957-58
Free Throws Attempted	808	George Yardley, 1957-58
Free Throw Percentage	.894	Bill Laimbeer, 1986-87
Most Rebounds	1205	Bob Lanier, 1972-73
Offensive Rebounds	329	Bill Laimbeer, 1983-84
Defensive Rebounds	805	Bob Lanier, 1973-74
Assists	*1123	Isiah Thomas, 1984-85
Personal Fouls	344	Joe Strawder, 1966-67
Disqualifications	22	Walter Dukes, 1958-59
Steals	204	Isiah Thomas, 1983-84
Most Turnovers	343	Isiah Thomas, 1986-87
Blocked Shots	247	Bob Lanier, 1973-74

Individual — One Game or Portion

Most Points

— Game	56	Kelly Tripucka (vs. Chicago)	Jan. 29, 1983
— Half (1st)	28	Kelly Tripucka (vs. Chicago)	Jan. 29, 1983
	28	Kelly Tripucka (vs. Golden State)	Mar. 12, 1982
— Half (2nd)	37	Dave Bing (vs. Boston)	Apr. 1, 1968
— Quarter (1st)	20	Kelly Tripucka (vs. Kansas City)	Nov. 12, 1983
— Quarter (2nd)	20	Kelly Tripucka (vs. Golden State)	Mar. 12, 1982
— Quarter (3rd)	24	Isiah Thomas (vs. Cleveland)	Feb. 26, 1984
— Quarter (4th)	24	Isiah Thomas (vs. Atlanta)	Mar. 12, 1983

Most Field Goals

— Game	22	Dave Bing (vs. Chicago)	Feb. 21, 1971
— Half	16	Dave Bing (vs. Boston) (2nd H playoffs)	Apr. 1, 1968
— Quarter	11	Isiah Thomas (vs. Cleveland) (3rd Q)	Feb. 26, 1984

Most Field Goals Attempted

— Game	41	Bob Lanier (vs. Milwaukee)	Dec. 25, 1971
— Half	28	Dave Bing (vs. Boston) (2nd H playoffs)	Apr. 1, 1968
— Quarter	17	Dave Bing (vs. Boston) (4th Q playoffs)	Apr. 1, 1968

All-Time Pistons Individual Records

Most Free Throws

— Game	20	George Yardley (@ St. Louis)	Dec. 26, 1957
	20	Walter Dukes (@ Los Angeles)	Jan. 19, 1961
	20	Kelly Tripucka (vs. Chicago)	Jan. 29, 1983
— Half	17	Adrian Dantley (vs. Sacramento) (2nd H)	Dec. 10, 1986
— Quarter	14	Adrian Dantley (vs. Sacramento) (4th Q)	Dec. 10, 1986

Most Free Throws Attempted

— Game	24	George Yardley (@ St. Louis)	Dec. 26, 1957
	24	Walter Dukes (@ Los Angeles)	Jan. 19, 1961
	24	Bob Lanier (vs. New Jersey) (2nd H)	Oct. 13, 1978
— Half	20	Isiah Thomas (@ Chicago) (2nd H)	Oct. 26, 1985
— Quarter	15	George Yardley (vs. Minneapolis @ Olympia) (3rd Q)	Dec. 25, 1957
		Adrian Dantley (vs. Sacramento)	Dec. 10, 1986

Most Total Rebounds

— Game	33	Bob Lanier (vs. Seattle)	Dec. 22, 1972
— Half	21	Bailey Howell (vs. Los Angeles @ Olympia) (1st H)	Nov. 25, 1960
— Quarter	14	Ray Scott (vs. Philadelphia) (1st Q)	Dec. 20, 1961

Most Offensive Rebounds

— Game	13	Earl Williams (@ Boston)	Jan. 23, 1976
— Half	7	Willie Norwood (vs. Los Angeles) (1st H)	Dec. 12, 1973
	7	Bob Lanier (@ Golden State) (2nd H)	Nov. 2, 1976
	7	Bill Laimbeer (vs. Indiana) (2nd H)	Apr. 10, 1984
	7	Earl Cureton (vs. New York) (2nd H)	Feb. 22, 1984
— Quarter	6	Willie Norwood (vs. Los Angeles) (2nd Q)	Dec. 12, 1973
	6	Lindsay Hairston (vs. Golden St.) (4th Q)	Dec. 17, 1975
	6	Earl Cureton (vs. New York) (4th Q)	Feb. 22, 1984

Most Defensive Rebounds

— Game	18	Bob Lanier (@ Washington)	Jan. 18, 1974
	18	Bob Lanier (@ Boston)	Nov. 8, 1974
	18	Bob Lanier (vs. Milwaukee)	Nov. 13, 1974
— Half	13	Bob Lanier (vs. Milwaukee) (1st H)	Nov. 15, 1975
— Quarter	8	Bob Lanier (vs. Milwaukee) (2nd Q)	Nov. 13, 1974
	8	Bob Lanier (vs. Portland) (3rd Q)	Dec. 8, 1973
	8	Leon Douglas (vs. Houston) (4th Q)	Jan. 19, 1980
	8	Terry Tyler (vs. New York) (1st Q)	Mar. 5, 1980
	8	Earl Cureton (vs. Atlanta) (4th Q)	Dec. 2, 1983

All-Time Pistons Individual Records

Most Assists
— Game	25	Kevin Porter (vs. Boston)	Mar. 9, 1979
	25	Kevin Porter (vs. Phoenix)	Apr. 1, 1979
	25	Isiah Thomas (vs. Dallas)	Feb. 23, 1985
— Half	16	Isiah Thomas (vs. Dallas) (1st H)	Feb. 23, 1985
— Quarter	11	Isiah Thomas (vs. Golden State) (1st Q)	Jan. 24, 1985

Most Personal Fouls
— Half	6	Terry Dischinger (@ Philadelphia)	Dec. 12, 1969
— Quarter	6	Roger Brown (vs. Golden State)	Mar. 25, 1977
	6	Paul Mokeski (vs. Cleveland)	Jan. 24, 1981
	6	Joe Dumars (vs. Atlanta)	Feb. 28, 1986

Most Turnovers
— Game	12	Kevin Porter (@ Philadelphia)	Feb. 7, 1979
— Half	8	Isiah Thomas (vs. Indiana) (2nd H)	Apr. 10, 1985

Most Steals
— Game	9	Earl Tatum (@ Los Angeles)	Nov. 28, 1978
	9	Ron Lee (vs. Houston)	Mar. 16, 1980
— Half	6	Chris Ford (@ Chicago) (2nd H)	Mar. 26, 1976
	6	Isiah Thomas (vs. Washington) (1st H)	Nov. 25, 1983
— Quarter	5	Chris Ford (vs. Golden State)	Mar. 25, 1977
	5	Ron Lee (vs. Washington) (3rd Q)	Nov. 19, 1981
	5	John Long (vs. Indiana) (1st Q)	Dec. 3, 1983

Most Blocked Shots
— Game	10	Edgar Jones (vs. Indiana)	Dec. 17, 1981
— Half	7	Edgar Jones (vs. Indiana) (2nd H)	Dec. 17, 1981
	7	Terry Tyler (vs. Chicago) (1st H)	Nov. 3, 1982
— Quarter	5	Terry Tyler (vs. Chicago) (1st Q)	Nov. 10, 1978
	5	Terry Tyler (vs. Seattle) (4th Q)	Feb. 7, 1980
	5	Terry Tyler (vs. Philadelphia) (3rd Q)	Feb. 15, 1980

Three Point Field Goals Attempted
— Game	12	Ron Lee (vs. Houston)	Mar. 16, 1980
— Half	7	Ron Lee (vs. Houston) (2nd H)	Mar. 16, 1980
— Quarter	5	Ron Lee (vs. Houston) (1st & 3rd Q)	Mar. 16, 1980

Consecutives

Season
Consecutive Free Throws Made	51	John Long (21 games)	Mar. 2, 1984 to Apr. 10, 1984
Consecutive Games Played	646	Bill Laimbeer	Feb. 17, 1982 to Apr. 24, 1988

Game or Portion
Consecutive Field Goals	13	Isiah Thomas (vs. Cleveland)	Feb. 26, 1984
Consecutive Free Throws	16	George Yardley (vs. Syr. @ Olympia)	Feb. 4, 1958
	16	Gene Shue (@ New York)	Nov. 10, 1961
	16	Isiah Thomas (vs. Atlanta)	Feb. 28, 1986

Detroit Pistons Select Circle

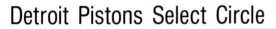

50 Points or More Club

Player	Opponent/Date	FG	FT	PTS
Kelly Tripucka	vs. Chicago, Jan. 29, 1983	18	20	56
Dave Bing	vs. Chicago, Feb. 21, 1971	22	10	54
George Yardley	vs. Syracuse, Feb. 4, 1958	18	16	52
George Yardley	at Boston, Jan. 15, 1958	19	13	51

Most Points by Position

— Forward	56	Kelly Tripucka (vs. Chicago)	Jan. 29, 1983
— Center	48	Bob Lanier (vs. Portland)	Nov. 28, 1972
— Guard	54	Dave Bing (vs. Chicago)	Feb. 21, 1971

All-Time Opponent Records vs. Pistons

Team — One Season

Most Points Against	9889	1967-68
Most Field Goals Attempted Against	8106	1971-72
Most Field Goals Against	3847	1979-80
Most Free Throws Attempted Against	2703	1970-71
Most Free Throws Against	2040	1970-71
Most Offensive Rebounds Against	1319	1979-80
Most Defensive Rebounds Against	2917	1973-74
Most Rebounds Against	4377	1971-72
Most Assists Against	2407	1978-79
Most Steals Against	902	1977-78
Most Turnovers Against	1828	1976-77
Most Blocked Shots Against	585	1980-81
Most Three-Point Field Goals Against	133	1986-87
Most Three-Point Field Goals Att. Against	419	1986-87

All-Time Opponents Records vs. Pistons

Team — One Game or Portion

Most Points Against
—	Game	184	at Denver (3 OT)	Dec. 13, 1983
—	Half (1st)	86	at Syracuse	Feb. 21, 1961
—	Half (2nd)	91	at Boston (Providence)	Feb. 10, 1960
			at Syracuse	Jan. 13, 1963
—	Quarter (1st)	48	at St. Louis	Dec. 6, 1960
—	Quarter (2nd)	48	at Syracuse	Feb. 12, 1961
—	Quarter (3rd)	52	at Baltimore	Dec. 18, 1965
—	Quarter (4th)	51	at Los Angeles	Mar. 31, 1962

Most Field Goals Against
—	Game	68	at Denver	Dec. 13, 1983
—	Half	40	vs. Syracuse	Jan. 13, 1963
—	Quarter	23	at St. Louis	Dec. 6, 1960

Most Field Goals Attempted Against
—	Game	136	by Boston at New York (OT)	Nov. 15, 1960
—	Half	70	vs. Syracuse	Jan. 24, 1962
—	Quarter	37	at Boston	Feb. 5, 1984

Most Free Throws Against
—	Game	47	at Syracuse + at Denver (3 OTS)	Jan. 12, 1958 Dec. 13, 1983
—	Half	26	at Philadelphia	Jan. 5, 1969
			at Buffalo (2nd H)	Nov. 26, 1976
—	Quarter	20	at Denver (3rd Q)	Jan. 27, 1981
			at Sacramento (4th Q)	Dec. 17, 1985

Most Free Throws Attempted Against
—	Game	60	by Baltimore	Nov. 4, 1964
—	Half	37	by Philadelphia (2nd H)	Nov. 24, 1976
—	Quarter	25	at Sacramento (4th Q)	Dec. 17, 1985

Most Rebounds Against
—	Game	112	at Boston	Dec. 24, 1960
—	Half	55	vs. Los Angeles	Dec. 12, 1962
—	Quarter	31	vs. New York	Dec. 12, 1962

Most Offensive Rebounds Against
—	Game	33	by Chicago	Nov. 10, 1978
—	Half	18	by Atlanta (2nd H-2 OT)	Oct. 18, 1980
—	Quarter	12	by Philadelphia (1st Q)	Dec. 19, 1975

Most Defensive Rebounds Against
—	Game	54	by Boston	Nov. 8, 1975
—	Half	28	by Boston (1st H)	Nov. 8, 1975
—	Quarter	16	by Boston (2nd Q)	Nov. 8, 1975

Most Assists Against
—	Game	53	at Milwaukee	Dec. 26, 1978
—	Half	30	at Milwaukee	Dec. 26, 1978
—	Quarter	19	at Milwaukee	Dec. 26, 1978

Most Steals Against
—	Game	24	at Philadelphia	Nov. 11, 1978
—	Half	13	at Philadelphia	Nov. 11, 1978
—	Quarter	9	at Phoenix (3rd Q)	Jan. 13, 1978

Most Turnovers Against
—	Game	41	by New Jersey	Nov. 16, 1980
—	Half	25	by San Antonio (2nd H)	Oct. 16, 1980
—	Quarter	17	by San Antonio (4th Q)	Oct. 16, 1980

Field Goal Pct.	.699	at Chicago	Jan. 22, 1980

All-Time Opponents Records vs. Pistons

Team — One Game or Portion

Most Blocked Shots Against
—	Game	19	at Los Angeles	Oct. 26, 1973
—	Half	10	at Los Angeles (1st H)	Oct. 26, 1973
		10	at Atlanta (1st H)	Mar. 21, 1980
		10	by Milwaukee (2nd H)	Nov. 12, 1980
—	Quarter	8	by Golden State (4th Q)	Dec. 17, 1975

Three Point Field Goals Made
—	Game	6	vs. Dallas	Dec. 18, 1987
—	Half	4	at Boston (2nd H)	Dec. 4, 1980
			at Washington (2nd H)	Feb. 2, 1984
—	Quarter	3	at Boston (4th)	Dec. 4, 1980
		3	at New York (4th)	Feb. 22, 1984
		3	at Washington (4th)	Feb. 2, 1984
		3	vs. Dallas (4th)	Dec. 18, 1987

All-Time Individual Opponents Records Against Detroit Pistons

Most Points
— Game	73	David Thompson, Denver	Apr. 9, 1978
— Half (1st)	53	David Thompson, Denver	Apr. 9, 1978
— Half (2nd)	37	Michael Jordan, Chicago	Mar. 4, 1987
— Quarter (1st)	32	David Thompson, Denver	Apr. 9, 1978
— Quarter (2nd)	22	Hal Greer, Philadelphia	Mar. 3, 1969
— Quarter (3rd)	20	Hal Greer, Philadelphia	Dec. 21, 1967
— Quarter (4th)	26	Michael Jordan, Chicago	Mar. 4, 1987

Most Field Goals
— Game	28	David Thompson, Denver	Apr. 9, 1978
— Half	20	David Thompson, Denver (1st H)	Apr. 9, 1978
— Quarter	13	David Thompson, Denver (1st Q)	Apr. 9, 1978

Most Field Goals Attempted
— Game	50	Wilt Chamberlain, San Fran. (overtime)	Feb. 11, 1964
— Half	29	Wilt Chamberlain, San Fran. (overtime)	Feb. 11, 1964
— Quarter	18	Wilt Chamberlain, at Philadelphia	Mar. 3, 1960

Most Free Throws
— Game	23	Nate Archibald, at Cincinnati (overtime)	Feb. 5, 1972
— Half	13	Ken Sears, New York (1st H @ Olympia)	Nov. 7, 1958
	13	Nate Archibald, at Cincinnati (overtime)	Feb. 5, 1972
	13	David Thompson, Denver (1st H)	Apr. 9, 1978
— Quarter	12	Calvin Natt, Portland (4th Q)	Feb. 23, 1980
	11	Frank Ramsey, Boston (3rd Q @ Olympia)	Dec. 3, 1957

Most Free Throws Attempted
— Game	26	Earl Monroe, at Baltimore	Feb. 24, 1968
— Half	17	Wilt Chamberlain, Philadelphia (@ Olympia)	Jan. 23, 1960
	17	Wilt Chamberlain, Philadelphia (@ Olympia)	Dec. 3, 1960
	17	Wilt Chamberlain, San Fran. (2nd H) (overtime)	Feb. 11, 1964
— Quarter	12	Jerry West, Los Angeles (3rd Q) (playoff)	Apr. 3, 1962
	12	Earvin Johnson, Los Angeles (4th Q)	Mar. 4, 1984

Most Total Rebounds
— Game	49	Bill Russell, Boston at Providence, R.I.	Mar. 11, 1965
— Half	23	Bill Russell, Boston (1st H)	Jan. 2, 1965
— Quarter	15	Wilt Chamberlain, San Fran. (4th Q)	Feb. 12, 1963

Most Offensive Rebounds
— Game	15	Mark Landsberger, Chicago	Nov. 10, 1978
— Half	8	George McGinnis, at Philadelphia (1st H)	Oct. 19, 1977
— Quarter	7	Sidney Wicks, Portland (1st Q)	Dec. 8, 1973

All-Time Individual Opponents Records Against Detroit Pistons

Most Defensive Rebounds
— Game	20	Dave Cowens, Boston	Nov. 8, 1975
— Half	14	Buck Williams, at New Jersey (1st H)	Jan. 21, 1984
— Quarter	8	Buck Williams, at New Jersey (1st Q)	Jan. 21, 1984

Most Assists
— Game	24	Kevin Porter, at Washington	Mar. 20, 1980
— Half	13	Kevin Porter, at Washington (2nd H)	Mar. 20, 1980
— Quarter	11	John McCarthy, at St. Louis (1st)	Mar. 8, 1960

Most Personal Fouls
— Quarter	6	Paul Mokeski, Milwaukee (4th Q)	Dec. 2, 1987

Most Steals
— Game	9	Larry Steele, at Portland	Mar. 14, 1976
— Half	5	LeRoy Ellis, Philadelphia	Mar. 23, 1974
	5	Larry Steele, Portland (2nd H)	Jan. 16, 1976
	5	Larry Steele, at Portland (2nd H)	Mar. 14, 1976
— Quarter	4	Many Players	

Most Turnovers
— Game	11	Orlando Woolridge, Chicago	Nov. 3, 1982

Most Blocked Shots
— Game	11	Kareem Abdul-Jabbar, Los Angeles	Dec. 3, 1975
	11	Elvin Hayes, Washington	Mar. 3, 1978
— Half	7	George Johnson, Golden State (2nd H)	Dec. 17, 1975
	7	Elvin Hayes, Washington (1st H)	Mar. 3, 1978
— Quarter	7	George Johnson, Golden State (4th Q)	Dec. 17, 1975

3-Point Field Goal Attempts
	7	Joe Hassett, Golden State	Dec. 15, 1981
	7	Mark Aguirre, Dallas	Dec. 18, 1987

Home Team Records

Home records in this section will be dealt with in three categories: Home High in the Detroit area, the Silverdome Arena High and the Detroit Pistons High. Some records would cover all three categories.

One Team — Game

Most Points
— Home High	162	Syracuse vs. Pistons	Feb. 8, 1963
— Silverdome High	160	Pistons vs. Boston	Mar. 9, 1979
— Pistons High	160	Pistons vs. Boston	Mar. 9, 1979

Most Field Goals
— Home High	69	Pistons vs. Boston	Mar. 9, 1979
— Silverdome High	69	Pistons vs. Boston	Mar. 9, 1979
— Pistons High	69	Pistons vs. Boston	Mar. 9, 1979

Most Field Goals Attempted
— Home High	142	Pistons vs. Boston (2 OT @ U-D)	Nov. 17, 1959
— Silverdome High	117	Pistons vs. New York	Feb. 17, 1983
	117	Pistons vs. Golden State	Feb. 10, 1984
— Pistons High	142	Pistons vs. Boston (2 OT @ U-D)	Nov. 17, 1959

Most Free Throws
— Home High	50	Minneapolis vs. Cincinnati (@ Olympia)	Nov. 27, 1957
— Silverdome High	45	Pistons vs. New Jersey	Feb. 29, 1980
— Pistons High	45	Pistons vs. New Jersey	Feb. 29, 1980

Most Free Throws Attempted
— Home High	60	Baltimore vs. Pistons	Nov. 4, 1964
— Silverdome High	57	Pistons vs. New Jersey	Feb. 29, 1980
— Pistons High	57	Pistons vs. New Jersey	Feb. 29, 1980

Home Team Records

Most Rebounds
— Home High	105	Pistons vs. St. Louis (@ Olympia)	Jan. 7, 1958
	105	Pistons vs. St. Louis (@ Olympia)	Dec. 7, 1960
— Silverdome High	70	Pistons vs. Golden State	Feb. 10, 1984
— Pistons High	105	Pistons vs. St. Louis (@ Olympia)	Dec. 7, 1958
	105	Pistons vs. St. Louis (@ Olympia)	Jan. 7, 1960

Most Offensive Rebounds
— Home High	34	Pistons vs. Los Angeles	Dec. 12, 1973
	34	Chicago vs. Pistons	Nov. 10, 1978
— Silverdome High	34	Chicago vs. Pistons	Nov. 10, 1978
— Pistons High	34	Pistons vs. Los Angeles	Dec. 12, 1973

Most Defensive Rebounds
— Home High	54	Boston vs. Pistons	Nov. 8, 1975
— Silverdome High	46	Pistons vs. Milwaukee	Mar. 18, 1983
	46	Washington vs. Pistons	Oct. 24, 1979
	46	Pistons vs. Atlanta	Dec. 2, 1983
— Pistons High	46	Pistons vs. Atlanta	Dec. 2, 1983

Most Assists
— Home High	45	Pistons vs. New York	Nav. 28, 1962
— Silverdome High	40	Pistons vs. Chicago	Nov. 3, 1982
	40	Pistons vs. Washington	Feb. 29, 1984
— Pistons High	45	Pistons vs. New York	Nov. 28, 1962

Most Personal Fouls
— Home High	43	Pistons vs. New Jersey	Feb. 29, 1980
— Silverdome High	43	Pistons vs. New Jersey	Feb. 29, 1980
— Pistons High	43	Pistons vs. New Jersey	Feb. 29, 1980

Most Disqualifications
— Home High	4	Los Angeles vs. Pistons (playoffs)	Apr. 3, 1962
	4	Pistons vs. New Jersey	Feb. 29, 1980
— Silverdome High	4	Pistons vs. New Jersey	Feb. 29, 1980
— Pistons High	4	Pistons vs. Buffalo	Nov. 11, 1974
	4	Pistons vs. New Jersey	Feb. 29, 1980

Most Steals
— Home High	20	Golden State vs. Pistons	Mar. 25, 1977
	20	Pistons vs. Phoenix	Feb. 1, 1978
— Silverdome High	17	Pistons vs. Seattle	Nov. 2, 1978
	17	Pistons vs. Boston	Dec. 5, 1978
	17	Indiana vs. Pistons	Oct. 12, 1979
	17	Pistons vs. Milwaukee	Nov. 23, 1979
— Pistons High	20	Pistons vs. Phoenix	Feb. 1, 1978

Most Turnovers
— Home High	38	vs. Atlanta (2 OT)	Oct. 18, 1980
— Silverdome High	38	vs. Atlanta (2 OT)	Oct. 18, 1980
— Pistons High	38	vs. Atlanta (2 OT)	Oct. 18, 1980

Most Blocked Shots
	20	Pistons vs. Chicago (regulation)	Nov. 3, 1982
— Home High	21	Pistons vs. Atlanta (2 OT)	Oct. 18, 1980
— Silverdome High	21	Pistons vs. Atlanta (2 OT)	Oct. 18, 1980
— Pistons High	21	Pistons vs. Atlanta (2 OT)	Oct. 18, 1980

Home Team Records

Most Consecutive Points
— Home High	18	Los Angeles vs. Pistons	Jan. 11, 1971
	18	Pistons vs. Cleveland	Dec. 7, 1978
	18	Philadelphia vs. Pistons	Nov. 5, 1982
	18	Pistons vs. Indiana	Dec. 3, 1983
— Silverdome High	18	Pistons vs. Cleveland	Dec. 7, 1978
	18	Pistons vs. Indiana	Dec. 3, 1983
— Pistons High	18	Pistons vs. Cleveland	Dec. 7, 1978
	18	Pistons vs. Indiana	Dec. 3, 1983

Most Consecutive Free Throws
— Home High	35	Chicago vs. Pistons	Mar. 3, 1968
— Silverdome High	20	Pistons vs. Milwaukee	Mar. 20, 1981
— Pistons High	26	Pistons vs. Kansas City	Mar. 23, 1976

Most 3-Point Field Goals Att.
— Home High	17	Milwaukee vs. Pistons	Nov. 28, 1986
— Silverdome High	17	Milwaukee vs. Pistons	Nov. 28, 1986
— Pistons High	14	Pistons vs. Kansas City	Mar. 3, 1983

Most 3-Point Field Goals Made
— Home High	6	Pistons vs. Houston	Mar. 16, 1980
	6	Pistons vs. Dallas	Dec. 18, 1987
— Silverdome High	6	Pistons vs. Houston	Mar. 16, 1980
	6	Milwaukee vs. Pistons	Oct. 31, 1986
	6	Pistons vs. Dallas	Dec. 18, 1987
— Pistons High	6	Pistons vs. Houston	Mar. 16, 1980
	6	Pistons vs. Dallas	Dec. 18, 1987

One Team — One Half

Most Points
— Home High	87	Syracuse vs. Pistons (2nd H)	Feb. 8, 1963
	87	Pistons vs. Cincinnati (2nd H)	Jan. 7, 1972
— Silverdome High	82	Pistons vs. Boston (1st H)	Mar. 9, 1979
— Pistons High	87	Pistons vs. Cincinnati (2nd H)	Jan. 7, 1972

Most Field Goals
— Home High	37	Pistons vs. Boston (1st H)	Mar. 9, 1979
— Silverdome High	37	Pistons vs. Boston (1st H)	Mar. 9, 1979
— Pistons High	37	Pistons vs. Boston (1st H)	Mar. 9, 1979

Most Field Goals Attempted
— Home High	77	New York vs. Pistons (2nd H @ Olympia)	Jan. 22, 1958
— Silverdome High	63	Pistons vs. Los Angeles (2nd H)	Nov. 15, 1978
	63	Pistons vs. Utah (1st H)	Nov. 18, 1983
— Pistons High	65	Pistons vs. Boston (1st H @ U-D)	Nov. 17, 1959

Most Free Throws
— Home High	34	Pistons vs. New Jersey (2nd H)	Feb. 29, 1980
— Silverdome High	34	Pistons vs. New Jersey (2nd H)	Feb. 29, 1980
— Pistons High	34	Pistons vs. New Jersey (2nd H)	Feb. 29, 1980

Most Free Throws Attempted
— Home High	45	Pistons vs. Baltimore (2nd H @ Olympia)	Jan. 15, 1966
— Silverdome High	41	Pistons vs. New Jersey (2nd H)	Feb. 29, 1980
— Pistons High	45	Pistons vs. Baltimore (2nd H)	Jan. 15, 1966

Most Rebounds
— Home High	60	New York vs. Pistons (1st H @ Olympia)	Jan. 22, 1967
— Silverdome High	38	Seattle vs. Pistons (2nd H)	Feb. 7, 1980
	38	Pistons vs. Atlanta (1st H)	Dec. 2, 1983
	38	Pistons vs. Golden State (2nd H)	Feb. 10, 1984
— Pistons High	52	Pistons vs. Seattle (2nd H)	Jan. 19, 1968

Most Offensive Rebounds
— Home High	19	Pistons vs. Los Angeles (1st H)	Dec. 12, 1973
— Silverdome High	18	Pistons vs. Golden State	Feb. 10, 1984
— Pistons High	19	Pistons vs. Los Angeles (1st H)	Dec. 12, 1973

Most Defensive Rebounds
— Home High	28	Boston vs. Pistons (1st H)	Nov. 8, 1975
— Silverdome High	26	San Diego vs. Pistons (1st H)	Dec. 29, 1978
— Pistons High	27	Pistons vs. Kansas City (1st H)	Nov. 6, 1974

Most Assists
— Home High	26	Pistons vs. Chicago	Nov. 3, 1982
— Silverdome High	26	Pistons vs. Chicago	Nov. 3, 1982
— Pistons High	26	Pistons vs. Chicago	Nov. 3, 1982

Most Personal Fouls
— Home High	25	St. Louis vs. New York (1st H @ Olympia)	Oct. 23, 1957
— Silverdome High	23	Pistons vs. New Jersey (2nd H)	Oct. 13, 1978
	23	Atlanta vs. Pistons (2nd H)	Nov. 24, 1978
— Pistons High	23	Pistons vs. St. Louis (1st H)	Jan. 1, 1962
	23	Pistons vs. New Jersey	Oct. 13, 1978

Most Steals
— Home High	14	Pistons vs. Phoenix (2nd H)	Feb. 1, 1978
— Silverdome High	13	Pistons vs. Philadelphia (2nd H)	Feb. 21, 1979
— Pistons High	14	Pistons vs. Phoenix (2nd H)	Feb. 1, 1978

Home Team Records

Most Turnovers
— Home High 25   San Antonio vs. Pistons (2nd H)   Oct. 16, 1980
— Silverdome High 25   San Antonio vs. Pistons (2nd H)   Oct. 16, 1980
— Pistons High 21   Pistons vs. Atlanta (2nd H)   Oct. 18, 1980

Most Blocked Shots
— Home High 15   Pistons vs. Washington (2nd H)   Nov. 19, 1981
— Silverdome High 15   Pistons vs. Washington (2nd H)   Nov. 19, 1981
— Pistons High 15   Pistons vs. Washington (2nd H)   Nov. 19, 1981

Most Consecutive Free Throws
— Home High 23   Chicago vs. Pistons (2nd H)   Mar. 3, 1968
— Silverdome High 16   Pistons vs. Chicago (2nd H)   *May 18, 1988
— Pistons High 16   Pistons vs. Chicago (2nd H)   *May 18, 1988
*Playoffs

One Team — One Quarter

Most Points
— Home High 53   Pistons vs. Cincinnati (4th Q)   Jan. 7, 1972
— Silverdome High 47   Pistons vs. Chicago (4th Q)   Nov. 6, 1985
— Pistons High 53   Pistons vs. Cincinnati (4th Q)   Jan. 7, 1972

Most Field Goals
— Home High 22   Pistons vs. Chicago (4th Q)   Mar. 23, 1969
— Silverdome High 20   Pistons vs. Boston (1st Q)   Mar. 9, 1979
— Pistons High 22   Pistons vs. Chicago (4th Q)   Mar. 23, 1969

Most Field Goals Attempted
— Home High 45   Pistons vs. Los Angeles (4th Q)   Nov. 28, 1965
— Silverdome High 36   Pistons vs. Los Angeles (4th Q)   Nov. 15, 1979
                                  36   Pistons vs. Golden State (4th Q)   Feb. 10, 1984
— Pistons High 45   Pistons vs. Los Angeles (4th Q)   Nov. 28, 1965

Most Free Throws
— Home High 24   St. Louis vs. Syracuse (4th Q @ Olympia)   Dec. 21, 1957
— Silverdome High 19   Los Angeles vs. Pistons (4th Q)   Mar. 4, 1984
— Pistons High 21   Pistons vs. Philadelphia @ Olympia)   Dec. 14, 1960
                                  21   Pistons vs. Cincinnati (4th Q)   Jan. 7, 1972

Most Free Throws Attempted
— Home High 29   St. Louis vs. Syracuse (4th Q @ Olympia)   Dec. 21, 1957
— Silverdome High 24   Washington vs. Pistons (4th Q)   Nov. 25, 1983
— Pistons High 25   Pistons vs. Cincinnati (4th Q)   Jan. 7, 1972

Most Rebounds
— Home High 38   Pistons vs. St. Louis (2nd Q @ Olympia)   Dec. 7, 1960
— Silverdome High 28   Seattle vs. Pistons (4th Q)   Feb. 7, 1980
— Pistons High 38   Pistons vs. St. Louis (2nd Q @ Olympia)   Dec. 7, 1960

Most Offensive Rebounds
— Home High 12   Philadelphia vs. Pistons (1st Q)   Dec. 19, 1975
                                  12   Seattle vs. Pistons (4th Q)   Feb. 7, 1980
— Silverdome High 12   Seattle vs. Pistons (4th Q)   Feb. 7, 1980
                                  12   Pistons vs. Golden State (2nd Q)   Feb. 10, 1984
— Pistons High 12   Pistons vs. Golden State (2nd Q)   Feb. 10, 1984

Most Defensive Rebounds
— Home High 16   Pistons vs. Seattle (1st Q)   Jan. 26, 1974
                                  16   Boston vs. Pistons (2nd Q)   Nov. 8, 1975
                                  16   Pistons vs. Houston (4th Q)   Jan. 19, 1980
                                  16   Seattle vs. Pistons (4th Q)   Feb. 7, 1980
— Silverdome High 16   Pistons vs. Houston (4th Q)   Jan. 19, 1980
                                  16   Seattle vs. Pistons (4th Q)   Feb. 7, 1980
— Pistons High 16   Pistons vs. Seattle (1st Q)   Jan. 26, 1974
                                  16   Pistons vs. Houston (4th Q)   Jan. 19, 1980

Most Assists
— Home High 16   Pistons vs. Boston (1st Q)   Apr. 13, 1983
                                  16   Pistons vs. Milwaukee (1st Q)   Nov. 28, 1986
— Silverdome High 16   Pistons vs. Milwaukee (1st Q)   Nov. 28, 1986
— Pistons High 16   Pistons vs. Milwaukee (1st Q)   Nov. 28, 1986

Most Personal Fouls
— Home High 16   Pistons vs. Nets (4th Q)   Oct. 13, 1978
                                  16   Pistons vs. Nets (4th Q)   Feb. 23, 1985
— Silverdome High 16   Pistons vs. Nets (4th Q)   Oct. 13, 1978
                                  16   Pistons vs. Nets (4th Q)   Feb. 23, 1985
— Pistons High 16   Pistons vs. Nets (4th Q)   Oct. 13, 1978
                                  16   Pistons vs. Nets (4th Q)   Feb. 23, 1985

Most Steals
— Home High 8   Pistons vs. New Orleans (1st Q)   Jan. 10, 1976
                                  8   Pistons vs. Washington (3rd Q)   Feb. 20, 1976
                                  8   Pistons vs. Phoenix (4th Q)   Feb. 1, 1978
— Silverdome High 6   Several Times
— Pistons High 8   Pistons vs. New Orleans (1st Q)   Jan. 10, 1978
                                  8   Pistons vs. Washington (3rd Q)   Feb. 20, 1976
                                  8   Pistons vs. Phoenix (4th Q)   Feb. 1, 1978

Most Turnovers
— Home High 17   San Antonio vs. Pistons (4th Q)   Oct. 16, 1980
— Silverdome High 17   San Antonio vs. Pistons (4th Q)   Oct. 16, 1980
— Pistons High 12   Pistons vs. Seattle (1st Q)   Mar. 13, 1981

Home Team Records

Most Blocked Shots
—	Home High	10	Washington (4th Q)	Nov. 19, 1981
—	Silverdome High	10	Washington (4th Q)	Nov. 19, 1981
—	Pistons High	10	Washington (4th Q)	Nov. 19, 1981

Home Individual Records

Home records in this section will be dealt with in three categories. Home High in the Detroit area, the Silverdome High and the Detroit Pistons High. Some records would cover all three categories.

Individual — Game

Most Points
—	Detroit	73	David Thompson, Denver vs. Pistons	Apr. 9, 1978
—	Silverdome	61	Michael Jordan, Chicago	Mar. 4, 1987
—	Pistons	56	Kelly Tripucka vs. Chicago	Jan. 29, 1983

Most Field Goals
—	Detroit	28	David Thompson, Denver vs. Pistons	Apr. 9, 1978
—	Silverdome	21	Ray Williams, New Jersey vs. Pistons	Apr. 17, 1982
—	Pistons	22	Dave Bing vs. Chicago	Feb. 21, 1971

Most Field Goals Attempted
—	Detroit	50	Wilt Chamberlain, San Fran. vs. Pistons (OT)	Feb. 11, 1964
—	Silverdome	39	Michael Jordan, Chicago	Mar. 4, 1987
—	Pistons	41	Bob Lanier vs. Milwaukee	Dec. 25, 1971

Most Free Throws
—	Detroit	20	Jerry West, Los Angeles vs. Pistons (playoff)	Apr. 3, 1962
—	Silverdome	20	Kelly Tripucka vs. Chicago	Jan. 29, 1983
—	Pistons	20	Kelly Tripucka vs. Chicago	Jan. 29, 1983

Most Free Throws Attempted
—	Detroit	25	Wilt Chamberlain, Philadelphia vs. Pistons (@ Olympia)	Jan. 23, 1960
—	Silverdome	24	Bob Lanier, Pistons vs. New Jersey	Oct. 13, 1978
—	Pistons	24	Bob Lanier, Pistons vs. New Jersey	Oct. 13, 1978

Most Rebounds
—	Detroit	37	Jerry Lucas, Cincinnati vs. Pistons	Jan. 20, 1965
—	Silverdome	23	Mark Landsberger, Chicago vs. Pistons	Nov. 10, 1978
—	Pistons	33	Bob Lanier vs. Seattle	Dec. 22, 1972

Most Offensive Rebounds
—	Detroit	15	Mark Landsberger, Chicago vs. Pistons	Nov. 10, 1978
—	Silverdome	15	Mark Landsberger, Chicago vs. Pistons	Nov. 10, 1978
—	Pistons	10	Bob Lanier, Pistons vs. Portland	Dec. 8, 1973
		10	Leon Douglas, Pistons vs. Utah	Mar. 23, 1977

Most Defensive Rebounds
—	Detroit	20	Dave Cowens, Boston vs. Pistons	Nov. 8, 1975
—	Silverdome	19	Robert Parrish, Golden State vs. Pistons	Nov. 4, 1978
—	Pistons	18	Bob Lanier vs. Milwaukee	Nov. 13, 1974
		18	Phil Hubbard vs. Cleveland	Feb. 27, 1981

Most Assists
—	Detroit	25	Kevin Porter, Pistons vs. Boston	Mar. 9, 1979
		25	Isiah Thomas vs. Dallas	Feb. 23, 1985
—	Silverdome	25	Kevin Porter, Pistons vs. Boston	Mar. 9, 1979
		25	Isiah Thomas vs. Dallas	Feb. 23, 1985
—	Pistons	25	Kevin Porter, Pistons vs. Boston	Mar. 9, 1979
		25	Isiah Thomas vs. Dallas	Feb. 23, 1985

Most Steals
—	Detroit	9	Ron Lee, Pistons vs. Houston	Mar. 16, 1980
—	Silverdome	9	Ron Lee, Pistons vs. Houston	Mar. 16, 1980
—	Pistons	9	Ron Lee vs. Houston	Mar. 16, 1980

Most Turnovers
—	Detroit	11	Orlando Woolridge, Chicago vs. Pistons	Nov. 3, 1982
		11	Isiah Thomas, Pistons vs. Indiana	Apr. 10, 1985
—	Silverdome	11	Orlando Woolridge, Chicago vs. Pistons	Nov. 3, 1982
—	Pistons	11	Isiah Thomas, Pistons vs. Indiana	Apr. 10, 1985

Most Blocked Shots
—	Detroit	11	Abdul-Jabbar, Los Angeles vs. Pistons	Dec. 3, 1975
		11	Elvin Hayes, Washington vs. Pistons	Mar. 3, 1978
—	Silverdome	10	Edgar Jones, Pistons vs. Indiana	Dec. 17, 1981
—	Pistons	10	Edgar Jones, Pistons vs. Indiana	Dec. 17, 1981

Most Consecutive Field Goals
—	Detroit	13	Isiah Thomas breaks Detroit, Silverdome, and Pistons record vs. Cleveland	Feb. 26, 1984

Three Point Field Goals
—	Detroit	6	Ron Lee, Pistons vs. Houston	Mar. 16, 1980
—	Silverdome	6	Ron Lee, Pistons vs. Houston	Mar. 16, 1980
—	Pistons	6	Ron Lee, Pistons vs. Houston	Mar. 16, 1980

Three Point Field Goals Attempted
—	Detroit	12	Ron Lee, Pistons vs. Houston	Mar. 16, 1980
—	Silverdome	12	Ron Lee, Pistons vs. Houston	Mar. 16, 1980
—	Pistons	12	Ron Lee, Pistons vs. Houston	Mar. 16, 1980

Home Individual Records

Individual — One Half

Most Points
— Detroit 53   David Thompson, Denver vs. Pistons (1st H)   Apr. 9, 1978
— Silverdome 37   Michael Jordan, Chicago (2nd H)   Mar. 4, 1987
— Pistons 37   Dave Bing vs. Boston (2nd H)   Apr. 1, 1968

Most Field Goals
— Detroit 20   David Thompson, Denver vs. Pistons (1st H)   Apr. 9, 1978
— Silverdome 15   Isiah Thomas vs. Cleveland (2nd H)   Feb. 26, 1984
— Pistons 16   Dave Bing vs. Boston (2nd H) (playoff)   Apr. 1, 1968

Most Field Goals Attempted
— Detroit 29   Wilt Chamberlain, San Fran. vs. Pistons (2nd H)   Feb. 11, 1964
— Silverdome 26   Michael Jordan, Chicago (2nd H)   Mar. 4, 1987
— Pistons 28   Dave Bing vs. Boston (2nd H) (playoff)   Apr. 1, 1968

Most Free Throws
— Detroit 17   Adrian Dantley, Pistons vs. Sacramento, (2nd H)   Dec. 10, 1986
— Silverdome 17   Adrian Dantley, Pistons vs. Sacramento, (2nd H)   Dec. 10, 1986
— Pistons 17   Adrian Dantley, Pistons vs. Sacramento, (2nd H)   Dec. 10, 1986

Most Free Throws Attempted
— Detroit 18   Bob Lanier, Pistons vs. New Jersey (2nd H)   Oct. 13, 1978
— Silverdome 18   Bob Lanier, Pistons vs. New Jersey (2nd H)   Oct. 13, 1978
— Pistons 18   Bob Lanier, Pistons vs. New Jersey (2nd H)   Oct. 13, 1978

Most Rebounds
— Detroit 23   Bill Russell, Boston vs. Pistons (1st H)   Jan. 2, 1965
— Silverdome 14   Wes Unseld, Washington vs. Pistons (1st H)   Oct. 24, 1979
                  14   Bill Laimbeer, Pistons vs. Indiana (1st H)   Mar. 12, 1986
— Pistons 22   Bill Laimbeer, Pistons vs. Indiana   Mar. 12, 1986

Most Offensive Rebounds
— Detroit 8   Mark Landsberger, Chicago vs. Pistons (1st H)   Nov. 10, 1978
— Silverdome 8   Mark Landsberger, Chicago vs. Pistons (1st H)   Nov. 10, 1978
— Pistons 7   Willie Norwood, Pistons vs. Los Angeles (1st H)   Dec. 12, 1973

Most Defensive Rebounds
— Detroit 13   Bob Lanier, Pistons vs. Milwaukee (1st H)   Nov. 15, 1975
— Silverdome 13   Robert Parrish, Golden State vs. Pistons (2nd H)   Nov. 4, 1978
— Pistons 13   Bob Lanier vs. Milwaukee (1st H)   Nov. 15, 1975

Most Assists
— Detroit 16   Isiah Thomas, Pistons vs. Dallas (1st H)   Feb. 23, 1985
— Silverdome 16   Isiah Thomas, Pistons vs. Dallas (1st H)   Feb. 23, 1985
— Pistons 16   Isiah Thomas, Pistons vs. Dallas (1st H)   Feb. 23, 1985

Most Steals
— Detroit 6   Chris Ford, Pistons vs. Golden State (2nd H)   Mar. 25, 1977
                  6   Isiah Thomas, Pistons vs. Washington (1st H)   Nov. 25, 1983
— Silverdome 6   Isiah Thomas vs. Washington (1st H)   Nov. 25, 1983
— Pistons 6   Chris Ford, Det. vs. Golden St. (2nd H)   Mar. 25, 1977
                  6   Isiah Thomas vs. Washington (1st H)   Nov. 25, 1983

Most Turnovers
— Detroit 9   Orlando Woolridge, Chicago vs. Pistons (1st H)   Nov. 3, 1982
— Silverdome 9   Orlando Woolridge, Chicago vs. Pistons (1st H)   Nov. 3, 1982
— Pistons 8   Isiah Thomas, Pistons vs. Indiana (2nd H)   Apr. 10, 1985

Most Blocked Shots
— Detroit 7   George Johnson, Golden St. vs. Pistons (2nd H)   Dec. 17, 1975
                  7   Sam Lacey, Kansas City vs. Pistons   Oct. 29, 1978
                  7   Edgar Jones, Pistons vs. Indiana (2nd H)   Dec. 17, 1981
                  7   Terry Tyler, Pistons vs. Chicago (1st H)   Nov. 3, 1982
— Silverdome 7   Sam Lacey, Kansas City vs. Pist. (1st H)   Oct. 27, 1978
                  7   Edgar Jones, Pistons vs. Indiana (2nd H)   Dec. 17, 1981
                  7   Terry Tyler, Pistons vs. Chicago (1st H)   Nov. 3, 1982
— Pistons 7   Edgar Jones, Pistons vs. Indiana (2nd H)   Dec. 17, 1981
                  7   Terry Tyler, Pistons vs. Chicago (1st H)   Nov. 3, 1982

Most Consecutive Field Goals
— Detroit 13   Isiah Thomas, Pist. vs. Cleveland (2nd H)   Feb. 26, 1984
— Silverdome 13   Isiah Thomas, Pist. vs. Cleveland (2nd H)   Feb. 26, 1984
— Pistons 13   Isiah Thomas, Pist. vs. Cleveland (2nd H)   Feb. 26, 1984

Three-Point Field Goals
— Detroit 5   Isiah Thomas, Pistons vs. Dallas (1st)   Dec. 18, 1987
— Silverdome 5   Isiah Thomas, Pistons vs. Dallas (1st)   Dec. 18, 1987
— Pistons 5   Isiah Thomas, Pistons vs. Dallas (1st)   Dec. 18, 1987

Home Individual Records

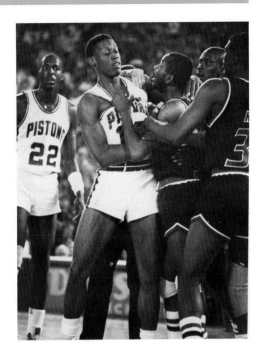

Three-Point Field Goal Attempts
— Detroit	7	Ron Lee, Pistons vs. Houston (2nd H)	Mar. 16, 1980
— Silverdome	7	Ron Lee, Pistons vs. Houston (2nd H)	Mar. 16, 1980
— Pistons	7	Ron Lee, Pistons vs. Houston (2nd H)	Mar. 16, 1980

Individual — One Quarter

Most Points
— Detroit	32	David Thompson, Denver vs. Pist. (1st Q)	Apr. 9, 1978
— Silverdome	26	Michael Jordan, Chicago (4th Q)	Mar. 4, 1987
— Pistons	24	Isiah Thomas, Pist. vs. Atlanta (4th Q)	Mar. 12, 1983
	24	Isiah Thomas, Pist. vs. Cleveland (3rd Q)	Feb. 26, 1984

Most Field Goals
— Detroit	11	Isiah Thomas, Pist. vs. Cleveland (3rd Q)	Feb. 26, 1984
— Silverdome	11	Isiah Thomas, Pist. vs. Cleveland (3rd Q)	Feb. 26, 1984
	11	Michael Jordan, Chicago (4th Q)	Mar. 4, 1987
— Pistons	11	Isiah Thomas, Pist. vs. Cleveland (3rd Q)	Feb. 26, 1984

Most Field Goals Attempted
— Detroit	17	Dave Bing, Pistons vs. Boston (4th Q) (playoff)	Apr. 1, 1968
— Silverdome	13	Isiah Thomas, Pistons vs. Atlanta (4th Q)	Mar. 12, 1983
— Pistons	17	Dave Bing, Pistons vs. Boston (4th Q) (playoff)	Apr. 1, 1968

Most Free Throws
— Detroit	14	Adrian Dantley vs. Sacramento (4th Q)	Dec. 10, 1986
— Silverdome	14	Adrian Dantley vs. Sacramento (4th Q)	Dec. 10, 1986
— Pistons	14	Adrian Dantley vs. Sacramento (4th Q)	Dec. 10, 1986

Most Free Throws Attempted
— Detroit	15	George Yardley, Pistons vs. Minneapolis (3rd Q @ Olympia)	Dec. 25, 1957
	15	Adrian Dantley vs. Sacramento (4th Q)	Dec. 10, 1986
— Silverdome	15	Adrian Dantley vs. Sacramento (4th Q)	Dec. 10, 1986
— Pistons	15	George Yardley, Pistons vs. Minneapolis (3rd Q @ Olympia)	Dec. 25, 1957
	15	Adrian Dantley vs. Sacramento (4th Q)	Dec. 10, 1986

Most Rebounds
— Detroit	15	Wilt Chamberlain, S.F. vs. Pistons (4th Q)	Feb. 12, 1963
— Silverdome	10	John Lambert, Cleveland vs. Pist. (2nd Q)	Feb. 13, 1980
	10	Greg Ballard, Wash. vs. Pistons (2nd Q)	Nov. 25, 1983
— Pistons	14	Ray Scott vs. Philadelphia (1st Q)	Dec. 20, 1961

Most Offensive Rebounds
— Detroit	7	Sidney Wicks, Portland vs. Pistons (1st Q)	Dec. 8, 1973
— Silverdome	6	Mark Landsberger, Chi. vs. Pist. (3rd Q)	Nov. 10, 1978
— Pistons	6	Willie Norwood, Pistons vs. LA (2nd Q)	Dec. 12, 1973
	6	Lindsay Hairston, Pist. vs. Gold. St. (4th Q)	Dec. 17, 1975

Most Defensive Rebounds
— Detroit	9	C. Jones, Philadelphia vs. Pistons (3rd Q)	Feb. 15, 1980
— Silverdome	9	C. Jones, Philadelphia vs. Pistons (3rd Q)	Feb. 15, 1980
— Pistons	8	Bob Lanier vs. Portland (3rd Q)	Dec. 8, 1973
	8	Bob Lanier vs. Milwaukee (2nd Q)	Nov. 13, 1974
	8	Leon Douglas vs. Houston (4th Q)	Jan. 19, 1980
	8	Terry Tyler vs. New York (1st Q)	Mar. 5, 1980

Most Assists
— Detroit	11	Isiah Thomas vs. Golden State (1st Q)	Jan. 24, 1985
— Silverdome	11	Isiah Thomas vs. Golden State (1st Q)	Jan. 24, 1985
— Pistons	11	Isiah Thomas vs. Golden State (1st Q)	Jan. 24, 1985

Most Personal Fouls
— Detroit	6	Roger Brown, Pistons vs. Gold. St. (4th Q)	Mar. 25, 1977
	6	Paul Mokeski, Pist. vs. Chicago (4th Q)	Jan. 22, 1981
— Silverdome	6	Paul Mokeski, Pist. vs. Chicago (4th Q)	Jan. 22, 1981
	6	Paul Mokeski, Milwaukee (4th Q)	Dec. 2, 1987
— Pistons	6	Roger Brown, Pist. vs. Gold. St. (4th Q)	Mar. 25, 1977
	6	Paul Mokeski, Pist. vs. Chicago (4th Q)	Jan. 22, 1981

Most Steals
— Detroit	5	Chris Ford, Pistons vs. Gold. St. (4th Q)	Dec. 17, 1975
	5	Ron Lee, Pistons vs. Washington (3rd Q)	Nov. 19, 1981
— Silverdome	5	Ron Lee, Pistons vs. Washington (3rd Q)	Nov. 19, 1981
— Pistons	5	Chris Ford, Pistons vs. Gold. St. (4th Q)	Dec. 17, 1975
	5	Ron Lee, Pistons vs. Washington (3rd Q)	Nov. 19, 1981
	5	John Long, Pistons vs. Indiana (1st Q)	Dec. 3, 1983

Most Blocked Shots
— Detroit	7	George Johnson, Gold. St. vs. Pist. (4th Q)	Dec. 17, 1975
— Silverdome	5	Terry Tyler, Pistons vs. Chicago (1st Q)	Nov. 10, 1978
	5	Terry Tyler, Pistons vs. Phil. (3rd Q)	Feb. 15, 1980
	5	Terry Tyler, Pistons vs. Seattle (4th Q)	Feb. 7, 1980
	5	Edgar Jones, Pistons vs. Indiana (4th H)	Dec. 17, 1981
— Pistons	5	Terry Tyler, Pistons vs. Chicago (1st Q)	Nov. 10, 1978
	5	Bob Lanier, Pist. vs. New York (4th Q)	Oct. 18, 1979
	5	Terry Tyler, Pistons vs. Seattle (4th Q)	Feb. 7, 1980
	5	Terry Tyler, Pistons vs. Phil. (3rd Q)	Feb. 15, 1980
	5	Edgar Jones, Pistons vs. Indiana (4th Q)	Dec. 17, 1981

NBA SCHEDULE

National Basketball Association 1988-89 Schedule
(starting times local)

Friday, November 4
New York at Boston, 7:30
Atlanta at New Jersey, 7:30
LA Clippers at Philadelphia, 7:30
Cleveland at Charlotte, 7:30
Milwaukee at Indiana, 7:30
Detroit at Chicago, 7:30
LA Lakers at Dallas, 7:00 (TBS)
Houston at Denver, 7:30
Seattle at Utah, 7:30

Saturday, November 5
New York at New Jersey, 7:30
Boston at Philadelphia, 7:30
Chicago at Washington, 7:30
LA Clippers at Miami, 7:30
Charlotte at Detroit, 7:30
Cleveland at Indiana, 7:30
Atlanta at Milwaukee, 8:00
Dallas at Houston, 7:30
LA Lakers at San Antonio, 7:30
Phoenix at Golden State, 7:30
Sacramento at Portland, 7:30
Denver at Seattle, 7:00

Tuesday, November 8
Chicago at New York, 8:00 (TBS)
Washington at New Jersey, 7:30
Detroit at Philadelphia, 7:30
LA Clippers at Charlotte, 7:30
Indiana at Atlanta, 7:30
San Antonio at Houston, 7:30
Miami at Dallas, 7:30
LA Lakers at Golden State, 7:30
Seattle at Sacramento, 7:30

Wednesday, November 9
Chicago at Boston, 7:30
New York at Washington, 7:30
LA Clippers at Charlotte, 7:30
Atlanta at Detroit, 7:30
Philadelphia at Milwaukee, 7:30
Miami at San Antonio, 7:30
Sacramento at Utah, 7:30
Dallas at Phoenix, 7:30
Denver at LA Lakers, 7:30
Golden State at Seattle, 7:00

Thursday, November 10
Utah at Houston, 7:30
Portland at Denver, 7:30

Friday, November 11
Detroit at Boston, 8:00
Atlanta at Philadelphia, 7:30
Charlotte at Washington, 8:00
Houston at Miami, 7:30
New York at Indiana, 7:30
New Jersey at Chicago, 7:30
San Antonio at Dallas, 7:30
Golden State at Phoenix, 8:30 (TBS)
Seattle at LA Lakers, 7:30

Saturday, November 12
Washington at New York, 7:30
Chicago at New Jersey, 7:30
Charlotte at Atlanta, 7:30
Indiana at Cleveland, 7:30
Boston at Milwaukee, 8:00
Sacramento at Dallas, 7:30
Utah at San Antonio, 7:30
Seattle at Denver, 7:30
Phoenix at LA Clippers, 7:30
Portland at Golden State, 7:30

Sunday, November 13
Sacramento at Houston, 7:30
Denver at Portland, 7:00

Monday, November 14
Golden State at New Jersey, 7:30

Tuesday, November 15
New Jersey at Charlotte, 7:30
Boston at Miami, 7:30
Atlanta at Cleveland, 8:00 (TBS)
Philadelphia at Chicago, 7:30
New York at Houston, 7:30
Detroit at Dallas, 7:30
LA Lakers at Denver, 7:30
Indiana at Utah, 7:30
Phoenix at Sacramento, 7:30
LA Clippers at Portland, 7:30

Wednesday, November 16
Golden State at Boston, 7:30
Chicago at Philadelphia, 7:30
Detroit at San Antonio, 7:30
Indiana at Phoenix, 7:30
Sacramento at LA Clippers, 7:30

Thursday, November 17
New Jersey at Milwaukee, 7:30
Miami at Houston, 7:30
Charlotte at Dallas, 7:30
San Antonio at Denver, 7:30
Portland at Utah, 7:30
LA Lakers at Seattle, 7:30

Friday, November 18
Washington at Boston, 7:30
Cleveland at New Jersey, 7:30
New York at Philadelphia, 7:30
Golden State at Miami, 7:30
Atlanta at Chicago, 7:00 (TBS)
Detroit at Phoenix, 7:30
Portland at LA Lakers, 7:30
Indiana at LA Clippers, 7:30

Saturday, November 19
Philadelphia at New York, 8:30
Boston at Washington, 7:30
Golden State at Atlanta, 7:30
Milwaukee at Cleveland, 7:30
Detroit at Houston, 7:30
Charlotte at San Antonio, 7:30
LA Clippers at Denver, 7:30
Phoenix at Utah, 7:30
Indiana at Sacramento, 7:30
Dallas at Seattle, 7:00

Sunday, November 20
New Jersey at Portland, 5:00

Monday, November 21
Atlanta at Houston, 7:30
LA Clippers at Utah, 7:30

Tuesday, November 22
Cleveland at Boston (Hartford), 7:30
LA Lakers at New York, 8:00 (TBS)
Philadelphia at Washington, 7:30
Detroit at Charlotte, 7:30
Milwaukee at Indiana, 7:30
New Jersey at Denver, 7:30
Chicago at Sacramento, 7:30
Portland at Seattle, 7:00

Wednesday, November 23
Charlotte at Boston, 7:30
Cleveland at Philadelphia, 7:30
LA Lakers at Miami, 7:30
New York at Detroit, 7:30
Washington at Milwaukee, 7:30
Denver at Dallas, 7:00 (TBS)
Atlanta at San Antonio, 7:30

Houston at Utah, 7:30
New Jersey at Phoenix, 7:30
Chicago at LA Clippers, 7:30 (TBS)
Seattle at Golden State, 7:30

Friday, November 25
Milwaukee at Boston, 7:30
Charlotte at Philadelphia, 7:30
Washington at Indiana, 7:30
Atlanta at Dallas, 7:00 (TBS)
San Antonio at Utah, 7:30
New Jersey at LA Clippers, 7:30
Houston at Portland, 7:30

Saturday, November 26
Cleveland at New York, 1:30
Indiana at Philadelphia, 7:00
Washington at Charlotte, 7:00
Boston at Atlanta, 7:00
LA Lakers at Detroit, 8:30 (CBS)
Miami at Milwaukee, 8:00
Utah at Dallas, 7:30
Phoenix at San Antonio, 7:30
Chicago at Denver, 8:00
Houston at Golden State, 7:30
New Jersey at Sacramento, 7:30

Sunday, November 27
Miami at Cleveland, 7:30
Golden State at Portland, 7:00

Monday, November 28
LA Lakers at Philadelphia, 7:30

Tuesday, November 29
Boston at New Jersey, 7:30
Miami at Charlotte, 7:30
San Antonio at Atlanta, 7:30
Detroit at Indiana, 7:30
Portland at Milwaukee, 7:00 (TBS)
Phoenix at Houston, 7:30
New York at Denver, 7:30
Chicago at Golden State, 7:30
LA Clippers at Sacramento, 7:30
Utah at Seattle, 7:00

Wednesday, November 30
New Jersey at Boston, 7:30
Portland at Philadelphia, 7:30
San Antonio at Miami, 7:30
Indiana at Detroit, 7:30
Houston at Dallas, 7:30
Chicago at Utah, 7:30
Seattle at LA Lakers, 7:30
New York at LA Clippers, 7:30

Thursday, December 1
Philadelphia at Charlotte, 7:30
Washington at Atlanta, 7:30
Cleveland at Milwaukee, 7:30
Denver at Sacramento, 7:30

Friday, December 2
Milwaukee at New Jersey, 7:30
Detroit at Washington, 8:00
Portland at Miami, 7:30
Boston at Cleveland, 8:00 (TBS)
New York at Dallas, 7:30
Golden State at Denver, 7:30
Houston at Phoenix, 7:30
Utah at LA Lakers, 7:30
LA Clippers at Seattle, 7:00

Saturday, December 3
Portland at Atlanta, 7:30
Philadelphia at Indiana, 7:30
Charlotte at Houston, 7:30
Chicago at Dallas, 7:30
New York at San Antonio, 7:30
LA Clippers at Phoenix, 7:30

Utah at Sacramento, 7:30
Golden State at Seattle, 7:00

Sunday, December 4
Detroit at New Jersey, 7:30
Denver at Cleveland, 7:30
Washington at LA Lakers, 7:30

Tuesday, December 6
Denver at New York, 7:30
Portland at New Jersey, 7:30
Sacramento at Atlanta, 7:30
Boston at Chicago, 7:00 (TBS)
Detroit at Milwaukee, 7:30
Cleveland at Houston, 7:30
Seattle at San Antonio, 7:30
Washington at Phoenix, 7:30
LA Lakers at LA Clippers, 7:30
Utah at Golden State, 7:30

Wednesday, December 7
Atlanta at Boston, 7:30
Denver at Philadelphia, 7:30
Sacramento at Miami, 7:30
Chicago at Detroit, 7:30
Portland at Indiana, 7:30
Seattle at Dallas, 7:30
Washington at Utah, 7:30
Phoenix at LA Lakers, 7:30

Thursday, December 8
Milwaukee at New York, 7:30
Cleveland at San Antonio, 7:30
Houston at LA Clippers, 7:30

Friday, December 9
Philadelphia at Boston, 7:30
New Jersey at Charlotte, 7:30
Denver at Miami, 7:30
Detroit at Atlanta, 8:00 (TBS)
Sacramento at Indiana, 7:30
Milwaukee at Chicago, 7:30
Dallas at Utah, 7:30
Golden State at Phoenix, 7:30
Washington at Portland, 7:30

Saturday, December 10
Sacramento at New York, 7:30
Charlotte at New Jersey, 7:30
Denver at Atlanta, 7:30
Philadelphia at Detroit, 7:30
LA Lakers at Indiana, 7:30
Miami at Chicago, 7:30
Seattle at Houston, 7:30
Cleveland at Dallas, 7:30
Utah at LA Clippers, 7:30
Washgington at Golden State, 7:30

Sunday, December 11
LA Lakers at Milwaukee, 7:30
San Antonio at Portland, 5:00

Monday, December 12
Miami at Utah, 7:30

Tuesday, December 13
New Jersey at New York, 8:00
Milwaukee at Philadelphia, 7:30
Boston at Washington, 7:30
LA Lakers at Cleveland, 7:30
Charlotte at Indiana, 7:30
Atlanta at Chicago, 7:30
Golden State at Dallas, 7:30
Houston at Denver, 7:30
San Antonio at Sacramento, 7:30
LA Clippers at Portland, 7:30
Phoenix at Seattle, 7:00

Wednesday, December 14
Utah at Boston, 7:30
LA Lakers at New Jersey, 7:30
Indiana at Charlotte, 7:30
Philadelphia at Atlanta, 7:30
Milwaukee at Detroit, 7:30
Miami at LA Clippers, 7:30
San Antonio at Seattle, 7:00

Friday, December 16
LA Lakers at Boston, 8:00 (TBS)
Philadelphia at New Jersey, 7:30
Dallas at Charlotte, 7:30
Milwaukee at Atlanta, 7:30
Indiana at Chicago, 7:30
Portland at Phoenix, 7:30
Denver at LA Clippers, 7:30

Saturday, December 17
Washington at New York, 7:30

Utah at Philadelphia, 7:30
Dallas at Miami, 7:30
Atlanta at Cleveland, 7:30
Charlotte at Detroit, 7:30
New Jersey at Indiana, 7:30
Chicago at Milwaukee, 8:00
Golden State at San Antonio, 7:30
LA Clippers at Denver, 7:30
Phoenix at Portland, 7:30
Sacramento at Seattle, 7:00

Sunday, December 18
New York at Boston, 7:30
LA Lakers at Washington, 7:30
San Antonio at Houston, 7:30

Tuesday, December 20
Indiana at New York, 7:30
Dallas at Philadelphia, 7:30
Seattle at Atlanta, 7:30
Utah at Cleveland, 7:30
LA Lakers at Chicago, 7:00 (TBS)
Charlotte at Milwaukee, 7:30
Sacramento at Houston, 7:30
Portland at Denver, 7:30
San Antonio at Phoenix, 7:30
LA Clippers at Golden State, 7:30

Wednesday, December 21
Cleveland at Boston, 7:30
Dallas at New Jersey, 7:30
Utah at Washington, 7:30
Milwaukee at Charlotte, 7:30
Seattle at Miami, 7:30
Sacramento at San Antonio, 7:30

Thursday, December 22
Detroit at New York, 7:30
LA Clippers at Houston, 7:30
Phoenix at Denver, 7:30
Portland and Golden State, 7:30

Friday, December 23
Chicago at Charlotte, 8:00 (TBS)
Utah at Miami, 7:30
Indiana at Atlanta, 7:30
Seattle at Cleveland, 7:30
Dallas at Milwaukee, 8:00
LA Clippers at San Antonio, 7:30
Denver at Phoenix, 7:30
Sacramento at LA Lakers, 7:30
Golden State at Portland, 7:30

Sunday, December 25
Washington at Philadelphia, 7:00 (TBS)
LA Lakers at Utah, 1:30 (CBS)

Monday, December 26
Washington at New Jersey, 7:30
Houston at Charlotte, 7:30
San Antonio at Miami, 7:30
LA Lakers at Phoenix, 7:30

Tuesday, December 27
Houston at Miami, 8:00 (TBS)
New York at Atlanta, 7:30
Cleveland at Chicago, 7:30
Indiana at Milwaukee, 7:30
San Antonio at Dallas, 7:30
Boston at Denver, 7:30
Seattle at LA Clippers, 7:30
Philadelphia at Golden State, 7:30
Portland at Sacramento, 7:30

Wednesday, December 28
Indiana at New Jersey, 7:30
Charlotte at Cleveland, 7:30
Phoenix at Detroit, 7:30
Sacramento at Utah, 7:30
Philadelphia at LA Lakers, 7:30

Thursday, December 29
Houston at Washington, 7:30
New York at Chicago, 7:30
Boston at Dallas, 7:30
Miami at Seattle, 7:00

Friday, December 30
Phoenix at New Jersey, 7:30
New York at Charlotte, 7:30
Washington at Cleveland, 7:30
Houston at Detroit, 8:00
Chicago at Indiana, 7:30
Atlanta at Milwaukee, 8:00
Boston at San Antonio, 7:30
Miami at Denver, 7:30
Philadelphia at Utah, 7:30

LA Clippers at LA Lakers, 7:30

Monday, January 2
Phoenix at Washington, 7:30

Tuesday, January 3
Boston at New York, 8:00 (TBS)
New Jersey at Charlotte, 7:30
Detroit at Atlanta, 7:30
Indiana at Cleveland, 7:30
LA Clippers at Chicago, 7:30
Utah at Houston, 7:30
Denver at San Antonio, 7:30
Dallas at Sacramento, 7:30
Miami at Portland, 7:30
LA Lakers at Seattle, 7:00

Wednesday, January 4
Phoenix at Boston, 7:30
New York at New Jersey, 7:30
Charlotte at Washington, 7:30
Atlanta at Indiana, 7:30
LA Clippers at Milwaukee, 7:30
Portland at LA Lakers, 7:30
Miami at Golden State, 7:30

Thursday, January 5
Chicago at Cleveland, 7:30
Philadelphia at San Antonio, 7:30
Golden State at Denver, 7:30
Sacramento at Seattle, 7:00

Friday, January 6
Charlotte at Boston, 7:30
Milwaukee at Washington (Balt.), 8:00
Atlanta at Detroit, 8:00 (TBS)
LA Clippers at Indiana, 7:30
Utah at Chicago, 7:30
Dallas at Phoenix, 7:30
Miami at LA Lakers, 7:30
Sacramento at Portland, 7:30

Saturday, January 7
Washington at Charlotte, 7:30
New Jersey at Atlanta, 7:30
New York at Cleveland, 1:30
Detroit at Indiana, 7:30
Utah at Milwaukee, 8:00
Philadelphia at Houston, 7:30
Dallas at Denver, 7:30
Miami at Phoenix, 7:30
San Antonio at Golden State, 7:30
Portland at Seattle, 7:00

Sunday, January 8
LA Clippers at New York, 7:30
San Antonio at LA Lakers, 7:30

Monday, January 9
LA Clippers at Boston, 7:30
Utah at Charlotte, 7:30
Philadelphia at Dallas, 7:30
Phoenix at Golden State, 7:30
Cleveland at Seattle, 7:00

Tuesday, January 10
Denver at Washington, 7:30
Utah at Miami, 7:30
Chicago at Atlanta, 7:30
LA Lakers at Sacramento, 5:00 (CBS)
Seattle at Portland, 7:30

Wednesday, January 11
Indiana at Boston, 7:30
New Jersey at Philadelphia, 7:30
Chicago at Charlotte, 7:30
New York at Detroit, 7:30
Denver at Milwaukee, 7:30
Houston at San Antonio, 7:30
Cleveland at Phoenix, 7:30
Sacramento at LA Clippers, 7:30
Dallas at Golden State, 7:30

Thursday, January 12
Charlotte at New York, 7:30
Boston at New Jersey, 7:30
Miami at Washington, 7:30
Portland at Houston, 7:30
San Antonio at Utah, 7:30
Dallas at Seattle, 7:00

Friday, January 13
Atlanta at Philadelphia, 7:30
Milwaukee at Miami, 7:30
Washington at Detroit, 8:00
Denver at Chicago, 7:00 (TBS)
Sacramento at Phoenix, 7:30
Cleveland at LA Lakers, 7:30

Golden State at LA Clippers, 7:30

Saturday, January 14
Atlanta at New York, 7:30
New Jersey at Indiana, 7:30
Dallas at Houston, 7:30
Portland at San Antonio, 7:30
Cleveland at Denver, 7:30
Utah at Golden State, 7:30
Seattle at Sacramento, 7:30

Sunday, January 15
Philadelphia at Charlotte, 2:00
Indiana at Miami, 7:30
Boston at Chicago, 2:30
Detroit at Milwaukee, 1:30
Portland at Dallas, 7:00
LA Lakers at LA Clippers, 3:00

Monday, January 16
San Antonio at New York, 1:30
Charlotte at Philadelphia, 1:00
Atlanta at Washington, 1:00
Phoenix at Cleveland, 2:30
Boston at Detroit, 7:30
Sacramento at Denver, 2:00
Houston at LA Lakers, 2:00
Seattle at Golden State, 7:30

Tuesday, January 17
San Antonio at New Jersey, 7:30
Phoenix at Miami, 7:30
Milwaukee at Atlanta, 8:00 (TBS)
Indiana at Cleveland, 7:30
Houston at Sacramento, 7:30
Utah at Portland, 7:30
LA Clippers at Seattle, 7:00

Wednesday, January 18
Boston at Philadelphia, 7:30
New Jersey at Detroit, 7:30
Charlotte at Milwaukee, 7:30
Denver at Dallas, 7:30
LA Clippers at LA Lakers, 7:30
New York at Golden State, 7:30

Thursday, January 19
San Antonio at Washington, 7:30
Phoenix at Charlotte, 7:30
Chicago at Miami, 7:30
Cleveland at Indiana, 7:30
New York at Sacramento, 7:30
Houston at Seattle, 7:00

Friday, January 20
Philadelphia at Boston, 7:30
Indiana at Detroit, 8:00 (TBS)
Milwaukee at Utah, 7:30
Dallas at LA Lakers, 7:30 (TBS)
Houston at Golden State, 7:30

Saturday, January 21
Philadelphia at Washington, 7:30
Charlotte at Atlanta, 7:30
New Jersey at Cleveland, 7:30
Phoenix at Chicago, 7:30
Milwaukee at Denver, 7:30
Golden State at Sacramento, 7:30
New York at Seattle, 7:00

Sunday, January 22
Detroit at Boston, 12:00 (CBS)
New York at Portland, 7:00

Monday, January 23
Golden State at Cleveland, 7:30
Denver at Indiana, 7:30
Miami at San Antonio, 7:30

Tuesday, January 24
Denver at New Jersey, 7:30
Cleveland at Atlanta, 7:30
Dallas at Chicago, 7:30
Miami at Houston, 7:30
Charlotte at Phoenix, 7:30
New York at LA Lakers, 7:30
Milwaukee at Sacramento, 7:30
Seattle at Portland, 5:00 (TBS)

Wednesday, January 25
Chicago at Philadelphia, 7:30
Golden State at Detroit, 7:30
Boston at Indiana, 7:30
LA Clippers at Dallas, 7:30
Utah at San Antonio, 7:30

Thursday, January 26
Sacramento at New Jersey, 7:30
Indiana at Washington, 7:30

Denver at Miami, 7:30
LA Clippers at Houston, 7:30
Charlotte at Utah, 7:30
Milwaukee at Portland, 7:30

Friday, January 27
Sacramento at Boston, 7:30
Golden State at Philadelphia, 7:30
Cleveland at Detroit, 8:00
Washington at Chicago, 7:30
San Antonio at Dallas, 7:00 (TBS)
New York at Phoenix, 7:30
Charlotte at LA Lakers, 7:30
Atlanta at Seattle, 7:00

Saturday, January 28
Philadelphia at New Jersey, 8:00
Golden State at Indiana, 7:30
Houston at San Antonio, 7:30
Phoenix at Denver, 7:30
New York at Utah, 7:30
Milwaukee at LA Clippers, 7:30
Atlanta at Portland, 7:30

Sunday, January 29
Miami at Boston, 3:30
Cleveland at Washington (Balt.), 1:00
Sacramento at Detroit, 7:00
LA Lakers at Dallas, 12:00 (CBS)
Milwaukee at Seattle, 7:00

Monday, January 30
Golden State at Miami, 7:30
Denver at Phoenix, 7:30
Atlanta at LA Clippers, 7:30
Charlotte at Portland, 7:30

Tuesday, January 31
Indiana at New York, 7:30
Boston at Washington, 7:30
Philadelphia at Cleveland, 7:30
Detroit at Chicago, 7:00 (TBS)
Sacramento at Milwaukee, 7:30
LA Lakers at Houston, 7:30
Utah at Dallas, 7:30
Denver at San Antonio, 7:30
New Jersey at Seattle, 7:00

Wednesday, February 1
Washington at Philadelphia, 7:30
Boston at Charlotte, 7:30
Miami at Detroit, 7:30
Atlanta at Utah, 7:30
LA Lakers at Phoenix, 7:30
Portland at LA Clippers, 7:30

Thursday, February 2
Cleveland at New York, 7:30
Seattle at Miami, 7:30
Sacramento at Chicago, 7:30
Atlanta at Denver, 7:30
New Jersey at Golden State, 7:30

Friday, February 3
Washington at Boston, 7:30
Detroit at Philadelphia, 8:00 (TBS)
Seattle at Charlotte, 7:30
Sacramento at Cleveland, 7:30
Milwaukee at Indiana, 7:30
Chicago at Houston, 7:30
Phoenix at Dallas, 7:30
New Jersey at Utah, 7:30
Portland at LA Lakers, 7:30
San Antonio at LA Clippers, 7:30

Saturday, February 4
Milwaukee at Washington, 7:30
New York at Indiana, 7:30
Utah at Denver, 7:30
Atlanta at PHoenix, 7:30
LA Clippers at Golden State, 7:30
San Antonio at Portland, 7:30

Sunday, February 5
Seattle at Boston, 7:30
Cleveland at Charlotte, 2:00
Sacramento at Miami, 7:30
Chicago at Detroit, 2:00 (CBS)
Denver at Houston, 7:30
New Jersey at LA Lakers, 7:30

Monday, February 6
Utah at Phoenix, 7:30
Dallas at LA Clippers, 7:30

Tuesday, February 7
Washington at New York, 7:30
Seattle at New Jersey, 7:30

Charlotte at Chicago, 7:30
Cleveland at Milwaukee, 7:00 (TBS)
Miami at Utah, 7:30
San Antonio at Sacramento, 7:30
Dallas at Portland, 7:30

Wednesday, February 8
Indiana at Boston, 7:30
Seattle at Philadelphia, 7:30
New York at Atlanta, 7:30
Milwaukee at Detroit, 7:30
Golden State at LA Lakers, 7:30
Houston at LA Clippers, 7:30

Thursday, February 9
New Jersey at Washington, 7:30
Atlanta at Charlotte, 7:30
Indiana at Cleveland, 7:30
Chicago at San Antonio, 7:30
Miami at Denver, 7:30
Dallas at Utah, 7:30
LA Clippers at Phoenix, 7:30
Golden State at Sacramento, 7:30
Houston at Portland, 7:30

Saturday, February 11
NBA ALL-STAR SATURDAY
at Houston, TBA (TBS)

Sunday, February 12
39th ANNUAL NBA ALL-STAR GAME
at Houston, 2:00 (CBS)

Tuesday, February 14
New York at Charlotte, 7:30
Cleveland at Miami, 7:30
Philadelphia at Indiana, 7:30
Atlanta at Chicago, 7:30
New Jersey at Milwaukee, 7:30
Boston at Houston, 7:00 (TBS)
LA Clippers at Dallas, 7:30
Denver at Utah, 7:30
Detroit at LA Lakers, 7:30 (TBS)
Washington at Sacramento, 7:30
San Antonio at Seattle, 7:00

Wednesday, February 15
Atlanta at New Jersey, 7:30
Indiana at Philadelphia, 7:30
New York at Cleveland, 7:30
Washington at Denver, 7:30
Seattle at Phoenix, 7:30
San Antonio at Golden State, 7:30

Thursday, February 16
Milwaukee at Chicago, 7:30
Miami at Dallas, 7:30
Boston at Utah, 7:30
Golden State at LA Clippers, 7:30
Detroit at Sacramento, 7:30
LA Lakers at Portland, 7:30

Friday, February 17
New Jersey at Philadelphia, 7:30
Charlotte at Miami, 7:30
Cleveland at Atlanta, 8:00 (TBS)
Denver at Houston, 7:30
Boston at Phoenix, 7:30
Washington at Seattle, 7:00

Saturday, February 18
New Jersey at New York, 7:30
Indiana at Charlotte, 7:30
Philadelphia at Cleveland, 7:30
Houston at Dallas, 7:30
San Antonio at Utah, 7:30
Washington at LA Clippers, 7:30
Detroit at Golden State, 7:30
Phoenix at Sacramento, 7:30
Seattle at Portland, 7:30

Sunday, February 19
Atlanta at Miami, 7:30
Chicago at Milwaukee, 1:30
Boston at LA Lakers, 12:30 (CBS)

Monday, February 20
Miami at New Jersey, 7:30
LA Clippers at Atlanta, 7:30
Houston at Cleveland, 1:30 (CBS)*
Portland at Chicago, 12:30 (CBS)*
Dallas at San Antonio, 7:30
Detroit at Denver, 2:00
Phoenix at Utah, 7:30
LA Lakers at Sacramento, 7:30

Tuesday, February 21
Houston at New York, 7:30

LA Clippers at Washington, 7:30
Indiana at Milwaukee, 7:30
Golden State at Phoenix, 7:30
Boston at Seattle, 5:00 (TBS)
Wednesday, February 22
Chicago at Charlotte, 7:30
Philadelphia at Miami, 7:30
New Jersey at Cleveland, 7:30
Portland at Detroit, 7:30
Golden State at San Antonio, 7:30
Dallas at Denver, 7:30
LA Lakers at Utah, 7:30
Boston at Sacramento, 7:30
Thursday, February 23
Charlotte at New York, 7:30
LA Clippers at New Jersey, 7:30
Indiana at Atlanta, 7:30
Friday, February 24
Milwaukee at Boston (Hartford), 7:30
New York at Washington, (Balt.), 8:00
LA Clippers at Miami, 7:30
Portland at Cleveland, 7:30
San Antonio at Indiana, 7:30
Houston at Chicago, 7:30
Golden State at Dallas, 7:30
Utah at Denver, 6:00 (TBS)
Philadelphia at Phoenix, 7:30
Sacramento at LA Lakers, 7:30
Saturday, February 25
Detroit at New Jersey, 7:30
San Antonio at Charlotte, 7:30
Chicago at Atlanta, 7:30
Houston at Milwaukee, 8:00
Washington at Dallas, 7:30
Sacramento at Seattle, 7:00
Sunday, February 26
Boston at New York, 2:00 (CBS)
Portland at Miami, 7:30
LA Clippers at Detroit, 7:00
Utah at Indiana, 2:30
Philadelphia at Denver, 2:30
Phoenix at LA Lakers, 7:30
Monday, February 27
Utah at New Jersey, 7:30
Dallas at Atlanta, 7:30
San Antonio at Milwaukee, 7:30
Washington at Houston, 7:30
Denver at Golden State, 7:30
Seattle at Sacramento, 7:30
Tuesday, February 28
Boston at Charlotte, 7:30
Dallas at Miami, 7:30
Detroit at Cleveland, 8:00 (TBS)
San Antonio at Chicago, 7:30
Philadelphia at LA Clippers, 7:30
Phoenix at Portland, 7:30
Indiana at Seattle, 7:00
Wednesday, March 1
Atlanta at Boston, 7:30
New Jersey at Washington, 7:30
Utah at Detroit, 7:30
New York at Milwaukee, 7:30
Golden State at LA Lakers, 7:30
Philadelphia at Sacramento, 7:30
Thursday, March 2
Miami at New York, 7:30
Charlotte at New Jersey, 7:30
San Antonio at Cleveland, 7:30
Houston at Denver, 7:30
Sacramento at Phoenix, 7:30
Portland at LA Clippers
Indiana at Golden State, 7:30
Friday, March 3
Dallas at Boston, 8:00 (TBS)
Utah at Miami, 7:30
Charlotte at Atlanta, 7:30
Cleveland at Detroit, 8:00
Milwaukee at Chicago, 7:30
Indiana at LA Lakers, 7:30
Philadelphia at Portland, 7:30
Houston at Seattle, 7:00
Saturday, March 4
Chicago at New York, 7:30
Boston at New Jersey, 7:30
Dallas at Washington, 7:30
Denver at San Antonio, 7:30

LA Clippers at Phoenix, 7:30
Sacramento at Golden State, 7:30
Philadelphia at Seattle, 7:00
Sunday, March 5
Charlotte at Washington, 7:30
Detroit at Miami, 7:30
Utah at Atlanta, 1:00
Milwaukee at Cleveland, 1:30
LA Lakers at Houston, 2:30 (CBS)
Golden State at Sacramento, 6:00
Indiana at Portland, 5:00
Monday, March 6
Phoenix at Philadelphia, 7:30
Denver at Detroit, 7:30
New Jersey at Dallas, 7:30
Tuesday, March 7
Phoenix at New York, 7:30
LA Lakers at Atlanta, 8:00 (TBS)
Seattle at Indiana, 7:30
Philadelphia at Chicago, 7:30
Washington at Milwaukee, 7:30
Portland at San Antonio, 7:30
LA Clippers at Golden State, 7:30
Cleveland at Sacramento, 7:30
Wednesday, March 8
Chicago at Boston, 7:30
Atlanta at Washington, 7:30
Denver at Charlotte, 7:30
LA Lakers at Miami, 7:30
Seattle at Detroit, 7:30
Portland at Dallas, 7:30
Houston at Utah, 7:30
Thursday, March 9
Sacramento at Philadelphia, 7:30
New Jersey at San Antonio, 7:30
Cleveland at Golden State, 7:30
Friday, March 10
Sacramento at Washington, 8:00
LA Lakers at Charlotte, 7:30
Denver at Miami, 7:30
Phoenix at Indiana, 7:30
Seattle at Milwaukee, 8:00
Dallas at Houston, 7:30
Golden State at Utah, 7:30
Cleveland at LA Clippers, 7:30
Saturday, March 11
Indiana at New York, 8:30
Detroit at Philadelphia, 7:30
Miami at Atlanta, 7:30
Seattle at Chicago, 7:30
Phoenix at Milwaukee, 8:00
New Jersey at Houston, 7:30
Dallas at San Antonio, 7:30
Sunday, March 12
Denver at Boston, 12:00 (CBS)
Sacramento at Charlotte, 2:00
Washington at Detroit, 7:30
LA Lakers at Golden State, 2:00
Cleveland at Portland, 5:00
Monday, March 13
New Jersey at Boston (Hartford), 7:30
Seattle at Washington, 7:30
Phoenix at Miami, 7:30
Indiana at Chicago, 7:30
Milwaukee at Dallas, 7:30
LA Clippers at San Antonio, 7:30
Cleveland at Utah, 7:30
Houston at LA Lakers, 7:30
Tuesday, March 14
Seattle at New York, 7:30
Phoenix at Atlanta, 7:30
Detroit at Indiana, 7:30
Charlotte at Denver, 7:30
Houston at Sacramento, 7:30
Golden State at Portland, 7:30
Wednesday March 15
New Jersey at Philadelphia, 7:30
Chicago at Cleveland, 7:30
Milwaukee at San Antonio, 7:30
Portland at Utah, 6:00 (TBS)
Miami at LA Clippers, 7:30
Dallas at Golden State, 7:30
Thursday, March 16
Philadelphia at New York, 7:30
Boston at Indiana, 7:30
Milwaukee at Houston, 7:30

San Antonio at Denver, 7:30
Atlanta at Sacramento, 7:30
Charlotte at Seattle, 7:00
Friday, March 17
Washington at New Jersey, 7:30
Boston at Detroit, 8:00
New York at Chicago, 7:30
Miami at Utah, 7:30
Portland at Phoenix, 7:30
Dallas at LA Lakers, 7:30
Charlotte at LA Clippers, 7:30
Atlanta at Golden State, 7:30
Saturday, March 18
Philadelphia at Washington, 7:30
Chicago at Indiana, 7:30
Detroit at Milwaukee, 8:00
Portland at Houston, 7:30
Utah at San Antonio, 7:30
Miami at Denver, 7:30
Seattle at Phoenix, 7:30
Dallas at Sacramento, 7:30
Sunday, March 19
Milwaukee at New York, 7:30
Cleveland at New Jersey, 7:30
Atlanta at LA Lakers, 7:30
Charlotte at Golden State, 2:00
Monday, March 20
San Antonio at Boston, 7:30
New York at Philadelphia, 7:30
Washington at Cleveland, 7:30
Miami at Phoenix, 7:30
Charlotte at Sacramento, 7:30
Dallas at Portland, 7:30
Tuesday, March 21
Indiana at New Jersey, 7:30
Detroit at Atlanta, 8:00 (TBS)
Boston at Milwaukee, 7:30
Denver at Houston, 7:30
Chicago at LA Lakers, 7:30 (TBS)
Portland at Golden State, 7:30
Utah at Seattle, 7:00
Wednesday, March 22
Cleveland at Philadelphia, 7:30
New York at Miami, 7:30
San Antonio at Detroit, 7:30
Washington at Indiana, 7:30
Chicago at Phoenix, 7:30
Dallas at LA Clippers, 7:30
Thursday, March 23
Washington at Charlotte, 7:30
Milwaukee at Cleveland, 7:30
Phoenix at Golden State, 7:30
LA Lakers at Sacramento, 7:30
LA Clippers at Seattle, 7:00
Friday, March 24
New York at Boston, 7:30
San Antonio at Philadelphia, 7:30
New Jersey at Detroit, 8:00
Utah at Houston, 7:30
Denver at Dallas, 7:30
Chicago at Portland, 7:30
Saturday, March 25
Atlanta at New York, 8:30
Indiana at Washington, 7:30
Detroit at Charlotte, 7:30
San Antonio at Miami, 7:30
Cleveland at Milwaukee, 8:00
Golden State at Houston, 7:30
Denver at Utah, 7:30
Phoenix at LA Clippers, 7:30
Portland at Sacramento, 7:30
Chicago at Seattle, 7:00
Sunday, March 26
Philadelphia at Boston, 1:00
Phoenix at LA Lakers, 7:30
Monday, March 27
New York at Charlotte, 7:30
New Jersey at Miami, 7:30
Dallas at Detroit, 7:30
Cleveland at Indiana, 7:30
Golden State at Milwaukee, 7:30
Seattle at Houston, 7:00
Washington at San Antonio, 7:30
LA Lakers at Phoenix, 7:30
Wednesday, March 29
Portland at Boston, 7:30

Washington at Atlanta, 7:30
Miami at Indiana, 7:30
Chicago at Milwaukee, 7:30
Detroit at Utah, 7:30
Sacramento at LA Clippers, 7:30

Thursday, March 30
Dallas at New York, 8:30
Houston at New Jersey, 7:30
Golden State at Charlotte, 7:30
Seattle at Denver, 7:30
San Antonio at LA Lakers, 7:30
Phoenix at Sacramento, 7:30

Friday, March 31
Houston at Boston, 7:30
Golden State at New York, 8:30
Miami at Philadelphia, 7:30
Portland at Washington, 8:00
New Jersey at Atlanta, 7:30
Dallas at Indiana, 7:30
Cleveland at Chicago, 7:00 (TBS)
Milwaukee at Phoenix, 7:30
San Antonio at LA Clippers, 7:30
Detroit at Seattle, 7:00

Saturday, April 1
Portland at Charlotte, 7:30
LA Lakers at Denver, 7:30
Utah at Sacramento, 7:30

Sunday, April 2
Houston at Philadelphia, 1:00
Golden State at Washington, 3:30
Boston at Cleveland, 1:00
Atlanta at Indiana, 2:30
New Jersey at Chicago, 12:30
Miami at Dallas, 2:30
Milwaukee at LA Lakers, 7:30
Detroit at LA Clippers, 3:00

Tuesday, April 4
Philadelphia at New York, 8:30
New Jersey at Washington, 7:30
Atlanta at Cleveland, 7:30
Houston at Indiana, 7:30
Charlotte at Chicago, 7:30
Miami at San Antonio, 7:30
Sacramento at Denver, 7:30
Dallas at Utah, 7:30
Boston at LA Clippers, 7:30
Milwaukee at Golden State, 7:30
Detroit at Portland, 7:30
LA Lakers at Seattle, 7:00

Wednesday, April 5
Philadelphia at Atlanta, 7:30
Utah at Phoenix, 7:30

Thursday, April 6
Washington at Miami, 7:30
Chicago at Detroit, 7:30
New York at Milwaukee, 7:30
Sacramento at San Antonio, 7:30
Indiana at Denver, 7:30
Portland at LA Clippers, 7:30
Boston at Golden State, 7:30
Phoenix at Seattle, 7:00

Friday, April 7
New York at New Jersey, 7:30
Cleveland at Washington, 8:00
Philadelphia at Charlotte, 7:30
Houston at Atlanta, 7:30
Detroit at Chicago, 7:30
Sacramento at Dallas, 7:30
Utah at LA Lakers, 7:30
Boston at Portland, 7:30 (TBS)

Saturday, April 8
Houston at Miami, 7:30
Philadelphia at Milwaukee, 8:00
Seattle at Dallas, 7:30
Indiana at San Antonio, 7:30
Utah at Denver, 7:30
Phoenix at LA Clippers, 7:30
LA Lakers at Golden State, 7:30

Sunday, April 9
New York at Washington, 1:00
Chicago at Atlanta, 12:30
Charlotte at Cleveland, 1:30
Milwaukee at Detroit, 7:00
Denver at Portland, 7:00

Monday, April 10
New Jersey at Boston, 7:30

Detroit at Washington, 7:30
Atlanta at Charlotte, 7:30
Indiana at Dallas, 7:30
Seattle at San Antonio, 7:30
LA Clippers at LA Lakers, 7:30
Miami at Sacramento, 7:30

Tuesday, April 11
Philadelphia at Cleveland, 7:30
New Jersey at Milwaukee, 7:30
Indiana at Houston, 7:30
Miami at Golden State, 7:30
LA Clippers at Portland, 7:30

Wednesday, April 12
Charlotte at New York, 8:30
Milwaukee at Washington, 7:30
Cleveland at Detroit, 7:30
Phoenix at Dallas, 7:30
LA Lakers at San Antonio, 7:30
Denver at Utah, 7:30

Thursday, April 13
Boston at Atlanta, 8:00 (TBS)
Chicago at Indiana, 7:30
Phoenix at Houston, 7:30
Golden State at LA Clippers, 7:30
Denver at Sacramento, 7:30
Miami at Seattle, 7:00

Friday, April 14
Cleveland at Boston, 7:30
Detroit at New York, 8:00 (TBS)
Chicago at New Jersey, 7:30
Charlotte at Philadelphia, 7:30
Dallas at San Antonio, 7:30
Houston at Utah, 7:30
Miami at Portland, 7:30

Saturday, April 15
Milwaukee at Atlanta, 7:30
Charlotte at Indiana, 7:30
San Antonio at Phoenix, 7:30
Sacramento at Golden State, 7:30
Utah at Portland, 7:30
Denver at Seattle, 7:00

Sunday, April 16
Milwaukee at New Jersey, 7:30
New York at Philadelphia, 3:30
Chicago at Cleveland, 1:00 (CBS)*
Washington at Detroit, 7:00
Houston at Dallas, 12:00 (CBS)*
Miami at LA Lakers, 7:30

Monday, April 17
Boston at Charlotte, 7:30
New York at Chicago, 7:30
San Antonio at Houston, 7:30
Sacramento at Phoenix, 7:30
Utah at LA Clippers, 7:30

Seattle at Golden State, 7:30

Tuesday, April 18
Washington at Boston, 7:30
Charlotte at New Jersey, 7:30
Milwaukee at Philadelphia, 7:30
Dallas at Miami, 7:30
Detroit at Cleveland, 7:30
Atlanta at Indiana, 7:30
LA Clippers at Utah, 7:30
Denver at LA Lakers, 7:30
Portland at Sacramento, 7:30
Golden State at Seattle, 7:00

Wednesday, April 19
Indiana at Detroit, 7:30
Atlanta at Milwaukee , 7:30
Houston at San Antonio, 7:30

Thursday, April 20
Boston at New York, 7:30
Philadelphia at New Jersey, 7:30
Chicago at Washington, 7:30
San Antonio at Denver, 7:30
Sacramento at LA Lakers, 7:30
Portland at Seattle, 7:00

Friday April 21
Milwaukee at Charlotte, 7:30
Cleveland at Atlanta, 7:30
Philadelphia at Detroit, 8:00
Boston at Indiana, 7:30
Washington at Chicago, 7:30
Utah at Dallas, 7:00 (TBS)
Houston at Phoenix, 7:30
Seattle at LA Clippers, 7:30
Denver at Golden State, 7:30
LA Lakers at Portland, 7:30

Saturday, April 22
New Jersey at New York, 8:30
Indiana at Milwaukee, 8:00
Miami at Houston, 7:30
Phoenix at San Antonio, 7:30
Golden State at Utah, 7:30
LA Clippers at Sacramento, 7:30

Sunday, April 23
Charlotte at Boston, 1:00
Washington at Philadelphia, 1:00
Atlanta at Detroit, 3:30 (CBS)*
Cleveland at Chicago, 12:00
Dallas at Denver, 1:30 (CBS)*
Seattle at LA Lakers, 12:30 (CBS)*
Sacramento at Portland, 7:00

*CBS will make its selection for national broadcasts of Feb. 20, April 16 and April 23 thirteen days prior to the date of the game.